Prolific Ground

TRANSITS

LITERATURE, THOUGHT & CULTURE, 1650–1850

A landmark series in long-eighteenth-century studies, *Transits* publishes monographs and edited volumes that are timely, transformative in their approach, and global in their engagement with arts, literature, culture, and history. Books in the series have engaged with visual arts, environment, politics, material culture, travel, theater and performance, embodiment, connections between the natural sciences and medical humanities, writing and book history, sexuality, gender, disability, race, and colonialism from Britain and Europe to the Americas, the Far East, the Middle/Near East, Africa, and Oceania. Works that make provocative connections across time, space, geography, or intellectual history, or that develop new modes of critical imagining are particularly welcome.

Recent titles in the series:

Prolific Ground: Landscape and British Women's Writing, 1690–1790
Nicolle Jordan

Consuming Anxieties: Alcohol, Tobacco, and Trade in British Satire, 1660–1751
Dayne C. Riley

The Part and the Whole in Early American Literature, Print Culture, and Art
Matthew Pethers and Daniel Diez Couch, eds.

Teaching the Eighteenth Century Now: Pedagogy as Ethical Engagement
Kate Parker and Miriam L. Wallace, eds.

Women and Music in the Age of Austen
Linda Zionkowski with Miriam F. Hart, eds.

Louis Sébastien Mercier: Revolution and Reform in Eighteenth-Century Paris
Michael J. Mulryan

Alimentary Orientalism: Britain's Literary Imagination and the Edible East
Yin Yuan

Thomas Holcroft's Revolutionary Drama: Reception and Afterlives
Amy Garnai

For more information about the series, please visit www.bucknelluniversitypress.org.

Prolific Ground

LANDSCAPE AND BRITISH WOMEN'S WRITING, 1690–1790

NICOLLE JORDAN

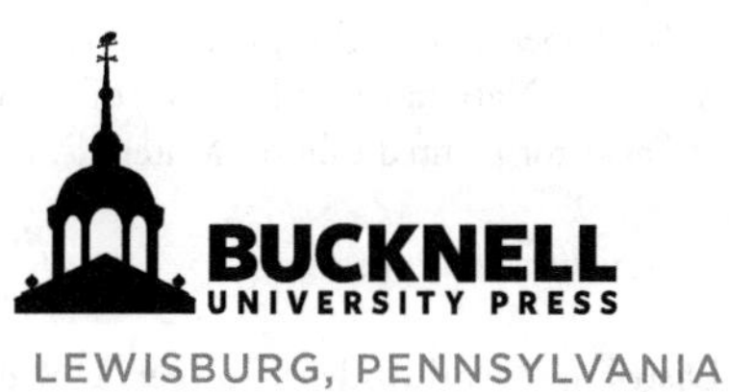

LEWISBURG, PENNSYLVANIA

978-1-68448-539-0 (paper)
978-1-68448-540-6 (cloth)
978-1-68448-541-3 (epub)

Cataloging-in-publication data is available from the Library of Congress.

LCCN 2024005135

A British Cataloging-in-Publication record for this book is available from the British Library.

∞ The paper used in this publication meets the requirements of the American National Standard for Information Sciences—Permanence of Paper for Printed Library Materials, ANSI Z39.48-1992.

bucknelluniversitypress.org

Distributed worldwide by Rutgers University Press

For Michele Anna Jordan
and
Thomas V. O'Brien

CONTENTS

List of Illustrations ix

Introduction: Landscape Studies and British Women's Literary History 1

1 Jane Barker's Liminal Landscapes 16

2 Stewarding the Country House: Anne Finch, Countess of Winchilsea 52

3 "And the Country Adjacent": Sarah Scott's Literary Landscaping 81

4 Elizabeth Montagu, Bluestocking Landscaper 114

Conclusion 152

Acknowledgments 163

Notes 165

Bibliography 179

Index 187

ILLUSTRATIONS

Figure 2.1 Eastwell in Kent, home of Anne Finch off and on, 1690–1720 58

Figure 2.2 Example of a mount, Dunham Massey, engraving in *Britannia Illustrata* (1707–1709) by Johannes Kip and Leendert Knyff 64

Figure 2.3 *Long Leate*, engraving in *Britannia Illustrata* (1707–1709) by Johannes Kip and Leendert Knyff 73

Figure 2.4 *View of Longleat* by Jan Siberechts, c. 1678 77

Figure 3.1 *Mount Morris*, near Hythe, engraving in *Britannia Illustrata* (1707–1709) by Johannes Kip and Leendert Knyff 82

Figure 4.1 *Elizabeth Montagu* (1776) by John Raphael Smith after Sir Joshua Reynolds 116

Prolific Ground

INTRODUCTION

Landscape Studies and British Women's Literary History

> The front of the House, & ye approach to it, remain just as when you were at Sandleford. The eating room & drawing room are compleated. The ground to the South is much improved, & a little rivulet that used to trickle between the ground on ye East & ye wood, is now enlarging, so that it will assume the appearance of a river by next spring. Then, according to the plan & intentions of Mr Brown, the improvements toward the front of ye house will be begun. Mr Wyatts people are now making such alterations as will give me a noble bed chamber, & dressing room, both of which will have a southern aspect & a most beautiful view. The other alterations must be delayed till another autumn, if I was to undertake more now the house would not be habitable next summer, & as I cannot flatter myself, at my age, with a long succession of summers, it wd be imprudent to banish myself from Sandleford when I most delight to spend that season.[1]

WRITING IN 1783 TO HER fellow Bluestocking hostess Elizabeth Vesey, Elizabeth Montagu (1718–1800) conjures an array of images and prospects-in-the-making, bringing to life the standard features one associates with landscape—a river, a wood, "a most beautiful view." The letter's visual rhetoric invites Vesey to recall her last visit to Sandleford Priory, the Montagu estate in Berkshire. Montagu then describes all that has changed since she undertook improvements to the property under the expert guidance of renowned landscape designer Lancelot "Capability" Brown and architect James Wyatt. The scene's bustling activity conveys commotion both in and out of doors as these professionals work to provide their client with a dwelling to suit her tastes. Less obvious, but no less important for the present study, is how the passage depicts the literal construction of a landscape. With the "ground to the South [being] much improved," the rivulet to the East "enlarged," and "improvements toward the front of ye house" undertaken, the scene captures the wholesale transformation of the exterior at the behest of the owner. Montagu did in fact own Sandleford, having inherited it from her husband upon his death in 1775.

This book explores how landownership, and engagements with land more broadly, constitute a crucial dimension of female independence. Montagu's command of the proceedings reveals how she derives her authority from a set of social relations grounded in landownership.[2] She presides over the property, directs the renovation of her home, and decides which plans will go forward and which will wait for another season. Indeed, her will is what makes the landscape; the passage shows her in the process of molding it to her specifications. The entire scenario evokes the multiplicity of landscape: on the one hand it consists in beautiful and natural scenery, but on the other it involves much more than the surface appearance of the land; it entails a spectrum of relations that arise from each person's relationship to the land in question, whether owner, employee, or dependent.

The distance between an understanding of landscape as natural scenery and as a more complex social arrangement is at the crux of this book. Landscape resists stable definition, in turn making selective definition a necessary yet daunting feature of scholarship in the field. As Isis Brook observes, "All that can be established with any certainty is that, like place, landscape is a vague concept and in reality has fuzzy edges. And yet we know what we mean and can spot when the term is being stretched, used metaphorically, or misapplied."[3] Such conceptual drift contributes to the abundant scholarship as well as its diffusion across disciplines, from the humanities (literature and history) and the arts to the social sciences (geography and material culture) and sciences (botany and medicine). Indeed, histories of British landscape abound; consider, for example, the work of Tom Williamson and Timothy Mowl.[4] Likewise, historical geographers and labor and agricultural historians have produced key texts that testify to the ongoing vitality of landscape studies. Briony McDonagh[5] and Nicola Verdon,[6] among others, provide invaluable historical and geographical context for this book, as do women's historians such as Bridget Hill and Amanda Vickery.[7] Building on this rich interdisciplinarity, the book demonstrates how reading British women's writing through the lens of landscape exposes the myriad ways in which gender relations emerge from the social relations governed by primarily male landownership. This approach, in turn, enables me to examine how in this the era, British women's writing necessarily condoned patriarchy while paradoxically contriving a form of independence through literary agency.

I build on the premise that landscapes are social constructs. Human perception is the sine qua non for the landscapes under scrutiny here; Galesia, Ardelia, Mrs. Maynard, and Elizabeth Montagu—among others—see the land, sometimes only in their mind's eye. This perception ignites subsequent perceptions and representations that culminate in a final product: a landscape. These female figures experience the land in decisive ways; they gaze upon, manage, versify, imagine, walk on, live within, and own it. As a result, they forge an identity that locates them in several ways: in the social and gender hierarchies of their time and place as well as within the manuscript and print cultures that mark their literary achievement as women writers. More broadly, then, the book also contributes to ongoing debates about female authority in a variety of contexts.[8] Focusing exclusively on landscape, I argue that exploring the status of women specifically through a problematics of land yields profound insight into the extent to which the possibilities for female identity are grounded in the social codes governing the land, and thus in landscape. Other renditions of British women's literary history uncover similar quandaries arising from contradictory codes of femininity; this book asserts the unique manifestation of these issues in and through the land.

The institution of landownership constitutes a key category of analysis here. Because of the singular relationship between male landownership and political authority in Britain, land—that is, grounded private property—becomes a crucial site for the construction of gender roles. For my purposes, then, land is material, while landscape is not. Furthermore, landscape itself, understood as a social construct, hinges on male landownership. I investigate the consequences of this arrangement for women writers during this period. How does a land-based sociopolitical regime impact their experience and circumscribe their identity? What does women's writing reveal about their negotiation of this regime, and how does this negotiation change over time? Finally, in what ways does women's writing participate in the discursive and material processes that turn land into landscape, and with what implications for female independence?

Answering these questions requires a long view of British literary history as it intersects with gender and landscape studies. In delineating the gambit of his book, *The Drama of Landscape: Land, Property, and Social Relations on the Early Modern Stage*, Garrett Sullivan notes what his project excludes: "A different project could take as its primary focus the crucially important ways in which landscapes are gendered."[9] I take this claim as my point of departure and focus on a period that begins a century after the one Sullivan studies. His historical narrative has great explanatory power when adapted to the situation of women writers because it exposes their subordination within the prevailing landscape regime and the alternative relationships to land—and thus, the landscapes—that emerge from such subordination. In brief, he posits that landscapes in their early modern iteration were not primarily visual in nature; rather, the landscapes of stewardship and custom united landowners and their dependents within a moral economy based on reciprocity. It was a lived-in landscape more than an observed one. Only in the seventeenth century, according to Sullivan, do aesthetic conceptions of landscape emerge, and he identifies these as "the landscape arts." Their corollary, "the landscape of absolute property," hinges exclusively on the owner's prerogative, thus nullifying the concerns of dependents.

As most landscape theorists agree, all models of landscape manifest the ideology that produces them.[10] Thus, the landscapes of stewardship and custom operate according to communitarian values, while the landscape arts bespeak an emergent capitalism wherein individualism gradually displaces its community-based forerunner. In the unified community of landowner and tenants, all members understand how their roles contribute to successful estate management. By contrast, with the emergence of the landscape arts, the key term refers not to the cohabited rural land and the reciprocal responsibilities of owners and laborers, but rather to the views appreciated by the landowner, his family, and his guests. Thus, the landscape arts serve the nation's elite, and not (except for the rare exception) the rural tenantry.

Building on Sullivan's three-part historical model of landscape, I argue that despite their subordinate status, some women managed to cultivate a certain authority, and to derive their very identity, from their distinctive practices of estate stewardship. I adapt his model by analyzing landscapes of stewardship when they are governed by principles of reciprocity between a landowning steward and *her* dependents. My analysis reveals the considerable moral authority that women garner from either their own exertions as stewards or their assessments of male stewardship. I also expose the ethical dilemmas they encounter when navigating the competing demands of communitarian stewardship and individualistic forms of landownership that aim to elevate and enrich the landlady rather than sustaining a landscape regime that is mutually beneficial to both owners and tenants.

In contesting the standard conception of landscape as visual, i.e., aesthetic in nature, I also challenge the commonplace assumption about *how* eighteenth-century England produced the landscape garden. My critical intervention here is twofold: First, I challenge the dominant narrative governing these histories of landscape in Britain. An exemplary text in this mold is Douglas Chambers's *The Planters of the English Landscape Garden*.[11] This work historicizes the English landscape garden as the work of a pantheon of elite visionary men: Lord Burlington, Viscount Cobham, Lord Bathurst, etc. A secondary cast of practitioners (nurserymen and landscape architects such as Henry Wise, William Kent, and Capability Brown) underscores the extent to which this history constructs landscape as a male domain. My second intervention challenges the very assumption that aestheticized land tells the full story of landscape, questioning how such histories reify the landscape arts. I explore the possibility that the alternative, nonaesthetic landscapes that traditional history covers over offer insight into how land relations help configure social relations, which in turn configure gender relations. I argue, therefore, that women's writing of the era offers a counternarrative that not only challenges the construction of landscape as a male domain, but also rejects the premise that literary engagements with land in the period are first and foremost matters of aesthetics.

Despite its hypermasculinity, the foregoing history of eighteenth-century British landscape has generated more recent scholarship that foregrounds the compelling relationship between landscape and literature. Cynthia Wall's *Grammars of Approach: Landscape, Narrative, and the Linguistic Picturesque* makes a brilliant argument about the era's intertwined topographical, typographical, and linguistic innovations. She links evolving tastes in landscape architecture to likewise evolving conventions of print and patterns of syntax. The picturesque serves as her governing model of landscape, leading her to engage most thoroughly with landscape theorists working in the late eighteenth and early nineteenth centuries. She organizes her engagement with these figures based on how they reject or adapt the style of Capability Brown (c. 1715/16–1783). Her pantheon of landscape theorists in the anti-Brown camp includes William Gilpin (1724–1804), Richard Payne Knight (1751–1824), and Uvedale Price (1747–1829); meanwhile, Humphry Repton (1752–1818) serves "as Brown's self-styled heir but also as innovator, folding aspects of the picturesque into the domesticity of common sense."[12] Repton's aesthetic and theoretical innovations make him the dominant landscaper in her book, and he appears in nearly every chapter.

The fact that Wall's primary actors are male does not, of course, discredit her argument, but it does perpetuate the long-standing tendency to see the history of landscape as an exclusively male domain. Given the constraints upon female conduct at the time, her history of landscape is accurate insofar as it assembles published writers and theorists as well as professional practitioners. Women's exclusion from the relevant professions necessarily renders these fields a male preserve. As we will see, however, women did participate in landscape design in significant if in informal (and fictional) ways.

I share Wall's implicit conviction that women writers make significant contributions to landscape discourse. To be sure, Wall's analysis of Frances Burney (1752–1840), Ann Radcliffe (1764–1823), and Jane Austen (1775–1817) demonstrates how women writers manifest the topographical, typographical, and aesthetic innovations under her scrutiny. I turn my gaze to those women writing during the century prior to the era when those female novelists wrote. Charting a course through landscapes of custom, stewardship, and absolute property (alongside its corollary, the landscape arts), my historicist conception of landscape hinges on the socioeconomic and political transformations underway during the long eighteenth century. Because partisan politics have a decisive and lasting impact on evolving landscape relations, especially around the turn of the eighteenth century, I devote the first half of the book to women writers whose partisanship constitutes a fundamental aspect of their identity. The manifestation of these political conflicts specifically in a problematics of land makes the works of Jane Barker (1652–1732) and Anne Finch (1661–1720) consummate expressions of the era's intertwined socioeconomic, political, and gender regimes. As renowned Jacobite women writers, who refused to swear loyalty to William III, they variously exemplify retrograde literary responses to the transformations in their culture's landscape relations.

After analyzing the partisan terrain within which Finch and Barker operate, I turn to two writers whose fictional and epistolary works instantiate a successive phase in landscape's history, as the landscape arts gradually (though fitfully) prevail over prior landscapes of custom and stewardship. Thus, I build the book's second half around Sarah Scott's *Millenium Hall* (1762) and selected epistles by her sister, Elizabeth Montagu, all of which testify to the ascendance of the landscape arts. Scott's novel constitutes the apotheosis of landscape's transformation over the long eighteenth century, for it captures the dynamic process by which landscape aesthetics came to displace, without entirely negating, the landscapes that preceded the new model. Meanwhile, Montagu provides a "real-world" enactment of the obsolescent and ascendant landscape regimes; as one of the wealthiest women of her era, and one of its most prolific letter writers, she provides a historical record of landscape's transformation over the course of her lifetime. As seen in her letter excerpt that opens this introduction, landscape has become, by the 1780s, primarily an aestheticized object savored by the landowner and her friends more than terrain within which the owner and her dependents operate according to a mutually beneficial arrangement.

LITERARY ALCHEMY AND THE HISTORY OF LANDSCAPE

An emphasis on literary form as the locus for women's negotiation of land relations distinguishes my synthesis of feminism and landscape. Stephen Bending's *Green Retreats: Women, Gardens, and Eighteenth-Century Culture* investigates female agency as enacted in the landscape gardens over which elite women exerted a measure of control. Our subtitles display our different methodological orientations; he locates *Eighteenth-Century Culture* in the archive, in the private letters these women wrote about their gardening experiences.[13] My emphasis on *British Women's Writing* privileges women's manuscript and print publication and thus foregrounds the literary distillation of women's investment in rural land. The translation of their experience into particular literary forms—country-house poetry and the novel—suggests the distinctive, one might say alchemical, process that turns land into landscape in these women's writing.[14] In turn, I treat Montagu as the culmination of the literary landscaping witnessed in the works of Barker, Finch, and Scott (1720–1795), analyzing the obsolescent and emergent landscapes encountered in these texts as they echo in Montagu's epistolary self-construction. The trajectory of my argument, from public to private literary production, insinuates an interest in the literary transformations that led women like Montagu to choose the landscape arts as the locus for their pursuit of self-determination. What did women of letters like Montagu read that conditioned them to translate their experience as owners and stewards of rural property into visual spectacles that encode their—triumphant, repentant, or ambivalent—self-invention?

The previous discussion of Bending's work hearkens back to the puzzle that opened this analysis: How does one craft a coherent narrative around the multiple ways in which landscape animates women's writing from this period? Related work such as Lisa L. Moore's exquisite *Sister Arts: The Erotics of Lesbian Landscapes* echoes Bending in signaling the period's pervasive interest in the landscape arts. Moore brings landscape into conversation with the history of sexuality, positing the notion of "lesbian genres" as a way to interpret the intimacy among women that emerged from their exchange of writings, plants, pictures, and garden designs.[15] As this amalgam of texts suggests, however, Moore reads sexuality in the landscape arts and thus amplifies the evidence of their stature at the time. *Prolific Ground* seeks rather to uncover the literary substratum that helped produce the countless artifacts perpetuating the value of aestheticized land, and to ask, what cultural processes conspired to refract that valuation of landed property in such kaleidoscopic variety? In order to access this literary substratum, I argue, one must disaggregate the multiple layers of landscape and thus disinter the discursive processes that established the landscape arts as the sole, decisive model in the first place.

To reconceptualize landscape within these broader historical parameters makes it possible, and even necessary, to draw connections between landscape relations and gender relations. Thus, the book also offers innovative interpretations of four female authors who figure prominently in eighteenth-century women's literary history. By examining Jacobite authors Barker, in chapter 1, and Finch, in chapter 2, I demonstrate the dynamic modulation of competing forms of landscape; from one vantage their characters and speakers inhabit landscapes of stewardship, while from another, those scenarios turn into beautiful scenery and signal the advent of early capitalism. The transformative processes at work in their texts exemplify the alchemy of turning land into landscape. Chapters 3 and 4 undertake similar, complementary readings that interpret the competing landscapes in Scott and Montagu, focusing on the evolving landscape relations that manifest in both women's devotion to philanthropy. As sisters whose contrasting material circumstances mirror their divergent conceptions of stewardship, they exemplify the forking paths of those who pursue communal versus individual modes of engaging with rural land.[16] The distinctions between the sisters' philanthropic visions demonstrate the tensions between landscapes of stewardship and the landscape arts, revealing how the principle of reciprocity that defines the landscape of stewardship obsolesces as the landscape arts co-opt it in the service of a more individualistic social paradigm.

BIASED SOURCES, FEMINIST CRITICISM, AND WOMEN'S COLLABORATION WITH PATRIARCHY

The decision to conclude this book with a study of Elizabeth Montagu arises from an interest in the lived experience of eighteenth-century British women writers.

But, as a work that synthesizes manuscript and print sources, *Prolific Ground* must reckon with the problematic and incomplete nature of the historical materials. They prove problematic because of male bias not only in archival sources but also in twentieth-century scholarship, which began to integrate women's perspectives in earnest only in the 1970s.[17] Because historical sources from the long eighteenth century sanctioned female philanthropy but not female estate management, then, women's historians have had to cultivate alternative methods for accessing details about women's lives at this time. The poetry, novels, and personal correspondence featured in this book, though obviously different from the historical sources studied by McDonagh and Vickery (among others), nonetheless reveal a great deal about those lives and how my featured writers judged them.

It would be naïve, however, to infer that the bias against recording elite women's landownership and stewardship makes them proto-feminists through and through. Indeed, McDonagh offers an incisive assessment of their implication in systems of both social and gender inequality:

> Propertied women's management of landed estates undoubtedly functioned to reproduce the elite's social and political power: for example, via building and landscaping works and their care of political constituencies as well as their astute management of the agricultural estate itself. It helped to preserve estates in the hands of the upper strata of English society, and thus not only bolstered the existing patriarchal social order but also contributed to the solidification of property rights, extinguishing of common rights and the rhetoric of possessive individualism which gradually emerged in the three and a half centuries up to c. 1850.[18]

Especially significant here is McDonagh's specification of possessive individualism. As previously noted regarding Sullivan's "landscape arts," their emergence alongside capitalism signals the obsolescence not only of common rights but also customary relations. Likewise, in the landscape of absolute property, landowners' aims are paramount and not beholden to any duty to their dependents' well-being.

It should therefore come as no surprise that McDonagh's claims about elite women who perpetuate patriarchy, evidence for which she bases on an array of historical documents but very few literary sources, nevertheless corroborate my own findings in the verse and fiction on which this book mostly focuses. This historical geographer studies Montagu in some depth, drawing similar conclusions about her self-construction through landownership and stewardship, and calling for a literary historical approach, one to which this book responds.[19] The poetry and novels featured here demonstrate how the practice of literary imagination led these writers to make strategic accommodations with the very system that subordinated them as women. Thus, they exemplify the ways in which women's complicity with patriarchy becomes possible (and perhaps instinctive and necessary) when they have something to gain besides gender equality—for instance, wealth, stature, and/or the prospect of economic independence. It proves fascinating, I argue, to witness the canny maneuvers these writers make in the process of forging their own agency and a modicum of independence. The ambivalence of contemporary feminist critics toward some of our foremothers is of course nothing new. In 1984, Bridget Hill observed of the Bluestockings, "All were exceptional women, some were outstanding scholars. [. . .] Few of them questioned the role of women, all women, in society. Even those who were writers and authors seemed content to accept the inferior position allotted to them because they were women. It was enough for the great majority of them to enjoy the recognition that they received in a limited sphere."[20]

One compelling consequence of studying female writers and characters who collaborate, if you will, with patriarchy is that doing so exposes the pitfalls that impede or slow the emergence of gender equality. Another consequence has to do with other forms of inequality, especially the social inequality that features prominently in some chapters but fleetingly in others. Accounting for such entangled forms of injustice requires us to reckon with the intersectional dimension of these issues. In the discussion in chapter 3 of Scott's *Millenium Hall*, for example, we glimpse the intersection of proto-feminism with disability studies and queer or lesbian studies. These idiosyncratic aspects of her novel have generated significant critical attention, though they deserve more given the current burgeoning of these methodologies.[21] The social inequality between the aristocracy and gentry, on the one hand, and the middling sort and laborers, on the other, appears much more frequently in the literature on which *Prolific Ground* focuses. Thus, its historical argument foregrounds the role of landscape as a tool for enforcing social inequality in various contexts. Hill offers another germane, and more recent, observation that, "Capitalism has always exploited gender conflict for its own purposes."[22] When we scrutinize how these women writers negotiate—and sometimes participate in—the emergent capitalist economy, we may better understand why they were often willing—or compelled—to maneuver strategically between that economy and their desire for independence. Ultimately, the dissonance between contemporary feminists and our forebears who cooperated with patriarchy proves instructive insofar as it mirrors the competing values that these women writers themselves faced as they navigated the obsolescent and emergent landscapes under scrutiny. Their encounters with competing landscapes—and the ambivalence these generated—reflect our own confrontation with competing models of feminism.

Although too numerous to discuss here, trailblazing scholars of the past thirty years have made decisive contributions to women's social, political, and economic history. For example, in "Women and Property: Women as Property," Patricia Crawford investigates early modern Englishwomen's vexed status within patriarchy and its property regime. Like McDonagh, she makes occasional reference to literary sources; the most germane observation for present purposes appears as she addresses the emergent category of intellectual property: "During the seventeenth century, the majority of women whose writings were published claimed the right to have their voices heard. A wealthy educated woman might delicately mock the pretensions of men to monopolize authorship: 'Alas! A woman that attempts the pen,' wrote Anne Finch, 'Such an intruder on the rights of men.' However, women asserted their rights as authors in a moral sense rather than at law."[23] This excerpt from one of Finch's most-often-quoted poems, "The Introduction," lends itself to appropriation by modern feminists; indeed, Crawford's reading complements the analysis of the Finch poems discussed in chapter 2. But it's also important to consider how the lines obscure the ways in which she made a strategic bargain with select patriarchs in order to pursue her poetic avocation. The tension between inspiration and degradation that today's feminists may feel in the face of such collaboration with patriarchy makes for provocative material in all four chapters, which extend this interrogation of the ambivalence that arises in the ideological chasm that separates twenty-first-century feminists from several proto-feminists writing circa 1690–1790.

Crawford also offers insight into women's status *as* property, illuminating a long-standing tendency to feminize the landscape: "Land was the main form of property, [. . .] and of particular importance for women, property was also one's body and labour."[24] Treating the landscape as a woman's body expresses the assumption of male ownership of both entities.[25] The rhetorical conflation of women and land has prompted scholars of British women's writing in the long eighteenth century to study the implications of this assumption, but they typically comment on the phenomenon in the course of studying another, broader or related topic. Carole Fabricant is an important exception to this tendency, making her landmark essay from 1979 a point of origin for this book.[26] She delineates the ways in which life on country estates inculcated certain forms of visuality that conflated women with the land, thus amplifying other tendencies to objectify women. Jennifer Keith and Kathryn King have also scrutinized the feminization of landscape; although they approach the topic in terms of the landscape arts, their compelling insights demonstrate the need for a monograph that delves into the social structures behind such rhetoric. Keith's *Poetry and the Feminine from Behn to Cowper* explores women writers who embrace the prospect view, a concept adapted from John Barrell's influential model of landscape (discussed hereafter). The pattern that emerges, Keith finds, is that the rhetoric of female objectification morphs into identification, a dynamic that effectively disrupts the voyeurism that typically animates male depictions of landscape.[27]

King offers a complementary, though much briefer, observation on the paucity of prospect views in women's poetry. In her essay on "Constructions of Femininity" in eighteenth-century British poetry, she notices a tendency for male poets to portray women's faces using the rhetoric of prospect poetry. Women poets, by contrast,

> produced few prospect poems and [. . .] such prospects as do appear in their work are to some degree ironized. Male poets, and the male speakers and characters they create, are at liberty to wander the landscape and subject its prospect-views to their commanding, sometimes appropriating gaze. [. . .] Women [. . .] are subjected to the gaze, their own included. They are seen, observed, watched, scrutinized, desired, admired, envied; scorned for the beauty they lack, chided for taking so seriously those fleeting beauties they do possess. Seldom, however, do they possess the kind of authority that would enable them to take command of the heights or to subdue a man to the status of landscape.[28]

King's proliferating vocabulary of surveillance and voyeurism emphasizes the degree to which women, whether writing or being written, operate within an economy of visuality. Inspired by King's attention to women writers who satirize or otherwise challenge degrading female objectification, I use her observation on the scarcity of women's prospect poetry as a point of departure. For it turns out that the instances of women writing prospects increase when we expand our inquiry beyond poetry and look also at novels and private letters, and when we subsume the term *prospect* within the broader category of landscape, which need not involve a bird's-eye perspective, as prospects typically do.

Crawford, Fabricant, Keith, and King all signal, from various angles, that the objectification of women constitutes a pervasive tendency in British literature of the long eighteenth century. By calling attention to the subordination effected by such rhetoric, they expose the textual strategies that some women writers concoct in order to resist a system that denies their subjectivity. Women's appropriation of the prospect view is a case in point. Yet I would also note that for my purposes, the fusion of landscape and the prospect view is provisional. Because important discussions of landscape in eighteenth- and early nineteenth-century British literature occur in the language of the prospect view, it is necessary to address them. *Prolific Ground* makes occasional reference to prospect views, but with the caveat that they serve as instances of the landscape arts and thus illuminate only the final phase of landscape's history as I conceive of it. The proliferation of prospect views in Romantic poetry attests to the triumph of the landscape arts as the very essence of landscape.

The assumption that prospects are a masculine prerogative derives from the pervasive sense that landownership and the intellectual and civic capacities inhering therein are likewise male. John Barrell's influential theory of the "man of taste" who exercises the prospect view is by now a commonplace in scholarly assessments of politicized landscape in Britain. The ability to distinguish the general from the particular, the argument goes, belongs exclusively to the landed gentleman, and a crucial expression of his qualification is his appreciation for a certain kind of landscape painting. Thus, Barrell argues that landscape "must be defended as an art capable of *calling forth* the ability to abstract substance from accident, the general from the particular."[29] That landscape assessment, of all cultural activities, was seen to measure a person's cultural and civic stature says a great deal about the decisive role it played in eighteenth-century British culture.

While Barrell acknowledges the gendered exclusivity of his topic, he does not elaborate on the manifestations or consequences of women's exclusion from the precincts of property ownership, political citizenship, abstract reason, or aesthetic discernment, all of which converge in the prospect view. Malcolm Andrews offers an addendum, of sorts, regarding the limited capacities typically ascribed to women according to the logic of the prospect view. In the midst of glossing Barrell, he asks, "Why not *woman* of taste too? The question focuses again on the degree to which landscape is bound up with issues of property and territorial control, the masculine command of a view. Women were credited with an aptitude for sensitive miniaturist portraits of cottages, village scenes, flowers, but were held to lack the intellectual virility to be able to organize a spacious, multifarious landscape."[30]

Alas, these provocative observations serve merely to entice readers to wonder how a woman of taste might have contributed to the landscape tradition, for Andrews goes on to discuss Ralph Waldo Emerson and other male observers of American landscape without further exploring the discourse's virtual exclusion of women. *Prolific Ground* aims, then, to fill the blank spaces left by scholars who, however unwittingly, perpetuate this exclusion. Women writers had much to gain, in terms of sociocultural and economic authority, by perpetuating long-held associations between women and land. It would be mistaken to suggest that the women writers I discuss are innocent of the objectifying language that perhaps originates in writing by men. At the same time, women's writing reveals much about the stultifying or otherwise limiting effects of femininity's role in the history of landscape and exposes how that history contributed to more diffuse patterns of women's cultural, economic, and political subordination.

In the effort to insert British women writers into a scholarly conversation that mostly excluded them, this book also benefits from an invaluable though chronologically limited range of feminist literary criticism that redresses their exclusion from landscape studies. By assessing landscape and its affiliated concepts through the lens of gender, Jacqueline Labbe's *Romantic Visualities: Landscape, Gender, and Romanticism* investigates a field that coincides perhaps most closely with my own. Analyzing women's writing mostly from the 1790s and thereafter, Labbe interrogates the material and aesthetic foundations for women's inferior status in landscape discourse. The prospect view—as theorized by Barrell—figures prominently in her investigation as she delineates women's typical placement within the prospect as objects of admiration and/or surveillance. She argues, furthermore, that the masculinity of the prospect view gathers momentum over the course of the eighteenth century, thus entrenching the feminization of detailed, occluded views that do not practice the abstracting, universalizing, disinterested modes of vision that define the prospect view. At the same time, Labbe discovers significant deviation from the foregoing pattern, for instance in Charlotte Smith's *Beachy Head* (1807), wherein the speaker bravely "take[s] possession" of the famed promontory. Labbe demonstrates that appropriating the view from the heights does not lead Smith to emulate her male forerunners in every particular: "The long view does not mean the indistinct generalized view in 'Beachy Head' [. . .] Details are not evidence of [Smith's] inability to reason but quite the opposite," as seen in the copious and learned footnotes subtending the poem.[31] Thus, Labbe tracks women's resistance to gendered conceptions of the prospect, and goes on to note these writers' occasional circumspection in the face of dominant narratives of masculine vision and authority.

Serving as a bookend for the landscapes studied in *Prolific Ground*, Labbe's work also presents a provocation of sorts, spurring eighteenth-century women's literary historians to consider whether—and if so, why—the dominion of masculine visuality strengthens over the course of the long eighteenth century. I interpret these issues in terms of women's strategic cooperation with patriarchy, the advantages of which are rewarding enough for the writers featured here to accept—to a greater or lesser degree—their subordinate status. As my four chapters demonstrate, however, structural and institutional barriers to female independence—e.g., patrilineality, primogeniture, and the legal doctrine of coverture—constitute formidable forces that sustain gender inequality. Thus, the book's various examples of women's relation to landownership lead me to consider the perhaps counterintuitive possibility that the obsolescent landscape of stewardship enabled women to sustain more just social relations than those in place under the capitalist landscape of absolute property. Though inherently unequal, the landscape of stewardship at least pursued an authentic mode of reciprocity and thus more equitable relations between landlady and dependents.

The chapters of *Prolific Ground* follow a roughly chronological order and make frequent observations about how and why landscape discourse differs from one historical moment to the next. One complication is that, since I discuss two sets of contemporaries, except for differences in lifespan it does not make sense to treat each pair as producing works consecutively. Thus, Jane Barker lived over a decade longer than Anne Finch, while Sarah Scott predeceased her elder sister, Elizabeth Montagu, by five years and was two years her junior. But Scott ceased to publish after *The Test of Filial Duty* in 1772 (though she continued to write letters nearly until her death). In any event, it would be inaccurate to suggest a causal relationship among these writers. Rather, the book situates them within a broader historical context—the history of landscape—and offers explanations for the changes that emerge when we compare women's landscape depictions from consecutive historical periods.

In chapter 1, Barker's semiautobiographical poet-narrator-protagonist in *The Galesia Trilogy* (1713, 1723, 1726) allows me to engage with both fictional and poetic landscapes, wherein the heroine gropes for independence amid a bevy of obstacles. Galesia makes for a compelling subject to open the book because of the many hats she wears in addition to *poet*: virtuous maiden, informal student of medicine, Jacobite, and estate manager. The trilogy's historical range prompts me to explore how the heroine's multifarious life experiences animate the competing landscapes that wax and wane over the long eighteenth century. I argue that her character and circumstances enact the liminal landscapes of stewardship and custom on the one hand, and the landscape of absolute property on the other. Her attachment to an obsolescent landscape, even as she confronts the vagaries of an economy based increasingly on mobile rather than landed property, testifies to both the appeal and the impermanence of the fading rural order.

Chapter 2 features the more famous but less extreme Jacobite poet Anne Finch, Countess of Winchilsea, whose remarkable generic variety and technical virtuosity make her a standard for women's poetic accomplishment in this era. As with Barker, Finch's competing landscapes signal how British culture navigates the uneven shift from landscapes of stewardship and custom to one of absolute property and its corollary, the landscape arts. Unlike Barker, however, Finch embraces country-house poetry as a means to confront matters of ideal estate ownership and stewardship. Two instances of the genre, entitled "Upon My Lord Winchilsea Converting the Mount in His Garden to a Terras" and "To the Honorable the Lady Worsley at Longleat," portray the estate grounds as a synecdoche for their lords, thus affirming a regime grounded in male landownership. This maneuver engenders a paradox of sorts in the way that Finch asserts her agency as a female poet and yet puts it in the service of an ideology that subordinates women.

Scott's novel *Millenium Hall*, the subject of chapter 3, builds on the rich and fruitful terrain of the country estate, which occasions detailed and moralistic landscape descriptions. In a novelistic country house rather than a poetic one, she constructs a complex social world that plays out its conflicts within the moral geography of dissipated London, on the one hand, and serene Cornwall and other unspecified provincial spaces, on the other. In the distance between Barker's last novel, *The Lining of the Patch Work Screen* (1726), and Scott's utopian tale of a philanthropic community of women who steward a thriving estate, we witness women's writing as it participates in the growing popularity of the novel form. Scott's focus on women's limited access to property—especially landed property—makes the novel in many ways the era's ultimate illustration of the interdependence of landownership and female self-determination. Moreover, the novel exemplifies a crucial moment in the history of landscape insofar as it purports to describe a landscape of stewardship while in fact creating a landscape of absolute property wherein nonelite women surrender to the demands of agricultural and industrial capitalism. In this way, *Millenium Hall* demonstrates how a new landscape regime appropriates the values of the obsolescent one and thus perpetuates social inequality, with the sole difference that now gentlewomen, too, may govern.

Chapter 4 turns from poetic and novelistic landscapes to the epistolary kind in the work of Montagu, a renowned patron and Bluestocking hostess. As the final installment in a series of chapters exploring the eighteenth-century literary history of landscape in Britain, this one considers the implications of the letters' facticity, which distinguishes them from the other texts featured in *Prolific Ground.* I demonstrate how Montagu's personal correspondence evidences her reliance on the conventions of visual landscape as she constructs a narrative of self-legitimation, compelled by her spectacular (some might say mercenary) marriage, in 1742, to Edward Montagu, grandson of the first Earl of Sandwich. Over a long lifetime, Montagu embraced various scholarly, sociable, commercial, and charitable activities, seeking to prove herself worthy of her fabulous wealth. As an industrialist who ran some of the nation's most profitable coal mines (like Sandleford, also inherited from her husband), she signals the advent of capitalism, which presents a discordant element in her frequently pastoral self-image. I interpret her several attempts to landscape her collieries as a way to cleanse them of the social degradation that she fears may compromise her gentility. Such canny, strategic conduct turns landscape into a means of accommodating herself socially and ideologically to a changing economy in which she finds opportunities to negotiate her independence while still maintaining an investment in the patriarchy.

As seen thus far, a survey of scholarship on landscape demonstrates how easily interpretations of landscape drift into other territory. Writing about landscape seems always to compel one to write about something else: property, prospects, country houses, gardens, the pastoral, Eden, and so forth. *Prolific Ground* aims to resist the conceptual drift that animates the topic while also profiting from its resonant proliferation of meaning. The book historicizes landscape, exposing its profound political and economic import, in order to illuminate how women factor into this history. The range of forms that it covers—poetry, fiction, private letters—attests to the pervasive nature of landscape discourse as well as its decisive impact on women's identity and agency. Finally, the four women featured herein exemplify various responses to patriarchy that testify to both the possibilities and compromises that it presented for women writers.

1
JANE BARKER'S LIMINAL LANDSCAPES

JANE BARKER (1652–1732), THE MOST versatile writer featured in this study, produced an oeuvre that animates the historically unstable meaning of landscape. A poet, novelist, and translator, she transmuted the raw materials of her life into texts that beguile readers who know better than to conflate the author with the voices in her work. Scholars have identified her literary self-invention as a kind of mythmaking, a strategy that suppressed aspects of her biography that she found problematic.[1] A staunch Jacobite and convert to Catholicism, Barker spent fifteen years in exile at Saint Germain-en-Laye outside Paris, where her beloved King James II retreated after the Revolution of 1688.[2] The poetry and fiction that emerged from these experiences bear witness to the artistic strategies that she devised in an evolving effort to denounce Britain's new Parliamentarian regime. Royalism, with an implicit Catholicism, undergirds her quasi-autobiographical project and entails a sociopolitical ethos grounded in landownership. Though not unique to royalists, this ethos manifests in Barker's work through artistic and politically fraught depictions of rural space, exposing a historical struggle over the intertwined sociopolitical and aesthetic significations of land.

The critical bibliography on Barker testifies to the persistent impact of historical contingency on interpretations of her works. As scholars disentangled her life from her work, they confronted the necessity to scrutinize the differences between the two as expressions of Barker's location within a tumultuous phase of British history, as the House of Hanover gradually prevailed over the ousted House of Stuart and Parliament superseded the monarchy.[3] At the same time, Barker's long-lasting and innovative career, which began in manuscript culture and evolved to enter the print marketplace, has variously positioned her as an important and unique voice in the history of British women's writing.[4] She published poetry first, in a 1688 volume entitled *Poetical Recreations*, which featured tributes to her by a Cambridge coterie of male poets. This affiliation, among other factors, has led Kathryn King, the most prolific Barker scholar, to voice skepticism regarding the facile assimilation of her oeuvre into feminist narratives of eighteenth-century British women's writing.[5] Misjudgments of this sort arise, King suggests, when scholars misread or overlook the historical forces that render Barker's conservatism incompatible with modern-day feminism despite her oeuvre's compelling assertion of writing as a means to female independence. Because she cleaved to a political ideology that obsolesced during her lifetime, then, studying Barker requires rigorous attention to historical context in order to understand her protofeminism in all its vexed ambivalence. I contend that landownership, with its gendered social relations and aesthetic adornments, operates in Barker's work as a crucial repository for the precepts that govern women's identity. Such a complex institution is, of course, laden with ideological struggle.

Scholars have also situated Barker within histories of both the romance and the novel, a liminal position that mirrors the transitional phase that her oeuvre exposes, as we will see, in the entwined histories of British landscape and women's writing.[6] Her novels' interpolation of poems—some adapted from the 1688 volume—also garners interest among critics attentive to her generic experimentation.[7] So, too, do they identify significant innovation in the "patchwork" aesthetic of her last two, distinctively episodic novels, *A Patch-Work Screen for the Ladies* (1723) and *The Lining of the Patch Work Screen* (1726).[8] While twentieth-century scholarship often situated Barker within the rise of the novel, more recent criticism expands the scope of her work to include adjacent discourses of Catholicism, sexuality, clothing, medicine, and natural philosophy.[9]

This chapter introduces the sociopolitical history of land into an ongoing critical effort to synthesize Barker's life and work within broader narratives about Britain's political history and evolving perceptions of its women writers. I focus on the three novels known as *The Galesia Trilogy*, which were published over the course of thirteen years, straddling the reigns of Queen Anne, the last Stuart monarch, and George I, the first Hanoverian. Together, the novels depict a decisive transition in the social significance of landownership, especially for women. Indeed, the trilogy's chronological span makes it uniquely suited to chart what I consider a crucial phase in women's relation to landed property. Barker's first novel, *Love Intrigues, or The History of the Amours of Bosvil and Galesia* (1713, 1719, 1736; hereafter *Bosvil and Galesia*) conjures an idyllic world wherein landownership guarantees social harmony among the landowner and his or her dependents.[10] In turn, the *Patch-Work* novels expose the obsolescence of this social order as alternative forms of wealth compete with landownership as the decisive marker of one's identity.[11] Seemingly negligible at first glance, the trilogy's depictions of rural land and the fantasies it propagates expose women's distinctive vulnerability to the evolving sociopolitical valence of landownership.

The generic experimentation that figures so prominently in Barker scholarship makes her trilogy almost impossible to summarize. It consists of a short first novel with a single narrative voice—the heroine's—followed by two longer novels whose multivocal and miscellany-like form includes a dizzying array of genres in prose and verse.[12] *Bosvil and Galesia* fuses a love story with a fictionalized memoir, in which the narrator navigates what appears to be her fate as a romance heroine destined for marriage but instead turns into the uncharted territory of life as an avowed virgin poet. Over the course of a tumultuous courtship with her inscrutable cousin Bosvil, Galesia salves her wounds by learning to manage the family estate and by immersing herself in the life of the mind, writing poetry and studying Latin, anatomy, botany, and herbal medicine with her beloved brother, a medical student. The story ends with the pious heroine reconciled to her unmarried state and confident in "the good Hand of Providence" to keep her from "fall[ing] into Ruin or Confusion."[13]

In the *Patch-Work* sequels, parables, romances, and realist vignettes jostle with a range of versified forms—landscape poetry, pastoral dialogue, and occasional and devotional verse—in addition to recipes, letters, and tales containing letters. These documents constitute the eponymous patches, which a frame narrative stitches together and, in the case of *A Patch-Work Screen,* designates as "Leaves." Readers unfamiliar with Barker's crypto-Jacobite way of storytelling tend to be baffled by the hodgepodge of texts bearing no apparent connection to the heroine's story. The second novel's unifying frame introduces its governing conceit, in which Galesia stumbles upon the country estate of a "good Lady" who asks her guest to join her in making a patchwork screen for the fireside. The papers that fall out of Galesia's trunk instead of clothing thus turn into the screen that the women sew while the heroine explains their provenance. *The Lining* relocates the scene of narration to the aged Galesia's London lodgings, where she receives various guests who tell their stories. Only on the final page does the outermost frame of the patchwork screen reappear, in a telling instance of wish fulfillment wherein the good lady sends her waiting woman to invite Galesia, then entangled in futile urban commerce, "to go into the Country."[14] Thus, in our last glimpse of Galesia, her rural benefactor cossets her in a sumptuous estate such that, although the property does not belong to the heroine, the denouement nevertheless reaffirms access to rural land as a fundamental determinant of her identity. Notwithstanding the trying circumstances that have kept Galesia in London, her return to the countryside endorses a social system that preserves rural landownership as an ideal means to female self-realization.

COMPETING LANDSCAPES

Bosvil and Galesia initiates Barker's three-volume project of constructing Galesia's identity as a poet who cultivates her selfhood through versified and material (agricultural) engagement with the land. The foregoing references to land and landownership demonstrate the need for a third term to specify land that bears the mark of its function in multifarious human endeavors. For my purposes, that term is *landscape*. Such a conception enables us to identify how the heroine hinges her identity, in several decisive ways, on landscape—a versatile concept that instrumentalizes and often aestheticizes land. What we might call her *landscaped* identity emerges most explicitly in the first novel, insofar as it features the uninterrupted narration of Galesia's youthful, ill-fated courtship and her tortuous transformation into a virgin poet and land steward. Seeking solace after an early encounter with Bosvil's mercurial, hot-and-cold conduct, she wanders the countryside and grows inspired to compose poetry that valorizes nature, even inscribing her artistic commitment in the bark of a tree.[15] After an even more egregious instance of Bosvil's inconstancy, she immerses herself in estate management, recuperating her self-worth through the land—that is, grounded private property. Each episode elicits an aspect of her profile, first as a poet and then as a steward surveying and optimizing the estate's productivity.

But it isn't only, or primarily, the convergence of these episodes under the banner of landscape that makes them so compelling. Rather, the tensions that emerge between them bespeak ambiguities that demand to be read historically. For instance, while Galesia the nature poet pursues self-affirmation through aesthetic appreciation for the land, Galesia the estate manager grounds her selfhood in the process of aligning it with the greater good of her community. The resulting contrast between individualist and communitarian values instantiates the competing models of landscape that are at the crux of my argument. The self-interest that undergirds her quest for poetic fame diverges from the selfless stewardship that she practices as an estate manager.

The difficulty of disentangling the threads of Galesia's identity, so far described in terms of tension, illuminates the sociopolitical struggle in Britain over why and how one's identity should be grounded in land. These questions are particularly vexed for women, who (with some spectacular exceptions) tended to be objects rather than owners of property.[16] Indeed, perhaps the most fundamental determinant of Galesia's identity is her gender. Few scholars scrutinize Barker's work without the gender lens, due to her status as a woman writer who narrates and versifies about the life of a woman writer.[17] In the context of these feminist interpretations, Galesia's complex identity and life experience reveal the crucial link between landscape and the pursuit of female independence in the early stages of the long eighteenth century. Because poets and estate managers of the time tended to be male more often than female, it becomes all the more important to scrutinize the two vectors of the heroine's profile in a way that accounts for her groundbreaking pursuit of female independence through engagement with the land.

Adding landscape to a critical conversation that has orbited around the proto-feminist implications of the trilogy illuminates heretofore unnoticed aspects of Galesia's character. While several scholars discuss her attachment to rural life, none delve into the issue in all its historical complexity. For example, Bronwen Price argues that "not until the sequel to Galesia's story, *A Patch-Work Screen for the Ladies* (1723), does she commit herself to [writing poetry] by 'passing my Time in my shady Walks, Fields, and Rural Affairs.'"[18] To be fair, Price focuses on the culturally constructed body and its role in the "retirement mode [of] women's poetry 1680–1723"; she asserts that "the site of retreat, while frequently pastoral, is usually presented in formulaic, undetailed terms, comprising shady groves, secret bowers and private glades. In this sense, it provides a topography which is implicitly feminized."[19] Without discounting the significance of the female body and its symbolic expressions, I take a different tack by asking, first of all, why *topography* and not *landscape*?[20] The "Rural Affairs" in question, and their grouping within one category, demonstrate the conceptual drift to which discussions of land are prone. One might argue that using *topography* as Price does emphasizes Galesia's lived experience of the land, whereas *landscape* shifts emphasis to the heroine's external perceptions—and readers' perceptions of her—as she engages with the land.[21] Regardless, the signal fact is that Galesia's interactions with rural land constitute a key component of her identity. In order to foreground this fact, I favor language that likewise includes the term *land*. Doing so sustains focus on the terrain itself rather than drifting into other territory, be it embodiment, retreat, or the pastoral—itself a freighted category that summons an array of related discourses demanding their own differentiation.

Second of all, I would complicate Price's suggestion that Galesia's "sites of retreat" tend to be formulaic. Elaborate and original landscape description does not occur frequently, to be sure; but when it does, it signifies in multiple ways, not least when prose gives way to verse in Galesia's depictions of her environment. By interpreting the formal modulations of her interactions with the land, and by identifying the historical inflection of these divergent interactions—poet or steward—I emphasize the land's evolving sociopolitical significations. In this way, I disinter the historical context that gives the formula in question its staying power. The prerogatives of landownership undergird Galesia's identity and thus necessitate the possessive pronoun in "*my* shady Walks, Fields, and Rural Affairs" (emphasis added).

The Galesia Trilogy animates the competition between individualist and communitarian landscapes by confronting the heroine with quandaries that require her to choose a course of action that privileges self or other. At the risk of oversimplifying her identity by implementing the individual/collective binary, I propose that this opposition has considerable explanatory power with regard to the meaning and history of British landscape. Moreover, the binary proves especially relevant to an analysis of women's identity formation, given that early modern social norms dictated that women be selfless and derive their identity from service to their family. When we trace how competing models of landscape map onto divergent political orientations, we apprehend how women navigated the material and social determinants of their identity. In sum, Galesia's identity emerges from the dilemma she encounters in being pulled between two distinct political orientations and their corresponding modes of landscape. In this way, the history of landscape also illuminates the history of British women's quest for independence.

History leaves its mark on Galesia's life experience, especially on her imagination, and these marks contribute to Barker's distinctive braiding of eighteenth-century women's writing and landscape. As previously noted, the trilogy's span from 1713 to 1726—encompassing the pivotal Jacobite defeat of 1715—imbues the novels with historic significance.[22] This is true not only for their direct references to historical events but also for the more subtle transformations in the heroine's relationship to rural land. For example, Galesia's identity as a country gentlewoman alters when, following her father's death, she and her mother move to London. Thus, when *A Patch-Work Screen* shifts from a bucolic setting to an urban "Wilderness," it prompts the heroine to imagine the solace and inspiration formerly provided by her rural home (Barker, *A Patch-Work Screen*, 107). Daydreams and other expressions of what she calls "my Fancy" bespeak Galesia's psychological attachment to the countryside (Barker, *A Patch-Work Screen*, 124). The shifting context in which these visions occur demonstrates how her imagination compensates for the loss of an obsolescent landscape. Despite her nostalgia for a retrograde social order, Galesia transforms the self-worth she derived from stewardship into a different form of self-affirmation, one that relies less on the presence of the actual countryside and more on her creative capacity to reproduce it in her mind's eye and in the poems she writes.

The previous references to nature poetry, estate stewardship, and depictions of British landscape signal the abundant terminology that enables us to distinguish subtleties within the realm of the natural world; yet these terms also introduce complications due to their multiple and often unstable meanings. It is notoriously difficult to define *landscape*, though perhaps not as difficult as defining "that amorphous chaos monster known in Western discourse as 'nature.'"[23] We see the potential for slippage among *nature*, *land*, and *landscape* in the preceding discussion, wherein readers may reasonably wonder whether the terms are interchangeable. My argument demands distinctive meanings for each one while also recognizing—and even benefiting from—their overlapping resonances. Stephen Daniels captures this dynamic instability when he identifies "the pressure exerted on landscape [. . .] by cognate concepts such as country, region, land, and nature and the countervailing pressure which landscape exerts upon them."[24] In the present context, *nature*, *land*, and *landscape* perform crucial roles in my argument, and their definitions are at once interdependent and similarly unstable. The trilogy presents a puzzle of sorts, prompting us to ask why it matters that nature and landscape, for instance, have overlapping meanings while also preserving their own unique definitions. For reasons often hard to explain, we know that British nature and British landscape resemble one another while not being quite the same thing.

Given its unique capaciousness, *nature* demands careful scrutiny. Raymond Williams's *Keywords* includes a three-part definition of the term, two of which are relevant for my purposes: "(ii) the inherent force which directs either the world or human beings or both; [and] (iii) the material world itself, taken as including or not including human beings."[25] Following on this definition, the term *land* then refers to the terrain that grounds "the material world" to which Williams refers. While land is characterized by its materiality, such is not the case with nature or landscape. Consequently, literary critics like Garrett Sullivan, art historians like Malcolm Andrews, and cultural geographers like Denis Cosgrove (among others) assert that nature and landscape—unlike land—are social constructs. Cosgrove famously defines landscape as a "way of seeing," and Sullivan complicates this definition by theorizing a nonvisual mode of landscape that constitutes a prehistory for the "social formations" that define Cosgrove's key term.[26] To build upon the truism that landscapes have histories, I use *The Galesia Trilogy* to explore how women participate in these histories in order to contest or complicate their limited access to landownership. By treating Barker's novels as an occasion to historicize landscape, I expose the provisional quality of the term's most common usage as a representation of rural land, or similarly, aestheticized land tout court. Galesia represents rural land in her poetry, but she also inhabits it and defines herself through it in ways that illuminate landscape as the product of a social system with specific prescriptions for women. Rurality is also a fundamental dimension of this phenomenon; Galesia's self-construction necessarily occurs in the countryside and in opposition to urban space. Although the pastoral is an obvious corollary to the various terminology in play, it makes only occasional appearances in my study so that I may develop a distinctive history of landscape rather than one of genre.[27]

Elaborating upon Sullivan's historical model of landscape enables us to situate Galesia's engagements with the land in a centuries-long transformation in the meaning of landscape. He distinguishes between "the landscape arts" (in essence, the landowner's perspective on land, a "landscape of absolute property") and two other key categories—the landscapes of stewardship and of custom. With its quasi-feudal commitment to mutual reciprocity, the landscape of stewardship honors social relations structured around an estate that sustains and is sustained by a benevolent lord and loyal tenants together. Similarly, "the landscape of custom is often compatible with that of stewardship, but it differs in that its emphasis is not on the landlord [but rather on the tenantry]." In both instances, land operates as "a site of customary relations" carried out in accordance with a seemingly natural hierarchical order, and differs from the landscape of absolute property, which entails "a mode of detachment from rather than immersion in the social relations of the estate."[28] *The Galesia Trilogy* offers a compelling addendum to Sullivan's theory by demonstrating that the various landscapes in question do not necessarily operate as successive stages but rather can occur in tandem, and even recursively. Thus, Galesia at times appears to inhabit a landscape of stewardship—or believes herself to do so—but her circumstances change in ways that relocate her to a landscape of absolute property, one that she is nevertheless incapable of recognizing as such. The dissonance that she experiences when the supposedly natural order of her rural home no longer provides her with stability exposes the fragility of what is in fact a changing social—and not natural—order.

This historical contingency undergirds my argument that the trilogy demonstrates how female identity and the history of landscape intersect. Building on previous claims about the link between landscape and female independence, this chapter proceeds by addressing two key factors. First, it traces how pivotal moments in Galesia's self-realization hinge upon her relationship to landscape. Second, it interprets these pivotal moments as instances of the competing landscapes in question and asserts that the rhythm of Galesia's engagements with the land demonstrates the ascendance of visual landscape and the obsolescence of experiential landscape. Operating as corollaries to Sullivan's theory of landscape, *visual landscape* and *experiential landscape* serve as terms that capture the difference between a landscape of absolute property on the one hand—which expresses itself in the landscape arts—and landscapes of custom and stewardship, on the other. Visual landscapes disentangle those privileged to exercise the owner's view of the estate from that estate and its inhabitants. Freed from the responsibility that a landscape of stewardship entails, participants in the landscape arts have the leisure to partake in visual landscape and feel no obligation to the estate's dependents, as they would have under prior models of social relations inhering in the land. By contrast, experiential landscapes lodge inhabitants who understand their status in society as a function of the role they play on a rural estate. Their identity depends on mutual reciprocity rather than individualistic self-construction. Broadly speaking, this schematic conception of landscape has the intricacy to identify subtle changes in its expression and operation, thereby offsetting the proliferation of terminology that the schema necessitates.

In Barker's trilogy, then, the tension between visual and experiential landscapes manifests in successive episodes wherein Galesia appears to inhabit a landscape of absolute property. Their status as such proves questionable, however, when details emerge that redefine her circumstances more properly as a landscape of stewardship and/or custom. As liminal landscapes, these situations engage multiple factors that make it difficult to classify what type of landscape she inhabits. An exemplary liminal landscapes emerges, as I have suggested, when Galesia asserts her authority and independence as an estate steward. Though the episode in question occurs well after she has embraced her identity as a poet, I turn to it first because it depicts the most discrete enactment of the landscape of stewardship in the first novel. Analyzing the circumstances that create such a landscape will enable us, in turn, to recognize its difference from the landscape arts, of which Galesia's poetry is the most decisive—though diffuse—example. Because the verses that I call nature poetry emerge only gradually, over the course of three novels, their legibility as examples of the landscape arts requires more contextualization and interpretation than the stewardship episode. By contrast, this episode consists of half a page wherein Galesia engages with the land in ways that emphasize the independence she derives from her role as steward and produces, then, a landscape of stewardship. At the same time, however, her description uses language that links the scene to a landscape of absolute power. The ambiguity that results from the tension between the two types of landscape exemplifies the liminal landscapes that make *The Galesia Trilogy* a compelling historical record of both the unstable meaning of landscape and women's relationship to it.

LANDSCAPES OF STEWARDSHIP AND ABSOLUTE PROPERTY

Turning to nature for solace may be Galesia's signature move, but only once in the trilogy does she embrace nature by assuming command of the agriculture and husbandry that sustain her family's estate. For over half the course of *Bosvil and Galesia*, she has struggled to maintain her dignity while treading the razor's edge between female propriety and enthusiasm for her suitor's attentions. The precipitating blow comes after Bosvil has promised his undying love for her and then gone home to seek his father's blessing of their marriage. Upon his return, though (and repeating his previous inconstancy), "He came with greater Coldness and Indifferency than ever! No Ray of Love darted from his Eyes, no Sigh from his Heart, no Smile towards me, nothing but a dusky cold Indifferency, as if Love had never shin'd in his Hemisphere" (Barker, *Bosvil and Galesia*, 28). Instead of making his own proposal, as promised, he now "propos[ed] his Friend to my Father as an Husband for me," to which Galesia responds in a letter asking him to "See me no more," meanwhile fantasizing about murdering him to avenge such a betrayal (Barker, 30, 33). When he promises to act "in submission to your Prohibition," she goes on:

> I retir'd into myself, and return'd to my Studies; the Woods, Fields, and Pastures, had the most of my Time, by which Means I became as perfect in rural Affairs as any Arcadian Shepherdess; insomuch, that my Father gave into my Power and Command all his Servants and Labourers; it was I that appointed them their Work, and paid them their Wages; I put in and put out who I pleas'd, and was as absolute over my Rusticks, as the Great Turk over his Subjects; and tho' this was a great Fatigue, yet it

> gratify'd my Vanity, that I was suppos'd able to perform Things above my Age and Sex, and tho' it was an Impediment to my Studies, yet it made Amends, it being itself a Study, and that a most useful one: The Rules to sow and reap in their Season; to know what Pasture is fit for Beeves, what for Sheep, what for Kine, with all their Branches, being a more useful Study than all the Grammar Rules, or Longitude or Latitude, Squaring the Circle, &c. (Barker, 34, 35)

A tour de force in establishing Galesia's resilience, resourcefulness, and ambition, the passage attests to both her versatility and the authority she derives specifically from her knowledge of the land. And because the passage adds a new dimension to her identity, investing her with the "Power and Command [over] all his Servants and Labourers," it also transmutes the land into a landscape, a set of social relations wherein the estate steward and her dependents inhabit identities determined by their relation to the land.

The case of Galesia as estate steward presents an instructive example of a landscape that could conceivably be seen as either one of absolute property or of stewardship—or even of both at once. Thus, the passage refracts the several meanings of landscape previously discussed, making it a compelling condensation of the competing versions that the novel engages. The uncertainty hinges on her supposition of a natural hierarchical order, which dictates both her "absolute" "Power and Command" and the submission of the "Servants and Labourers." Such a vision of the natural order assigns roles based on status rather than contract; being a gentleman's daughter qualifies her to issue orders to those beneath her in status. One might argue, then, that although her authoritarian pronouncements may strike us as overbearing (and absolutist), they also encode her unquestioned position in a fixed hierarchy that legitimates her actions, which aim for the proper functioning of the estate if not for the comfort of each and every "Rustick." A steward performing her proper role and ensuring that her dependents do theirs, Galesia enacts a conception of land as the source of both her and their identities. Profit does not enter into the equation, nor does the stature that might come with a newly thriving or improved estate. These factors indicate that stewardship prevails over absolute property in the episode's representation of landscape.[29]

Nevertheless, Galesia's own language complicates what appears to be a landscape of stewardship, making it plausible to read the scene instead as an instance of absolute property. She claims, "[I] was as *absolute* over my Rusticks, as the Great Turk over his Subjects," implying that her prerogative as the lord's (her father's) daughter and steward trumps any controverting claim to the land she is managing (emphasis added). Her explicit reference to the payment of wages locates her in a proto-capitalist economy in which wages have replaced customary rights and privileges as compensation for labor. Ultimately, neither stewardship nor absolute property adequately describes Barker's depiction of landscape in this scene, an ambiguity that arises in part from the ideological malleability of stewardship itself. The various implications of Galesia's stewarding practices reveal how both stewardship and absolute property avail themselves of the logic of a putatively natural social hierarchy, which assigns identity according to one's relation to the land. Thus, the landed authority that Galesia exerts over the family estate expresses her position in the social hierarchy while also exposing both obsolescent and emergent forms of social relations inhering in the land. The overlapping and often contradictory modes of landscape manifest the ideological volatility of landscape discourse. This insight positions us to grasp the conflicted process by which the landscape arts displaced and occluded other, less privileged expressions of landscape such as that of stewardship.

Turning to the poetic dimension of the Galesia novels, we encounter an array of scenes that likewise produce ambiguous and thus liminal landscapes. The scene where the heroine first embraces her identity as a poet exemplifies several of the milestones that collectively determine her identity. Set against the backdrop of her rural home, the incident conjoins Galesia's poetic and pastoral proclivities in ways that evoke both visual and experiential landscape. The liminality arises from the fact that contextual detail makes her landscape legible through both visual and experiential lenses. The rural setting that precipitates and marks her first poetic utterance initially emerges as a visual spectacle of natural beauty, thus rendering her a participant in the landscape arts. But later in the novel, as we have seen, the country estate featuring in this spectacle also incites her to steward the land in ways that call forth its instrumental (experiential) rather than aesthetic (visual) value. Furthermore, her performance as a steward of the land and its dependents signals her quest for independence ("I was suppos'd able to perform Things above my Age and Sex"). Yet, this component of the scene also fractures the landscape of stewardship because Galesia, while deriving authority from her management of the land, also avows an individualistic satisfaction in her mastery, thus evoking a landscape of absolute property wherein individuality trumps community-centered values.

In the final analysis, Galesia's estate management most often situates her in landscapes of stewardship and custom, while her poetry locates her in the realm of the landscape arts. These competing aspects of her identity—estate manager or nature poet—exemplify how landscape relations encode social relations, and how our perception of her social position changes depending on which aspect of her profile we privilege. Yet it is important to acknowledge the fleeting quality of Galesia's immersion in estate management. For all the fortitude and self-confidence she expresses as a land steward, her performance of this role does not last. Shortly after this scene, her brother returns from his studies in France and renews her interest in herbal medicine. But while leaving the impression that estate management was just a passing fancy, she still continues to write poetry. The last installment of verse in *Bosvil and Galesia* laments the disgrace she suffers at her beloved's betrayal and the hopelessness brought on by the realization that she will never marry. She despairs that

> *Heaven [. . .]*
> *Knows the just Schemes of my intended Life,*
> *To be the chast, the cheerful, faithful Wife:*
> *A vertuous Matron to my Household good,*
> *A helpful Neighbor in my Nighborhood.*[30]

A lamentation for such traditional female roles undermines any lingering impression that the heroine derives her identity from being "able to perform Things above [her] Age and Sex." By retreating from the authority of a land steward and instead conforming to expectation by embracing woman's ideal role as a housewife, Galesia forecloses the transgressive ambition that flickered on the horizon of her path to independence. Not until *A Patch-Work Screen* does she return her attention to the land in any depth. In sum, her interest in land stewardship fades from view while her poetic responsiveness to nature endures and grows even more potent in the second novel. Yet Galesia's retreat from estate management by no means invalidates the landscape of stewardship. She continues to valorize a social hierarchy grounded in rural landownership even when circumstances reduce her to a guest rather than an authority in such a landscape. In this sense, the competition between landscapes continues to play out over the trilogy, but from now on she endorses and benefits from landscapes of stewardship rather than presiding over one herself.

Politics, meanwhile, hovers over these competing landscapes and imbues them with the politically coded meanings that undergird Galesia's various assertions of social position. The tumultuous politics of the late seventeenth century appear in the first paragraph of Barker's 1713 novel: "King *James's* Affairs [had] so turn'd Things in *Europe*, that the War between *France* and the Allies was almost like a Civil War" (7). Similar comments throughout the trilogy remind us that the landscapes in question are historically contingent, and intimate that the heroine's family history effectively bequeaths her the Jacobite political orientation to which she repeatedly alludes. Thus, her self-perception as an inhabitant of a landscape of stewardship bespeaks her attachment to a retrograde political order, while the incursions of a landscape of absolute property conjure the Whig ascendancy that hovers on the horizon. Barker's well-documented Jacobitism marks the various landscapes of stewardship that her heroine inhabits, often but not always valorizing a political commitment to monarchy and the principles of legitimate succession.[31]

A brief turn to a contemporaneous source, Joseph Addison's *Spectator* number 414 (1712) offers a Whiggish example of landscape discourse that elevates the individual above the community. A consummate Whig, Addison frames his conception of the land such that a gentleman produces his identity through a process of shaping his private property so as to provide himself with visual pleasure. He articulates, then, a converse conception of landscape compared to the landscape of stewardship that Galesia most identifies with. While criticizing what he considers the excessive "Neatness and Elegancy" of English gardens, Addison asserts:

> It might, indeed, be of ill Consequence to the Publick, as well as unprofitable to private Persons, to alienate so much Ground from Pasturage, and the Plow, in many Parts of a Country that is so well peopled, and cultivated to a far greater Advantage. But why may not a whole Estate be thrown into a kind of Garden by frequent Plantations, that may turn as much to the Profit, as the Pleasure of the Owner? [. . .] Fields of Corn make a pleasant Prospect, and if the Walks were a little taken care of that lie between them, if the natural Embroidery of the Meadows were helpt and improved by some small Additions of Art, and the several Rows of Hedges set off by Trees and Flowers, that the Soil was capable of receiving, a Man might make a pretty Landskip of his own Possessions.[32]

Addison's public/private schema implies his sense of responsibility to weigh the two realms in relation to one another, and to perceive their interdependence in matters relating to the extent of untilled land. His conclusion that "a whole Estate [. . .] might make a pretty Landskip of his own Possessions" exemplifies the individualism (not to mention masculinity) that is a hallmark of Whiggism. Meanwhile, his now-obsolete spelling of "Landskip" signals his own participation in the historical evolution of landscape, locating himself at a moment when the term is hewing toward a visual more than experiential meaning. Finally, in its pursuit of landscape as a mode of self-interest, the Whig model brings to mind the enthusiasm for estate improvement that Jane Austen was to satirize in *Mansfield Park* (1814) through her portrayal of Henry Crawford, a modish but ultimately depraved estate improver.

Bearing in mind Barker's ardent Jacobitism in addition to a sense of its difference from Whig approaches to landscape, we return to Galesia's liminal landscapes with a refined perception of their ambiguous political valence. When the heroine embraces her role as an estate steward, she grounds both her own identity and that of her dependents in their mutually determining relationships to the land. The historical component of my argument thus situates Galesia's expressions of landed authority at a liminal moment in the genealogy of British landscape, when landscapes of stewardship and custom have not yet ceded to landscapes of absolute property, the socioeconomic corollary, in Sullivan's theory, to the landscape arts.

POLITICS, FORMAL HYBRIDITY, AND THE BELATED LANDSCAPE ARTS

When Galesia's rural home inspires her poetic creativity, she expresses an aesthetic sensibility that makes her a participant in the landscape arts. It is noteworthy that she chooses poetry as the ideal form for aesthetic expression—a choice that demands to be read historically given her inheritance of a centuries-long poetic tradition that valorizes and politicizes rural retirement.[33] Likewise significant is the trilogy's formal hybridity. Margaret Ezell suggests that Barker interpolated verse into her fiction as a way to both correct errors in her unauthorized volume of verse, *Poetical Recreations*, and to make her poetry available to a wider audience.[34] Status no doubt also motivates Barker's formal decisions; integrating verse into her fiction enables her to compensate for the degradation of the novel form.[35] As we will see, social anxiety also manifests in the specific contexts that prompt Galesia to shift from prose to verse—and to nature poetry specifically. These formal maneuvers demonstrate how her conflicted identity expresses itself through aestheticized landscape and its corollary landscape of absolute property. Moreover, the landscaped components of her profile align her with the modernity typically associated with capitalism. This alignment justifies adding landscape to the commercial and political factors, leading King to argue that "if anyone in this period sought to chart the emergent modern self in its sometimes baffling singularity, it was Jane Barker."[36] Modifying King's analysis in this way illuminates how the trilogy creates a complex relationship between historical contingency and literary form, particularly with regard to the land. The fluctuating landscape relations embedded in the texts' formal hybridity testify to the unique capacity for landownership to facilitate female independence. Whether stewarding her family estate or versifying about the land, Galesia's engagements with it signal her grasp of its sociopolitical value.

Consider once again how Barker's novels enact the transitional or liminal quality of landscape relations. These coincide with the novels' formal hybridity, linking historical and formal change so as to expose their mutual impact. In effect, the evolution in the meaning of landscape is imbricated with the evolution of Galesia's character. This imbrication in turn renders her self-expression in verse legible as a socially determined and aesthetic creation. Careful analysis of her poetry reveals how her indeterminate location within a landscape of absolute property, on the one hand, or of stewardship and custom on the other, produces a comparable indeterminacy in the text's form. A novelistic narrative with frequently interpolated verse demonstrates, in the most basic terms, that the textual rendition of Galesia's life story alternates between two different modes, which express the instability and ambivalence of the heroine's negotiation of evolving landscape relations.

The first instance of this formal shift occurs when Bosvil first disappoints Galesia. As she describes the circumstances of her devastation, she insinuates how a different mode of expression—verse instead of prose—enables her to withstand and perhaps overcome her grief. The sources of solace in this scene turn out to be both nature and versification, and the integration of the two indicates how engagement with the land both entices and eludes her. In other words, the land initially dazzles her, and this experience has a transformative effect on her mode of expression such that poetry displaces land as the primary source of wonder. These shifts expose her uncertainty about which element—nature or poetry—will serve as the fulcrum for her emergent identity and the focus of her art. Just as she vacillates, over the course of the novels, between inhabiting a landscape of stewardship or of absolute property, so, too, does she drift from one form of solace to another, revealing the instability in her identity formation.

Prior to the moment in question, Galesia has explained how Bosvil "consulted my Father about a certain Neighboring Gentlewoman, who was propos'd to him in Marriage." Stricken by this betrayal, she wants nothing more than to be alone.

> This Solitude I sought was not hard to be found, our Habitation being situate in a remote Country Village where one has full Opportunity to sooth and cajole Melancholy,'till it becomes rampant, and hardly to be restrain'd. Sometimes I endeavour'd to divert my Chagrin, by contemplating, in these shady Walks, the wonderful Works of the Creation. In the Spring methought the Earth was dress'd in new Apparel, the soft Meadow Grass was as a Robe of green Velvet imbroider'd with Pearls and Diamonds, compos'd of the Evening Dew, which the Sun's Morning Rays made bright and sparkling; all the Borders curiously lac'd with chequer'd Work of Sun and Shade, caus'd by the Trees and Hedges. It was in one of these solitary Walks that my rolling Thoughts turn'd themselves into these Verses.
>
> *Methinks these Shades strange thoughts suggest.* (13–14)

The passage constitutes a rare example of what we now call landscape in the most common sense—that is, a depiction of rural scenery. But consider how the passage also situates Galesia at a decisive juncture in her development—brokenhearted yet resourceful, melancholy yet able to use that feeling to conjure a new vista of possibility. Some uncertainty underlies the articulation of her emotions in this scene, the gist of which is to convey her desire to overcome the melancholy induced by Bosvil's betrayal. For example, "to sooth and cajole Melancholy" seemingly expresses two contrary strategies, since "soothing" would presumably lessen that feeling, while "cajoling" could heighten it. Such incoherent emotions, which catch her in dynamic suspension between resisting and reveling in her grief, express the quandary she faces as a lovelorn, talented, and versatile young gentlewoman. Her ambiguous language has both sociopolitical and emotional explanations. In order to grasp the former, we must treat the turn from prose to verse as a likewise politically inflected maneuver.

Galesia's nature poetry, I argue, arises in part from her location within a historical moment when partisan politics take poetic form in versified celebrations of rural retirement. *Bosvil and Galesia*'s allusions to royalist poets such as Katherine Philips and Abraham Cowley (Barker's fellow in exile) signal the heroine's mastery of a tradition that makes a virtue of rejecting tainted urban and courtly intrigue. Conversely, she earns virtue by fashioning her private selfhood in the pure environment of the countryside. Politics appear in the novel almost immediately, as it opens with a rueful explanation of her father's political misfortunes. The first paragraph of "The History of Galesia" (following an introductory paragraph told by an omniscient narrator) provides the political context in question: "My Father (said *Galesia*) and all his Family being of the Loyal Party, in the Time of King *Charles* the First, is a sufficient Demonstration of the Non–existence of Riches amongst them; for some were in Battel slain, and some in Prison dy'd; some ruin'd in their Estates, some in their Persons, and so (like most of the Adherents to the Royal Cause) were unhappy" (7–8). The distance between the two passages in question—Galesia's explanation of her family history and her landscape description (which appears some five pages later)—obscures the link between the historical and personal dimensions of her dilemma. But for Galesia to frame her tale with a description of its historical context compels readers to make a connection between political and personal experience. The "ruin'd [. . .] estates" of her kinsmen specify land as one site of contestation in this power struggle, a circumstance that impacts her personal experience even though she may not elaborate upon that impact herself. Though she never claims the Civil Wars ruined her immediate family's estate, the passage specifies that they witnessed such ruin in close proximity, and it informed her perception of their situation.

The next sentence delineates how the political tumult upended her own family: "My Father, in particular, lost a very honourable and profitable Place at Court; after which he retir'd into the Country, leading a very private, or rather obscure Life, just above the Contempt of Poverty, and below that Envy which attends Riches, of which he laid aside all Hopes" (8). Thus, Galesia situates her youth within the context of politically imposed rural retirement, a consequence of her father's allegiance to "the Loyal Party." The political turmoil has, in effect, destabilized the family's relationship to land such that they now inhabit a precarious "retir[ement in] the Country." The father's removal from court to country relocates himself and his family to a rural setting where their specific engagements with the land result in an evolving range of landscape relations. As we have seen, his daughter takes pride in her role in a landscape of stewardship, but intimations of absolutism ("[I] was as *absolute* over my Rusticks, as the Great Turk over his Subjects") bespeak the instability of this obsolescent relation to the land.

The text's exposition of the family's political circumstances also predisposes readers to see the subtext in Galesia's description of the scene that inspired her first verses. By dressing the land in the lavish adornments that a monarch would wear—"a Robe of green Velvet imbroider'd with Pearls and Diamonds"—she intimates her sympathy for the royalist cause (and offers an ironic spin on Addison's previously mentioned "natural Embroidery of the Meadows"). The passage parses, then, as an instantiation of the landscape arts wherein Whiggish values are inchoate, insofar as Galesia aestheticizes rural land and privileges the pleasure it offers over the responsibility it confers. Yet at the same time, the passage's figuration of royalism turns a beautiful spectacle into an avowal of loyalty to the crown. The "chequer'd Work of Sun and Shade" acquires new meaning in light of this political subtext, exposing the contrast in the heroine's backward- and forward-facing entanglements with the land.

Though family history and personal proclivity contribute to Galesia's various engagements with the land, at times she figures her poetic inspiration as an external force rather than a product of her own character. The final phrase in the passage preceding her first verse, when her "rolling Thoughts turn'd themselves into these Verses," suggests something transformative in the shift from prose to verse; investing her thoughts with the agency to generate a new mode of expression implies something almost magical in the process. Given her profound investment in being a poet (discussed hereafter), the notion of her thoughts taking on a life of their own and generating a precious product—poetry—conjures a preternatural force that takes possession of Galesia.

Whatever their source, her thoughts precipitate a similar transformation of the land she sees while hearing the muses ("Methinks I hear the Muses sing"), resulting in a poem that intimates her potential to put land at the center of her verses (14). In its visual orientation, Galesia's poetry gradually transmutes the land into the realm of the landscape arts, thus foregrounding a form of landscape with subtle differences from that of stewardship. These competing landscapes, which position visually oriented nature poetry (the landscape arts) against experience (stewardship), emerge more gradually than the narrative distillation of competing landscapes described above. Understanding how her poetry operates within this competition requires reading from a distance, as it were, rather than close up, as seen in the "chequer'd" landscape above. A distanced view of Galesia's poetry reveals the gradual displacement of visual for experiential landscapes. More precisely, her production of nature poetry complicates her location in a landscape of absolute property as evidenced in her participation in the landscape arts. The complication arises from the belated appearance of fully realized nature poetry until *A Patch-Work Screen for the Ladies*. The delay reveals, as we will see, that the heroine's versified visualization of land grows more pronounced only once she has left the scene that inspires her verses. The first novel's poetic rendition of the landscape arts therefore proves less decisive than the second novel's poems, suggesting the prevalence of nonvisual—and prosaic—landscapes early on in the heroine's development.

While Galesia's inaugural poem may evoke without sustaining the landscape arts, it also features her affinity for the land and propensity to ground her creativity in aesthetic responsiveness to landscape. "Methinks these Shades strange Thoughts suggest," the first full-fledged poem to appear in *Bosvil and Galesia*, consists of six three-line stanzas. The poem conjures the landscape arts insofar as they value the land for its capacity to provide visual pleasure and other forms of sensory fulfillment, as seen in the first two stanzas:

> *Methinks these Shades strange Thoughts suggest,*
> *Which beat my Head, and cool my Breast,*
> *And mind me of a Lawrel Crest.*
>
> *Methinks I hear the Muses sing,*
> *And see 'em all dance in a Ring,*
> *And call upon me to take Wing.*
> (14)

"[T]hese Shades" in line one limn a landscape without fully realizing it, eliciting "strange Thoughts" of artistic fame ("a Lawrel Crest"). But the natural imagery does not elaborate a rural scene that lends itself to visualization—unless one visualizes Galesia inscribing her vow to remain a virgin on the tree trunk, as the Muses later invite her to do ("Write, write thy Vow upon this Tree"). In sum, Galesia's first poem intimates how land may inspire aesthetic pleasure, but such pleasure ultimately resides in versification rather than land.

Initially, then, Galesia's first verses feature natural imagery without quite inhabiting the category of nature poetry. The timing of this transmutation of land into landscape proves significant, suggesting that the heroine has recourse to aesthetic appreciation in order to compensate for her removal—in *A Patch-Work Screen*—from the landscape that inspired her verses. Moreover, aestheticized landscape encodes not only her removal from rural land but also her downward movement in the social hierarchy, occasioned by her father's death in the second novel. These circumstances reinforce the seemingly natural alignment of rural gentility, virtuous femininity, and versification that, together, constitute the essence of her identity. *Bosvil and Galesia* establishes these traits and hints at Galesia's habitual use of visual landscape as the basis for her virgin-poet persona.

In the same way that *Bosvil and Galesia* swerves backward and forward, inhabiting a landscape of stewardship in one scene and the landscape arts in the next (and sometimes both simultaneously), so, too, do the poems in this novel depict fitful swerving from one set of relations with the land to another. One such foray into the landscape arts appears in another poem, which addresses Galesia's capacity to find solace in the landscape's beauty—her capacity, that is, to participate in the landscape arts. The poem thus complements the novel's representation of the liminal landscape that the heroine inhabits. Whereas "Methinks these shades strange thoughts suggest" depicts the landscape arts hovering, if you will, in her peripheral vision, the next substantial poem (consisting of more than three lines) foregrounds her aesthetic appreciation for nature by lamenting how her broken heart impedes her receptive capacity. Thus, her first poem describes her "contract with the muses," while her next one reveals how an appreciation for nature serves as her standard for measuring the extent of her happiness.[37] Ironically, the second poem positions Galesia within the landscape arts by depicting her inability to engage them when her beloved seems to have forsaken her yet again: "Nothing at present wonted Pleasure yields, / The Birds, nor Bushes, nor the gaudy Fields." Despite this purported incapacity, however, the components of aestheticized land—"gaudy Fields," copses ("Oiser Holts"), "soft Meadow Grass," and "flow'ry Banks of [the River] Glenn"—all coalesce to create a picture of Galesia straining to practice the landscape arts, such that her perception of failure nevertheless marks a more fundamental affinity for them (20).

LAYERED LANDSCAPES IN *A PATCH-WORK SCREEN FOR THE LADIES*

The second novel of the trilogy stages the landscape of stewardship prior to introducing subtle incursions of the proto-capitalist landscape of absolute property. Like *Bosvil and Galesia*, the sequel intertwines prose and verse in ways that simultaneously pull the heroine backward, toward a landscape of stewardship, and forward, toward the landscape arts, realized primarily through poetry. The sequel features the full flowering of the heroine's nature poetry, in an episode whose circumstances are the converse of "Nothing at present wonted pleasure yields." Whereas the earlier poem depicts Galesia's purported inability to find solace in nature, the first poem in *A Patch-Work Screen* shows her doing just that. The latter poem also perpetuates the competition between landscapes that emerges in the first novel, participating in the landscape arts by portraying land as a source of visual pleasure while also constructing a rural scene that valorizes an ostensibly natural hierarchical order embedded in estate stewardship.

The landscape arts may be peripheral in the first Galesia novel, but they prove more significant when we expand the scope of inquiry to include all three novels. From this vantage, we see that aestheticized land first occupies the periphery, when she versifies about becoming a poet while grounded in a rural setting. This landscape then moves to the center of her poetry when, having lived in London, she shares poetry about the countryside with her benevolent country-house hostess. The gradual focus on visual landscape evidences the shifting meaning of landscape itself. Over the course of three novels, readers witness the transformation of a heroine at first embedded in the landscape that moves her to write and then absent from it, remembering. Landscape's role in the emergence of Galesia's artistic identity thus proves most discernible when assessed as a trajectory rather than a singular, decisive moment. As mentioned above, the timing of the transmutation of land into landscape proves significant, suggesting that the heroine has recourse to aesthetic appreciation as compensation for her removal from the landscape that inspired her verses. By tracing the gradual emergence of poetic landscapes in the trilogy, we perceive the instantiation of landscape in poetic form as evidence of its increasingly aesthetic meaning.

Poems with rural settings constitute important "patches" in *A Patch-Work Screen for the Ladies*, bolstering Galesia's identity as a female poet whose selfhood is planted in the countryside. The novel resumes the heroine's story where the first one left off and features its narrator's status in its very title. The contrast between the structurally and thematically unified *Bosvil and Galesia*, on the one hand, and the episodic and seemingly scattershot *Patch-Work Screen*, on the other, makes the second novel's reliance on landscape discourse less prominent than that of the first. But the second novel's inclusion of "a Landskip in Verse," consisting of poems entitled "The *Grove*" and "The *Rivulet*," mitigates its thematic and formal deviation from the first novel. The novel's subtitle even calls attention to its poetic contents, presenting a series of "Instructive Novels [. . .] Interspersed with Rural Poems, / describing the Innocence of a Country-Life." By foregrounding its integration of poetry—and "Rural Poems" specifically—the title page signals the text's investment in rurality, drawing out its other key commitment, to female virtue (49). Thus, *A Patch-Work Screen* announces its grounding in the countryside and makes explicit the moral component that was implicit in the first Galesia novel, entwining rural life and female virtue such that neither one seems possible without the other. Furthermore, by surpassing the first novel's intimation of visual landscape in verse, the second novel extends Galesia's commitment to the landscape arts even though urban life threatens to smother it.

Although multiple layers of landscape in prose precede the appearance of "The *Grove*," taking an initial glimpse at its robust visual rendering of the land demonstrates how it offers the trilogy's most fully realized nature poem, and thus the texts' poetic realization of the landscape arts. The poem's visual figuration occurs—not coincidentally, to be sure—in sartorial and ceremonial imagery, thus reinforcing the trilogy's Jacobite orientation. While exalting the grove as "The sacred Mansion of some deity," the speaker invests the land with aesthetic value by dressing it in sumptuous garments and then transfiguring it into a space adorned with other accoutrements of royal splendor. The first stanza, on how the grove inspires the soul with fear and love, concludes with the first sartorial reference, and the next stanza elaborates on the image of the earth's clothing.

> The worst that can be said of it, 'tis *rude*.
> Yet *Nature's Culture* is so well express'd,
> That *Art* herself would wish to be so dress'd.
> Lo! here the *Sun* conspires with ev'ry Tree,

> To deck the *Earth* in Landskip-Tapistry:
> Then thro' some Space his brightest Beams appear,
> Erecting a bright golden Pillar there.
> Here a close Canopy of Boughs is made;
> There a soft grassy Cloth of State is spread;
> With Gems and gayest Flow'rs imbroider'd o'er,
> Fresh as those Beauties honest Swains adore.
> (77)

By dressing nature in the lavish adornments that a monarch would wear, Galesia ennobles the land while also naturalizing the nobility. Echoing the "Robe of green Velvet imbroider'd with Pearls and Diamonds" that she previously envisioned when contemplating the fields in springtime, the foregoing lines portray the land as decked "in Landskip-Tapistry" and then as "a soft grassy Cloth of State."[38] In conjuring such vivid images, the lines emphasize the play of light on the land, tracing and revering the very source of visual experience—something we will also see Anne Finch do in chapter 2. And by depicting the sunbeams shining through the trees, contrasting the "Brightest beams" and the "close Canopy of Boughs," the poem extends its play between light and dark, this time echoing the "chequer'd Work of Sun and Shade" that Galesia saw in the land just before composing her very first verses.[39] The second stanza thus summons a courtly spectacle in the forest, revealing the heroine's instinctive reliance on royal regalia as a means to honor the hallowed grove.[40] The way the poem stages this spectacle augments the novel's participation in the landscape arts, in part by planting the verses within a scene featuring visual complexity of a complementary, aesthetic kind.

Meanwhile, Barker extends the competition among landscapes initiated in *Bosvil and Galesia*, adding scenes to the sequel that evoke the entire landscape spectrum—stewardship, custom, and the arts. The bucolic scene in which Barker presents "The *Grove*" exemplifies the layering of landscape that evolves over the entire trilogy. We gain full appreciation for the aesthetic impact of "The *Grove*" only by studying Barker's framed and framing artistry. *A Patch-Work Screen*'s episodic structure uses the heroine as its through line but without featuring her in every episode. The novel begins with a preface "To the Reader," followed by an "Introduction" featuring five framed narratives that bear no apparent relevance to the heroine's rural life (and comprise just over a tenth of the novel's length) (51, 55). Next, we encounter the novel's governing framework: Galesia's reception at a country estate by the benevolent lady of the eponymous patchwork screens. In the prelude to this reception, Galesia gets lost in "a fine Park," only to be rescued by its lady, who welcomes her guest to stay and keep her company while working together on the screens. In response to the lady's invitation, the heroine settles upon the "Pieces of *Romances, Poems, Love-Letters,* and the like" when her trunk spills these out instead of the "Wearing Cloaths" she had intended to offer

(72, 74). The novel's subsequent four "Leaves" intermingle the consecutive stages of the heroine's life with other stories she recalls from her past or hears about while living in London. The arboreal imagery of the "Leaves" and "The *Grove*" refract that of the park where she loses her way, producing a mirroring effect that subsumes her own writing within the material traces of rural life. The interleaved narrative and verse likewise entwine the different types of landscape: the lady's warm reception of Galesia produces a landscape of stewardship within which the text layers several iterations of the landscape arts, in the form of patches featuring "rural Poems" such as "The *Grove*."

The tension between the idyllic life of the countryside and the turbulent experiences Galesia endures in the novel's interior Leaves thus produces the incommensurable strata of stewardship, on the one hand, and the landscape of absolute property, on the other. The landscape arts, meanwhile, play a liminal role, overlapping with and complementing the landscape of stewardship in a way that masks their affiliation with a contrary, proto-capitalist landscape of absolute property. Such a taxonomy of landscape may bewilder those struggling to reconcile the term's dominant usage with the historical distinctions of my three-part model. Bewilderment of this sort actually resembles the vertiginous effect of Barker's own patchwork strategy, suggesting how complex texts require comparable theoretical tools to make sense of them. As the robust scholarship demonstrates, the patchwork novels have generated a lively critical conversation. Karen Gevirtz, for example, positions the topic within the context of natural philosophy, providing a provocative complement to the purposeful layering effect between prelude and poem under discussion here. She interprets the complexity of Barker's frame structure as a manifestation of her insistence that knowledge is communally based rather than issuing from a stable and self-knowing individual: "Each framed narrative offers one perspective but only one; each is a piece of a larger puzzle that is more completely assembled when other framed narratives are used to illuminate the issue."[41]

For my purposes, the limitation of a single perspective proves especially germane with regard to landscape. In tracing the convergence, or coexistence, of several modes of landscape, I emphasize Galesia's limited perspective on the meaning and value of this phenomenon, as seen when she believes she inhabits one type of landscape while readers realize her occupation of another. Our wider vantage allows us to recognize how the trilogy uses the landscape of stewardship to valorize and naturalize a social hierarchy, all the while occluding objections, modifications, or threats to that hierarchy. Yet as we will see, certain features of the Galesia novels expose traces of an alternative landscape based less on reciprocity than on financial volatility. Thus, the trilogy produces multiple perspectives on landownership from which readers can infer the landscape of stewardship's vulnerability to co-optation.

The structural emphasis on a harmonious and beautiful landscape of stewardship manifests Barker's ideological commitment, foregrounding the landscapes she wishes and imagines her heroine to inhabit—that is, stewardship and custom—while relegating the threatening landscape of absolute property to peripheral and seemingly negligible episodes later in the novel. Featured prior to "Leaf I," *A Patch-Work Screen*'s outermost frame with its country-house setting occupies a privileged position by virtue of the fact that it contains most of the novel's contents (aside from the five initial frame narratives). Similar to the estate management scene in *Bosvil and Galesia*, then, the sequel's unifying frame situates the heroine in a landscape of stewardship that later proves to be ceding to a landscape of absolute property. The Introduction opens with this observation: "When we parted from Galesia last, it was in St. Germain's Garden; and now we meet with her in England, travelling in a Stage-Coach from London Northward" (55). Thus, the narrative glances backward, to the heroine's experience as a Jacobite exile, before turning toward her future, in a pastoral transition whereby she leaves the city to visit a place that resembles the rural scene of her youth.

Near the end of the stagecoach journey, Galesia's travels go awry when, as the last passenger, she is overturned from the coach into a river. The next day, having mostly recovered, she sets out on foot for the town where she can catch the next stage northward. Finding herself in "a fine Park, amongst Trees, Firs, Thickets, Rabbet-burrows," and at a loss what to do, she ambles through the park and overhears the sounds of a hunt underway. Meanwhile, the lady of the estate, who is participating in the hunt, resolves "to walk home over the Park, it being a fine smooth Walk betwixt two Rows of Lime trees, planted and grown in exact Form, agreeable to the Eye, pleasing to the Smell, and making a most delightful Shade" (72–73). At once pleasurable and purposeful, the Park exemplifies its owners' commitment to the Horatian principle of *utile dulci*, hinting at the congenial reception Galesia will find there while also insinuating the governing principle behind the scene's synthesis of stewardship and the landscape arts. The lady then happens upon Galesia, and thus begins the heroine's serendipitous welcome into a country house by a solicitous hostess who "diverted her, by shewing *Galesia* her Gardens, House, and glorious Appartments, adorn'd with rich Furniture of all Sorts; some were the Work of hers and her Husband's Ancestors, who delighted to imploy poor Gentlewomen, thereby to keep them from Distress, and evil Company, 'till Time and Friends could dispose Things for their better Settlement" (74). The episode thus begins with Galesia getting lost in the park and told by the birds to "*Sit thee down*" and "*Chear-up*," and then shows her being found there, offered shelter, and invited to assist in making a screen.

All told, the sequential events represent an assemblage of landscape-arts-in-the-making and a stewarded (and stewarding) landscape that, together, conjure a precapitalist world not yet corrupted by exploitation. The landscape of stewardship permeates the Introduction with its references to anthropomorphized birds and "the Rows of Lime trees, planted and grown in exact Form," depicting a cultivated space wherein avian and arboreal nature gives succor to its inhabitants, and so in turn does the lady when she invites Galesia to stay. Meanwhile, the landscape arts overlay these manifestations of stewardship and custom, making a beautiful spectacle of the rural scenery and interior design that dazzle Galesia and her hostess.

Taking a distanced survey of the complex representation of the lady's estate, we see how much energy Barker invests in constructing a pastoral enclave in which to secure her heroine from the vagaries of capital. The estate's natural economy promises to sustain Galesia prior to her meeting its lady, who presides over a natural order the benevolence of which is reinforced by the charitable ancestors who engage in the mutually beneficial enterprise of employing needy women in exchange for a worthwhile service. The chain of interdependence proceeds from the land itself to the fauna who provision their lord and lady, just as the poor gentlewomen do by working on the screens, in turn receiving sustenance themselves. Galesia participates in this microeconomy by agreeing to help complete the lady's screen, contributing items from her trunkful of manuscripts. The narrative prelude to "The *Grove*" thus situates the heroine in an environment where both animate and inanimate nature nurture one another, creating a landscape of stewardship, and a complementary landscape of custom, in which Galesia's poetry may thrive.

Further scrutiny reveals an even more complex interweaving of stewardship and the landscape arts, a result of "The *Grove*"'s participation in this layering effect. The accumulation of visual detail in both the prose and verse portions of the text thus amounts to a subtle but nevertheless crucial shift in the novel's representation of landscape, from experiential renditions such as stewardship to visual renditions such as the patchwork screens' nature poems. While the two renditions seem harmonious and simultaneous, subsequent details about Galesia's experience in London suggest that the iterations of the landscape arts play a compensatory role, comforting the heroine for the profound and unsettling loss of the social order that stabilized her world. Consider, first, how the text naturalizes the landscape of stewardship by generating an aesthetic harmony between the visually rendered landscape Park ("agreeable to the Eye"), the estate's "glorious Appartments," and the "Patch-Work, most curiously compos'd of rich Silks, and Silver and Gold Brocades" (74). The visual emphasis that we saw in Galesia's poem ("here the *Sun* conspires with ev'ry Tree, / To deck the *Earth* in Landskip-Tapistry") resonates with the narrative details of the estate's visual splendor, producing a dynamic that compels the reader to participate in the visual appreciation of rural land and thus in the landscape arts. Admiring the land's beauty more than being immersed in its agricultural productivity, the characters and the reader perceive land in terms of the sensual pleasure it provides; land is thus valued for its aesthetic rather than instrumental—and experiential—quality. The preponderance of visual landscape in the novel's early pages anchors the subsequent scenes of visual emphasis to these previous renditions of the landscape arts, revealing Galesia's reliance on a distinctive visual mode to screen her from the unpleasant aspects of her life in London.

WISHFUL SEEING: LANDSCAPE AS DREAMSCAPE

A Patch-Work Screen depicts the development of Galesia's visual imagination as grounded in political circumstance. She traces her disorienting experience of London to her sense of being uprooted from her natural home: "My Country Innocence render'd me a kind of *Solitary* in the midst of Throngs and great Congregations" (115). Though her imaginative life—primarily devoted to poetry—still dominates her self-image, she nevertheless intersperses her narrative with political allusions situating her at a historical juncture that makes her ideal landscape of stewardship less and less accessible. Rural land recedes from view in *A Patch-Work Screen* most decisively when Galesia is compelled to leave her home in the countryside. Her life takes a dramatic turn when, after a brief courtship with a gentleman turned thief, she suffers the death of her father. This loss in turn necessitates that she and her mother move to London. Deprived of the rural quiet that inspired and permeated her creative life at home, Galesia eventually finds a substitute refuge in the attic of her London lodgings. The persistence of her landscape "way of seeing" (and her ironic resistance to versifying) is evident in the opening of "To my Muse," a poem she writes to commemorate her return to poetry.

> Cease, prithee, Muse, thus to infest
> The barren Region of my Breast,
> Which never can an Harvest yield,
> Since Weeds of Noise o'er-run the Field.
> (123)

Once again Galesia avails herself of agricultural language, here treating herself as terrain in which inspiration takes root (or doesn't, as she pretends). Keeping in mind that *Bosvil and Galesia* established the heroine's political affiliation in the very first paragraph, it makes sense that the sequel would assume the reader's familiarity with this dimension of her character. Nevertheless, even when sustaining the narrative of how the muses beguile her in London, she refers to historical events that remind us of the recent tumult that shook her family and her nation. These references intimate that even as her circumstances change, she remains committed to an obsolescent political order.

To put it another way, Galesia's persistent tendency to survey her surroundings as if they consist of rural land, even when they do not, signals her habit of seeing in a way that naturalizes her political values. Just as Galesia seems incapable of describing intellectual or creative endeavors without recourse to natural imagery, so she imports her landscape way of seeing to the cityscapes of London. Following the poem to her muse, she turns her attention to the setting in which she surrendered to the Muse's ministrations, where her "Den of Parnassus" gives her access to a rooftop.

> Out of this Garret, there was a Door went out to the Leads; on which I us'd frequently to walk to take the Air, or rather the Smoke; for Air, abstracted from Smoke, is not to be had within Five Miles of London. Here it was that I wish'd sometimes to be of Don Quixote's Sentiments, that I might take the Tops of Chimneys, for Bodies of Trees; and the rising Smoke for Branches; the Gutters of Houses, for Tarras-Walks; and the Roofs for stupendous Rocks and Mountains. However, though I could not beguile my Fancy thus, yet here I was alone, or, as the Philosopher says, never less alone. Here I entertain'd my Thoughts, and indulg'd my solitary Fancy. (124)

Galesia's desire to transform the city, in effect to pastoralize it, attests to her nostalgia for the rural calm where she was in her element. More striking still is that she conveys this desire in the conditional mood ("I wish'd [. . .] that I might"). Her grammar implies hesitation or perhaps regrettable incapacity to see in the city what she would like to see. Given her instinctive ability to envision sartorial splendor in the rural landscape—her tendency, that is, to invest political meaning in a seemingly neutral scene—one must wonder what inhibits such vision now. Her circumstances have been reversed; where once rural scenery surrounded her, now, in its absence, she seeks to conjure it but cannot. Given how often Galesia "beguile[s her] Fancy" elsewhere in the trilogy, it behooves us to pause over the scenes that enact this mode of wishful seeing.

The novel's frame structure amplifies the impact of her way of seeing: when we recall that the events under scrutiny here—her father's death, her relocation to London, her retreat to a "Garret-Closet"—together comprise "Leaf II" of the *Patch-Work Screen*, then we realize that the dynamic visuality of the novel's outermost frame mirrors that of the rooftop scene. In retrospect, the reconfiguration of the cityscape into a rural scene (in common parlance, a landscape) becomes legible as a manifestation of the landscape arts. Galesia's view of the cityscape transforms the scene, turning banal items—chimneys, gutters, roofs—into sources of visual pleasure. It seems, then, that the heroine copes with adverse circumstances by subsuming them within a visualized rural idiom that cleanses them of their taint. From a certain vantage this coping mechanism might sustain Galesia's pastoral persona, providing a way for her to prolong her sense of living in a rural idyll. However, if we consider the tenuous quality of her city vision, alongside other details that further destabilize her circumstances, then it becomes necessary to apprehend the landscape way of seeing—the landscape arts—as compromising rather than sustaining an identity grounded in social relations inhering in rural land. From her London garret, her access to the rural idyll proves illusory.

A powerful indication of the adverse circumstances that Galesia faces in London emerges in the sentences immediately following her failed attempt to "beguile her fancy." She turns her gaze upon an adjacent scene, one featuring the iconic buildings that house Britain's unique mode of governance as a constitutional monarchy.

> Here I could behold the Parliament-House, Westminster-Hall, and the Abbey, and admir'd the Magnificence of their Structure, and still more, the Greatness of Mind in those who had been their Founders; one Place for the establishing good Laws; another for putting them in Practice; the Third for the immediate Glory of God; a Place for the continual singing his Praise, for all the Blessings bestow'd on Mankind. But with what Amazement did I reflect, how Mankind had perverted the Use of those Places design'd for a general Benefit: and having been reading the Reign of King *Charles* the First, I was amaz'd, to think how those *Law-Makers* cou'd become such *Law-Confounders*, as the History relates. (124–125)

The passage explains, then, what has thwarted her effort to "beguile fancy"; now that she gazes down upon the very foundation of the nation's intertwined political and religious life, she cannot summon the spirit for pastoralized transcendence thereof. Though moved by the ideals embodied in the scene, Galesia founders in her contemplation of her nation's revered institutions. Given her Jacobite loyalties, her despair no doubt arises from the fact that the trial of "King *Charles* the First," whose history she has been reading, was held in Westminster-Hall. Indeed, it was here that he received his death sentence. In effect, the forces of a new social order, the Parliamentarians (to whom one may trace the Whigs' genealogy) have disrupted the status quo that Charles I stood for, impeding Galesia's patriotic reverie by causing her to brood over the "Law-Confounders," who have (in her view) violated the monarchy by effecting Parliamentary ascendancy (not to mention committing regicide). In light of this historical context, the scene on the leads disrupts Galesia's landscape way of seeing; she cannot see continuity between the cityscape and the countryside of her imagination because political events have sundered that continuity.

The trilogy's most precise articulation of the continuity in question appears in *Bosvil and Galesia*, directly following the heroine's immersion in estate management. Her comments address the gradual decrease of the nobles' involvement in day-to-day management of their lands, which led to frequent proclamations from both the Elizabethan and Stuart courts that the lords should return to their country estates.[42] She thus advocates a natural order whereby the nobility embrace the stewardship of their demesnes rather than indulging in the life of absentee landlords: "The Farmer, according to the Utility of his Occupation, deserves to hold the first Rank amonst [*sic*] Mankind: That one may justly reflect with Veneration on those Times, when Kings and Princes thought it no Derogation to their Dignities. The Nobles, in ancient Times, did not leave their Country-Seats to become the Habitation of Jack-daws, and the Manufactory of Spiders, who, in Reproach to the Mistress, prepare Hangings, to supply those the Moth has devour'd, thro' her Negligence, or Absence" (35). In exercising the "Power and Command" of a steward, Galesia takes pride in putting herself among "the first Rank amonst Mankind," and her identification with an agrarian order that valorizes agricultural stewardship indicts those who shirk their duty. In effect, she proclaims her affiliation with a landscape of stewardship, and decries the landscape of absolute property exemplified by absentee landlords, who eschew reciprocal social relations and instead treat their estates as mere sources of wealth.

Conjuring a landscape of stewardship becomes a way for *A Patch-Work Screen* to signal its affiliation with an older, and putatively morally superior social order founded on a stable, land-based economy. Yet evidence of commodified land—the undoing of that older order—intrudes on the plot and threatens the serenity of the lady's estate. Thus, seemingly negligible details of life on the estate, which seemed so idyllic when first introduced in the novel's outer frame, now rear up to threaten Galesia's rural idyll. The intrusion occurs late in the novel, distant from Leaf I and thus seeming not to mar the aesthetic and formal integrity of the outer frame. For we learn at the beginning of Leaf IV that the lady's estate may be implicated in the most famous—and catastrophic—eighteenth-century instance of capitalist speculation, the South Sea Bubble. Hints of this imminent economic disaster appear when the lady's cook interrupts the continuation of Galesia's story with the news "That Two of the *South-Sea* Directors had sent his Master Word that they wou'd dine with him to Day" (151). After making a snide comment about the directors' presumption, the lady explains to Galesia, "My Husband is about to lay a Debt upon his Estate, to put into this profitable Fund: He has, with much ado, got the Promise of a Subscription for 10,000*l.* for this Purpose. Madam, reply'd *Galesia,* I beg you to use your utmost Endeavours to prevent this Proceeding: I beg you for God's Sake, your own Sake, your Childrens Sake, and for the Sake of all the Poor, that depend upon your Charity, to endeavour to disappoint this Design" (151–152). It would be easy to overlook this omen of financial catastrophe since, in the diegesis at least, it comes to naught. But as Samara Anne Cahill observes, Barker's readers would no doubt recall the 1720 crash while reading her novel: "Writing from a post-crash vantage point, Barker manipulated her narrative to present Galesia as prophetic while also leveraging the knowledge her readers in 1723 would have had of this recent financial disaster."[43]

The flickering of disaster on the margin of a text otherwise beholden to the stability of landed property reveals that this idealized estate could be lost in an instant if the owners encumber its value through imprudent financial investment. What looks like a landscape of stewardship proves to be a landscape of absolute property. Galesia's protestations frame the threat in terms of disrupted social relations; the landowners risk failing in their social duty if they treat their estate like mobile property. And though speaking selflessly "for the Sake of all the Poor," she signals her alignment with them insofar as she, too, benefits from inhabiting the landscape of custom that the lady's stewardship nourishes. Thus, commodified land, even *in potentia*, exposes the vulnerability of the landscapes of stewardship and custom that the text so artfully constructs.

Galesia's nostalgia for "ancient times," when "the Farmer [was] the first Rank amonst [*sic*] Mankind," also resounds in her meditation above London's cityscape, producing an abstract panorama of the obsolescent landscape of stewardship that she cannot see because the emergent landscape of absolute property obstructs it. In this way, Galesia's removal to London marks a transition from pastoral romance to gritty realism, literalized in her inability to see the London smoke as anything other than itself. When she admits, "I could not beguile my Fancy thus," she speaks with wisdom and self-ironizing affection for lost innocence not entirely to be regretted. In the heroine's fading pastoral vision, we encounter a more mature and understandably bitter persona. Overlooking the Westminster prospect, she expresses the landscape way of seeing—that is, the landscape arts—for nearly the last time in this volume.

The near-total absence of visual landscape from the rest of the novel confirms that Galesia indeed cannot "beguile her fancy" to see London as a terrestrial Elysium, as she is wont to see the countryside of her home. On the few occasions when rural views do appear, they do so in dreams that reiterate her subconscious attachment to the countryside. These dreams depict a generic paradise, and yet the specific visual features ascribed to them are the very ones Galesia first pictured in her "shady Walks [amid] the Wonderful Works of the Creation" (*Bosvil and Galesia*, 13). For example, not long after musing over the London rooftops, and directly following a scene in which she overhears a neighbor singing a hymn to the Duke of Monmouth, she dreams of a fantasy landscape, described in the poem "The *Children's*, or *Catechumen's Elysium*." Envisioning "the soft Abode / [of those] Who ignorantly serve the *Unknown God*," the dream catalogs familiar landscape elements ("Large Walks, tall Trees, Groves, Grots, and shady Bow'rs," etc.), demonstrating how, in her mind's eye, paradise looks like the English countryside, even for the unbaptized (160). For the duration of her London sojourn, then, Galesia's access to the pleasures of rural land is limited to her dream world.

In the landscapes of stewardship that precede (and follow) her removal to London, and her inability to visualize it as a rural paradise, we witness the consequences of Galesia's encounter with the evolving meaning of landscape. Once circumstances change so as to suspend her access to the privileged realm of stewardship, she falls back on the resources of her imagination to reinstate her lost world—with limited results. Bereft of the support of her male relatives (her beloved brother also having died), she expresses a vulnerability that informs her diminishing access to the modes of landscape most congenial to her. Clinging to a landscape of stewardship, she suffers the hardships endemic to a landscape of absolute property. Her dream world takes versified form in a poem that quickly follows upon "The *Children's, or Catechumen's Elysium*," after she awakens to find her bedridden mother still alive rather than dispatched to "that *happy Place*, where [. . .] I thought *I had seen my mother*" in her dream. The second poem, entitled "On *Dreams*," ends with a stanza that expresses Galesia's enduring vision of a natural order based on social relations inhering in rural land.

> But as a Country Lady, after all
> The Pleasures of th' *Exchange, Plays, Park,* and *Mall,*
> Returns again to her old *Rural Seat,*
> T'instruct her *Hinds,* and make 'em earn their Meat,
> So comes the Soul home to her *coarse Retreat.*
> (162)

For Galesia to choose an image of rural retreat from London ("th' *Exchange, Plays, Park,* and *Mall*") to figure the soul's return to paradise signals how thoroughly the landscape of stewardship inhabits her imagination. The tableau of "a Country Lady" managing the *Hinds* of her estate turns the soul itself into a steward, and thus sanctifies the landscape of stewardship animating the soul's "*Rural Seat.*" Likewise, paradise is itself a landscape of stewardship. The oneiric expression of this landscape indicates how it obsolesces, assuming imaginary rather than material form. Much of Leaf IV, where these poems appear, consists of Galesia lamenting the despair pervading London upon the death of Charles II, and "the Villainies of those Times" when her own ancestors died defending his father, Charles I (153). By depicting Galesia in London attending her mother's deathbed as they contemplate this tragic state of affairs, the text implies both that landscapes of stewardship have a Jacobite lineage and that such landscapes no longer seem possible.

London proves to be a place from which Galesia repeatedly seeks to escape, and she often does so in her dreams. The instability that precipitated her move to London in the first place continues to unsettle her as long as she lives there. *The Lining of the Patch Work Screen* (1726), the last Galesia novel, opens with the heroine sitting in her London lodgings, contemplating her circumstances, "when the Coldness of friends, or rather the want of Riches, deprives me of their Company these long Winter Evenings" (180). Like the first *Patch-Work* novel, *The Lining* uses Galesia's situation as a frame narrative within which to assemble various in-set narratives with no apparent connection to her story. Rural conceits are likewise scarce in this novel, which opens with the aged heroine sitting by the fireside in her London lodgings and receiving visitors who tell her stories, and sometimes stories within stories. Mostly of the romantic sort, they continue the previous novel's allegorical bent in tales of bigamy and other iterations of the broken vow theme.[44] Galesia remains mostly in the background until near the end, when an allegorical sequence revisits her identity as a writer. Landscape here makes a final appearance, in a symbolic form that echoes the way in which the heroine typically resorts to a rural idiom to express her most momentous experiences. But whereas previous symbolic landscapes conjured Jacobite finery or Eden after the Fall, our final encounter with a rural setting in *The Lining* appears in a dream allegorizing what kind of writer Galesia is. The symbolic and allegorical turn in the trilogy's last landscape reiterates how Galesia resorts to the landscape idiom when deprived of the actual rural life that she finds most congenial—as we saw her do while gazing over the rooftops of London.

The buildup to the dream occurs in this way: upon hearing several treacherous tales of young women tricked out of their fortunes and into prostitution, Galesia succumbs to melancholy over humanity's proliferating woes ("Distress, Distractions, Quarrels, Broils, Debts, Duels, Law-suits, Tricks, Cheats, Taxes, Tumults, Mobs, Riots, Mutinies, Rebellions, Battels, *&c*" (273). In this state of mind she falls asleep, embarking upon "Galecia's Dream," as this section is titled. It begins with her walking amid scenes of misery that echo the above litany of travails ("Horse-men thrown, Limbs broken, Robbers rifling, Ladies affronted, Maids deluded by false Lovers," etc. [274][45]). But the scene abruptly shifts thereafter.

> After many of these frightful Visions were past, she imagin'd she came into a pleasant Valley, fertile of Corn, Fruits and Pasturage; pleasant Brooks, Rills and Springs, such as are rarely to be found; for they never froze in Winter, nor abated of their Water in Summer. Woods replete with singing Birds, Shoals of Pigeons in the Dove-House, which cooed about the Yard, in amorous Addresses to their innocent constant Mates. Sure, said *Galecia* to her self, this is the *Eden* of old, or at least, the Land of Promise, flowing with more delicious Streams than those of Milk and Honey. She was extreamly delighted with this Valley, thought it almost a terrestrial Paradice. (274)

Such serenity recalls happier times, most recently when Galesia was similarly beset by her coach's fall into the river, but eventually wandered onto the estate of "the good Lady," who took her in and enlisted her help in making patches. Just as that earlier scene cosseted the heroine with rural tranquility ("she lost her Way, and got, she knew not how, into a fine Park, amongst Trees, Firs, Thickets, Rabbet-burrows, and such like"), so here the narrative uses a pastoral scene to deliver her from despair (*A Patch-Work Screen*, 72). Images of plenty and variety (water, fields, woods) display Barker's facility in composing a landscape replete with various elements whose harmonious mixture creates a sense of plenitude and peace through visual (and aural and olfactory) pleasure. It is as if Galesia's subconscious were designed to assuage her anxiety by conjuring such "a pleasant Valley."

The fact that this symbolic landscape appears in a dream rather than a poem, as did the ones previously discussed, locates it in an even more remote realm. As a product of Galesia's subconscious mind rather than her poetic craft, the dreamscape reproduces the rural tranquility and plenitude that mark her poems, but its ephemeral quality suggests that rural idylls have become less and less accessible to her. It is worth remembering the urban setting in which she has the dream, and the proliferating ills that precede it; these circumstances provide a sharp contrast to her dream world. Such an oneiric landscape would seem incommensurable with my argument for how *The Galesia Trilogy* limns the historical transformation of landscape; how, after all, does the dreamscape evidence an ascendant landscape of absolute property? If we interpret the "pleasant valley" as the nostalgic residue of an evanescent landscape of stewardship, however, it becomes possible to perceive its role in a broader historical process. The increasingly elusive quality of the novel's rural space bespeaks Barker's awareness of a receding social and moral order founded on the benevolent stewardship of landed property. When we scrutinize the entire dream sequence, which features "the Annual Coronation of Orinda" and Galesia's late arrival and early expulsion therefrom, then it makes even more sense to interpret the episode as Barker's tribute to a passing literary era and recognition of her place in "the fallen commercialized literary world."[46] The dreamscape functions, then, as a counterpart to the evanescent world of scribal literary culture, its idyllic qualities a token of lost rural serenity.

Invaluable readings such as King's help us to understand the dream episode as an allegory for the transition from manuscript to print culture, and Barker's nostalgic acknowledgment of her own position therein. By shifting focus from the transitional literary culture to the particular setting within which Barker stages that transition, I call attention to how depictions of landscape register cultural shifts of the sort we encounter in the dream. In other words, the setting for the scribal community that Galesia aspires to belong to (and achieves, during her sojourn at the lady's country estate) constitutes a landscape of stewardship. The fleeting traces of bucolic plenitude, combined with Galesia's subsequent encounter with hostile city women who cast aspersions on landed women, offer intimations of stewardship ceding to absolute ownership as the prevailing terms of social relations.

Under the dispensation of absolute property, land is a fungible commodity like any other. Though, until now, Galesia rarely mentions her own involvement in monetary exchange, the intrusion of money (gold) into the dream suggests that she is compelled to enter the realm of commerce once she loses her connection to a landed estate. As we go on to learn, the "pleasant valley" leads to Parnassus, where Galesia is led by "her good Genius" after being saved from a giant by "a good Philosopher." There follows a pageant of sorts featuring Orinda, "Queen of Female Writers" (275). Arriving late and tucked into a corner to watch the proceedings, Galesia enjoys the singing and dancing tributes to her revered Orinda, but the Fairy Queen (not Orinda) inexplicably dispatches her with a handful of gold, "command[ing] her away from thence" (277). The gold, and the dream itself, tend to elicit allegorical readings of Barker's ambivalence as she straddles the threshold between manuscript and print cultures—Orinda being the paragon of scribal culture, and the gold signifying money Galesia has been paid to print her work.[47]

Understandably, these readings focus more on the personages featured than the setting for the proceedings; we could not make sense of the allegory without doing so. But, as I have demonstrated by scrutinizing the persistent and purposeful attention to landscape as a significant component of Barker's novels, the detailed rural plenitude of Galesia's approach to Parnassus is not incidental. As "the *Eden* of old [. . .] the Land of Promise, flowing with more delicious Streams than those of Milk and Honey, [. . .] a terrestrial Paradice," the valley represents Barker's reliance on biblical imagery to conjure the perfect world. The scene may synthesize pagan and Christian realms by placing Eden adjacent to Parnassus, but its concrete details—"fertile of Corn, Fruits and Pasturage [and] Shoals of Pigeons in the Dove-House"—render the valley a recognizably earthly place as well, reminiscent of both Galesia's rural home and the benevolent lady's country estate. Galesia's dreamscape in *The Lining* celebrates "a terrestrial Paradice, excelling in fact, whatsoever the Fancies of Poets or Romances could represent" (274). Seemingly generic expressions of pastoral tranquility, these details nevertheless create a continuity between the heroine's depictions of her actual experience, on the one hand, and her imagined paradise on the other. Their correspondence to previous descriptions of the countryside expresses the rural ideal that Galesia has lost, and her resort to fantasy thus proves a compensatory measure—with likewise illusory results.

THE FINAL RETREAT

The ambiguities infusing the trilogy's treatment of gender never come to a resolution, instead lingering as perhaps insoluble questions regarding how a gentlewoman ought to achieve independence. Indeed, the elusiveness of female independence resembles the barely perceptible presence of land as the trilogy comes to a close. Though not encountered in a dream, the last reference to land occurs in passing such that readers would most likely not even notice it, demanding in turn considerable contextualization: The final pages of *The Lining of the Patch Work Screen* offer negative scenes to offset the pleasant valley's positive ones, detailing rampant urban vice in order to reiterate the appeal of pastoral retreat. Included herein is an indirect glimpse of the landscape of absolute property, in the form of an encounter staging the triumph of commodity capitalism over benevolent stewardship. The precipitating drama has to do with the "Female Vertues" that Galesia sets out to peddle in London after being woken from her dream by a real man who unaccountably brings her a real bag of gold (and after a friend visits and offers to sell her these goods). The episode serves as a map of urban iniquity, for Galesia finds each quarter of London uniquely uninterested in buying "*Female Vertues*"; "*Sincerity*" enlists no buyers at Court, nor "*Chastity*" any customers in "the Hundreds of Drury," the haunt of prostitutes (279–280). At this point she hopes the commercial district ("the City") will prove a reliable place for exchange, and so sends her agent there. But "those rich and haughty Dames" have no interest in the "good Parcel of *Humility*" she tries to sell them,

> for they would not so much as look on the Ware, nor permit the Factor to open her Parcel, telling her, they had greater store thereof in the City than they needed; which appears daily (said they) by giving your Ladies place every where, by following their Fashions at all times; Whereas our Riches give us a right to be fantastical, and setters-up of new Modes; But 'tis our *Humility* that pervails with us, and makes us their Apes, at the same time; many of them being but meanly descended, they often run in our Debt, for their gaudy Trappings; and their Husbands borrow of ours, to support their Equipage, on the credit of their Acres. (281)

The city dames' comments expose "Acres"—i.e., land—as one component of a credit economy that renders it a volatile object of exchange rather than a stable guarantor of status. The credit economy belongs to the same economic order as the landscape of absolute property in that both depend upon the unassailable claims of private property (absolute ownership). The country gentry's absolute ownership of their land allows them to alienate it in exchange for cash. Seen from the perspective of the city dames, rural land is merely a contemptible source of wealth for the "meanly descended," who hold no moral authority over their city creditors. Such people, the city dames imply, do not practice benevolent stewardship of their landed property but rather exploit it in order to indulge their vanity and pride. For Galesia, deeply committed to the social and moral stability derived from a landed economy, the city dames' conception of a capitalist social order is repulsive—and indeed repels the heroine back to her beloved countryside.

In the end, then, Barker dispatches her heroine to more congenial territory: "*Galecia* perceiving, she made no better return of her Merchandize in *London,* resolved to try the Country, in hopes the Women of all Ranks and Stations would be better Customers" (289). In the logic of coincidence commensurate with the novel's pattern of wish fulfillment, word arrives just then that the good lady who had taken Galesia in to her sumptuous country house in *A Patch-Work Screen* "very very earnestly desires your Company, now the Spring comes on" (290). Thus, we arrive at the novel's final instance of rural retreat, which brings the narrative full circle by returning Galesia to the bucolic setting in which she last enjoyed the pleasures most dear to her—writing in the countryside (for presumably the good lady will solicit Galesia's aid in stitching together the lining, as she did the patches during the heroine's first visit). Such a denouement effects a final reassertion of the landscape of stewardship, as the good lady extends her hospitality to Galesia, as she did before, and thus provides a final reprieve from the indignities of London and its ruthless credit economy. This outcome relies on conjecture, since Galesia's initial plan for retreat involves seeking customers in the country. Yet she accepts the good lady's invitation without a moment's hesitation, leaving readers to expect all the good that comes with living in rural tranquility.

Scholarly assessments of this conclusion focus on the political implications of retreat, detecting Barker's enduring commitment to an obsolescent moral and political order. Thus, Galesia's return to the country is a refusal rather than a defeat, sounding a note of Jacobite loyalty to the very end. Rivka Swenson, among others, interprets the heroine's failed enterprise as evidence of her belatedness: "Galesia's peddling of 'Vertues,' like Barker's peddling of her fiction, comprises an attempt to resurrect an earlier era associated with those virtues." Swenson detects a note of optimism in the final paragraph, as in this assertion: "This Invitation was an inexpressible Joy to our *Galecia*" (290). Swenson emphasizes the seasonal framing of the summons ("now the Spring comes on"), linking it to the entire trilogy's seasonal rhythms, which situate the heroine in "an essentially cyclical progression," historically linked to May Day and other rituals that the Stuarts embraced as symbols of their eventual return to the throne. Rather than "an admission of defeat," then, Galesia's springtime rural retreat signals her hewing to a cyclical conception of history that makes a Jacobite future appear more possible.[48]

In a complementary reading of the novels' Jacobite propensities, Constance Lacroix concurs that the *Lining*'s ending embeds optimism within its heroine's rural retreat. The terms of Lacroix's analysis expose the novel's moral and political geography, which is implicit rather than explicit in Swenson's discussion, though both critics concur that the proper setting for Jacobite triumphalism is in the countryside. Noting the novels' alignment of Jacobite, Tory, and Country party values, Lacroix argues, "Galesia's subsequent retreat to the country, though symbolic of a disillusioned waiving of pre-eminence, is far from desperate: her 'inexpressible Joy' [. . .] at the completion of a cycle that brings her back to an Arcadian existence leaves no doubt as to her faith in the vitality of the bucolic ideal that suffuses the conservative Augustan 'poetics of nostalgia.'"[49] Together, Swenson and Lacroix indirectly corroborate my own treatment of landscape as expressive of a worldview; just as Galesia sees her royalism in the fabric of the fields (and in the rooftops of Westminster), so the springtime return to her English Arcadia encodes her political orientation. While Lacroix focuses on Barker's hostility to "bourgeois capitalistic ideology," and Swenson privileges the seasons and cyclical history, all of our inquiries recognize rurality as a decisive component of Barker's moral universe.[50] The sense of evanescence and nostalgia detected by these critics applies equally to the landscape of stewardship that, as I have argued, underwrites other defining features of Barker's rural ideal. By intertwining her quest for independence as a woman writer and estate manager, and reading the evolution of landscape through the lens of that quest, I treat the modulations in Galesia's relationship to rural land as a unique measure of changing social relations as they gradually become unmoored from rural land.

In the distance between Galesia's youthful rural wanderings and her twilight return to the setting that feels most natural to her, we have witnessed a heroine whose attachment to the rural landscape never wavers. By using her persistent reliance on the landscape idiom to track its evolving meaning, I emphasize the appealing malleability of a discourse that purports to locate its adherents within a natural order. The heroine understands her social, intellectual, and artistic identity through a system of social relations inhering in landed property. Over the course of three novels, as we observe the uneven transition from a landscape of stewardship to one of absolute property, we also experience both the coherence of the older order as well as its exploitation by a new and different one. By imagining herself as inhabiting a landscape of stewardship, Galesia may shut out the disturbing evidence that the stability it supposedly provides has crumbled, or that it may not be as natural as she supposed. Acknowledging the landscape of absolute property would require her to admit that the social hierarchy she so rigidly adheres to is impermanent and changeable. Money, not land, serves as the decisive factor in the new order. By revealing how landscape rhetoric may be summoned to support both the old order and the new, *The Galesia Trilogy* demonstrates the versatility and staying power of this consummate ideological tool.

2

STEWARDING THE COUNTRY HOUSE

Anne Finch, Countess of Winchilsea

ONE STRIKING SIMILARITY BETWEEN Jane Barker and Anne Finch (née Kingsmill, 1661–1720) is that both writers embrace the country estate as the ideal setting for a woman's self-realization. Their example reveals how the conservative gentlewoman's identity formation necessitates access to landed private property; in short, her independence coalesces in and through the landscape. Their common interest in the country house arises partly from its associations with the rhetoric of retreat, which both women embraced when their Jacobite sympathies compelled them into exile, though Finch's retreat to rural England proves less drastic than Barker's self-imposed banishment to France. A telling difference between these Jacobite poets is that Finch retreated to the country houses of various relatives and friends, while Barker spent fifteen years (1689–1704) in more dire straits with the exiled Stuart court outside Paris, far from the rural stability and comfort that Finch experienced in her country-house sojourns.[1] Thus, Finch's higher social status, Anglicanism, and less strident Jacobite affinities make her a compelling counterpoint to the Catholic Barker; Finch's insulation from material hardship and religious persecution enabled her to embrace her poetic avocation in a way that Barker could not afford. These advantages surely helped Finch achieve her status as the most revered British woman poet of the long eighteenth century.

Yet it would be inaccurate to portray Finch simply as the beneficiary of aristocratic privilege. Orphaned by age three, she barely knew her parents, and her guardians had to undertake lengthy and contentious litigation in order to gain access to the patrimony bequeathed by her father but claimed by her stepfather.[2] Long after this contested inheritance, Finch also endured years of thwarted access to landownership when, from 1713 to 1720, she and her husband, Heneage, were involved in a lengthy legal ordeal in order acquire the Finch family estate at Eastwell.[3] These circumstances demonstrate the burdensome quality of her relationship to landed property, revealing in turn significant motivation for her to embrace the luxury and security of country-house discourse. She did have the good fortune, however, to receive the steadfast care of both a strong and independent paternal grandmother (Bridget, Lady Kingsmill) until age eleven, and then comparable support of from maternal uncle, Sir William Haslewood.[4] In short, Finch's biography provided her with enviable social and material advantage while also encumbering her with familial and political turmoil that contributed to the "spleen" (i.e., depression) that she occasionally experienced throughout her lifetime and described in perhaps her most famous poem.

Finch's biography also positioned her under the care (albeit sometimes indirect) of successive patriarchs—from her Uncle Haslewood to the Duke of York (later James II), whose consort, Mary of Modena, she served as maid of honor in 1682–1684; to her husband, Heneage, whom she married in 1684; to his nephew Sir Charles Finch, who welcomed the couple to Eastwell in late 1690.[5] Benefiting from the tutelage of both the future king and her male relatives, Finch experienced the convergence of monarchy and aristocracy with patriarchy as a matter of course. That both she and Barker endorse patriarchy even as they express frustration and outrage at women's subordination complicates this analysis. To be sure, a certain complicity in patriarchy is compulsory even for the most strident proto-feminist, given the nation's dominant patriarchal power structure. Yet Finch demonstrates the difference it makes to know supportive, congenial, and well-landed gentlemen who sanction and encourage her artistic talent. She strategically accepts patriarchy while using the country estates of various patriarchs as settings for her literary pursuit of female independence. Of course, as a married woman she experiences independence very differently than Barker does. Finch aims to craft a poetic voice unencumbered by male censure, whereas Barker's literary persona arises from her rejection of male duplicity and marriage. Given the relative advantage that Finch enjoys in her wide-ranging access to country estates, she offers a compelling example of female artistic self-realization that benefits from patriarchal landownership and stewardship. This profile manifests in verses celebrating several country estates and the lords who preside over them. Her poetic landscapes thus register both the importance of estate stewardship and the gradual shift away from it in favor of more individualistic values. Such a striking ethical transformation manifests in her poetry's divergent sociopolitical and aesthetic relations to the land.

Finch is known primarily as a poet, and she is often crowned the most talented female poet of the eighteenth century, although she also wrote two plays and undertook numerous translations. Decades of scholarship have shown how she commands attention for her remarkable technical dexterity and formal versatility. From fables and Pindaric odes to songs and pastoral dialogues, her oeuvre has demonstrated her talent and innovation across a range of neoclassical forms.[6] The rural orientation of her poetic persona—pen-named *Ardelia*—has prompted scholars to study the intricacies of her relationship to nature and its expression in various generic contexts. Given her affinity for the country estate, Finch unsurprisingly reveres the country-house poem as a vehicle for reckoning with the sorrows and joys she experienced after retreating from the deposed Stuart court in London. This genre therefore offers a powerful form through which to investigate how she participates in the historical transformation of landscape. Using the form as a ready-made device to both address her political plight and express gratitude to her hosts, she exploits and modifies its conventions as the occasion demands. The results attest not only to her innovation but also to important transformations in the meaning and function of landscape.

This chapter studies two country-house poems from Finch's oeuvre, focusing on how they make legible the historical shift in British culture's conception of landscape. They include "Upon My Lord Winchilsea's Converting the Mount in His Garden to a Terras" (c. 1693–1703) and "To the Honorable the Lady Worsley at Long-Leate" (c. 1690).[7] These texts present a compelling contrast insofar as the former one depicts a landscape of stewardship, while the latter features a protocapitalist landscape of absolute property. This formulation builds upon Garrett Sullivan's historical model of landscape, which argues that the latter landscape's emphasis on aesthetic pleasure aligns it with the landscape arts. Focusing on Finch's female speakers, this chapter evaluates how she appropriates a typically male genre to establish her artistic independence. We learn, then, how a distinguished female poet conspires with patriarchy without thoroughly compromising her artistic agency.

THE PARADOX OF FINCH'S PATRIARCHAL LANDSCAPES

We saw in chapter 1 how Barker exposes the competing landscapes that govern a gentlewoman's life during the centuries-long transition from feudalism to capitalism. A similar situation informs Finch's country-house poetry, but with significant differences related to her aristocratic (and later noble) milieu. She proves adept at manipulating a genre that typically lionizes Britain's landed patriarchs, and in the process exposes how aestheticized conceptions of land gain currency from around the turn of the eighteenth century, and how women participate in this process provided they pose only equivocal challenges to gender inequality.

Several other scholars have identified Finch's affinity for patriarchs and their rural estates and noted her seeming inconsistency, given her defense of women's education and artistic agency. As Jennifer Keith observes with regard to Finch's affiliation with country houses, "Her elevation of what to some might be regarded as oppressive landed patriarchy repeatedly asserts the importance of women and displaced Jacobites in this 'retreat.'"[8] Keith's qualification regarding the nature of patriarchy signals how our modern vantage leads some readers—including me—to wrestle with apparent contradictions in Finch's oeuvre. By linking the poet's proto-feminism and Jacobitism, Keith identifies the source of the contradiction: the patriarchal monarchy compels Finch's loyalty to this ideology, but part of her artistry inheres in her subtle assertions of women's agency despite the fact that gender inequality is an important Jacobite principle. Keith's observation builds upon a related concern in Michael Gavin's interpretation of Finch, which treats provincial life as a definitive component of her poetic identity. In his view, she advocates a provincial poetic and critical practice that eschews the treachery and cynicism of satire, typically associated with the city; the "patriarchal estate[s]" where she lives or visits are among the key sites in which this practice develops.[9] Poems addressed to her noble kinsmen and -women articulate an ethical geography whereby their rural seats provide the ideal circumstances for the production and appreciation of dignified neoclassical verse. These idyllic conditions diverge from the frivolity, vanity, and contempt that prevail in the city and its satires. Not only do Finch's estate poems endorse the aristocratic principle linking noble blood to virtuous character; they also engage a process of naturalization that, Gavin argues, collapses "the social, the biological, and the poetic. [. . .] This collapse is inscribed onto the patriarchal landscape itself."[10]

The precise nature of the landscape here remains obscure; its role as the site and manifestation of patriarchy emerges from the circumstances in which the poet wrote. The rural setting for much of Finch's writing surely informs Gavin's word choice; yet, to identify her preferred milieu as a landscape signals more than the poet's preference for rural life. She not only lived most of her life in the countryside but also depicted it in much of her verse. These depictions constitute landscapes in the most general sense as representations of natural scenery, but they also express the historical transformation of landscape's meaning that is the focus of this book. A comparison of Barker and Finch thus enriches our grasp of this transformation by tracing how they engage with landscape in strikingly different ways, even though they were contemporaries with the same political affiliation. Their divergence in matters of social and religious privilege demonstrates how a woman's experience of landscape evolves, depending on these variables (in addition to differences in disposition). Yet Barker and Finch remain fellow travelers in their dual—and ostensibly contradictory—commitment to proto-feminism and Jacobitism. Although they favor different literary genres, they still offer complementary testimony to the ambiguity and inconsistency that arise as a quasi-feudal model of landscape cedes to a proto-capitalist one.

The signature sites in which these authorial personae take shape speak to the aforementioned differences in stature, privilege, and generic choice. Barker depicts her heroine Galesia enjoying the generous hospitality and lush demesnes of a benevolent gentlewoman, but the aspirational quality of this fictional encounter differs from similar evocations of country-house hospitality in Finch's poetic oeuvre. The contrast between Galesia's imaginary reception at a stately home versus Finch's actual sojourns on several renowned estates—including the famous Longleat in Wiltshire—impresses upon us the different material circumstances of these writers. Without minimizing the emotional, political, and spiritual hardship that Finch's poetry often expresses, I argue that her social, religious, and marital privilege enables her to make a strategic bargain with patriarchy in order to pursue her literary ambition. The bargain is made palatable by her husband and other male relatives who appreciated, encouraged, and to some extent enabled her art. Moreover, the patriarchal landscapes of the poems in question demonstrate both forward- and backward-facing modes of landscape. These are likewise witnessed in Barker's oeuvre; yet Finch offers a generically distinct endorsement of the social hierarchy, encoding it in country-house poetry and thus naturalizing hierarchical social relations specifically in and through the land. Her appropriation of country-house poetry exemplifies the evolving meaning of landscape insofar as her iterations of the genre feature competing versions thereof. Thus, she complicates firm distinctions between backward-facing landscapes of stewardship and forward-facing, proto-capitalist instantiations of the landscape arts. The puzzling convergence of her socially conservative orientation and her progressive views on the status of women signals how her poetry conjures landscapes that register as either backward- or forward-facing, or both.

Sullivan's historical investigation of landscape offers a compelling framework within which to interpret the puzzle presented by Finch, for he identifies obsolescent and emergent forms of landscape that illuminate her simultaneously retrograde and progressive orientation. He argues that landscapes of stewardship and custom work as complementary forces that unite landowner-stewards and their dependents who lay claim to certain resources provided by the estate. The mutual dependence of this relationship constitutes a "moral economy," which gradually erodes as the landscape of absolute property, engendered by early capitalism, comes to dominate social relations inhering in the land.[11] As landed property turns into a commodity like any other, landowners extricate themselves from responsibilities to their tenants, and a wage economy gradually displaces the moral one. The signal manifestation of this historical shift, according to Sullivan, is the landscape arts, which express the landowner's privileged perspective and occlude the rights formerly held by the tenantry. These arts function as the corollary to the landscape of absolute property so that what we most commonly conceive of as landscapes—aestheticized rural land or representations thereof—obfuscates other versions of landscape that preceded the landscape of absolute property.

Although Sullivan's study of early modern English drama addresses the prehistory of the transformations under scrutiny here, he gestures toward the future in ways that apply his argument to the long eighteenth century. He acknowledges that the plays he studies "predate the emergence in England of both the category of landscape (as it is traditionally construed) and those artifacts identified as landscapes." The artifacts in question, he notes—Augustan georgic poetry, prospect painting, landscape gardening—coalesced during the long eighteenth century. A crucial observation here is that the landscape arts (including estate poetry) constitute, for Sullivan, "the institutionalization of landscape," and that these arts are a manifestation of the landscape of absolute property.[12] These insights reinforce my premise that Finch's estate poems constitute historically significant examples of landscape. Not only do they instantiate the landscape arts, but they also feature powerful depictions of the landscapes of stewardship and custom. Her layering of various landscapes affords us an opportunity to explore the historical and literary forces that propel the ascendance of one specific form of landscape—the landscape of absolute property as expressed through the landscape arts—alongside the obsolescence of the others.

The presence of several landscapes of stewardship in Finch's estate poems prompts an inquiry into how these retrograde landscapes have minimal impact on the Whig ascendancy, even as they advance women's literary agency.[13] A puzzle thus appears because the aesthetic dimension of these depictions would seem to locate them in the realm of the landscape arts; nevertheless, frequent attention to stewardship also plants them within an older model of landscape that hinges on reciprocity between landlord and tenants. The estate poems in question also demonstrate how the elusiveness of the term *landscape* is symptomatic of a cultural struggle over the values that the term ought to transmit. This struggle manifests in the tension between obsolescent and emergent landscapes; moreover, the poems in question feature only male stewardship, suggesting that Finch may ultimately condone patriarchy provided that it accommodate female poetic self-realization. Unlike Barker's multiple depictions of female stewardship, Finch's country-house poems leave us to interrogate the conditions—whether social, literary-conventional, or otherwise—that compelled her to foreground the male version, and with what implications.

The patriarchal landscapes that Gavin identifies in Finch's poetry acquire this designation, as we have seen, because of the several patriarchs who encourage and inspire her literary pursuits. One key site for this landscape is Eastwell, the estate to which Finch and her husband retreated from London in the wake of the Revolution of 1688 (see figure 2.1). That Anne was surrounded by virtuous and congenial patriarchs is indisputable, also evidenced in the fact that her husband served, in Gavin's words, as "archivist and curator" of the fair-copy manuscript of her "Miscellany Poems with Two Plays by Ardelia" (also known as the Folger Manuscript).[14] He treats Finch's decorous self-alignment with patriarchal estates such as Eastwell and Longleat (home of Sir Thomas and Lady Frances Thynne, her brother- and sister-in-law) as a means to authorize her own literary agency. In so doing, Gavin captures Finch's tactical fusion of female transgression and aristocratic affiliation: "She instrumentalizes the commonplace of the

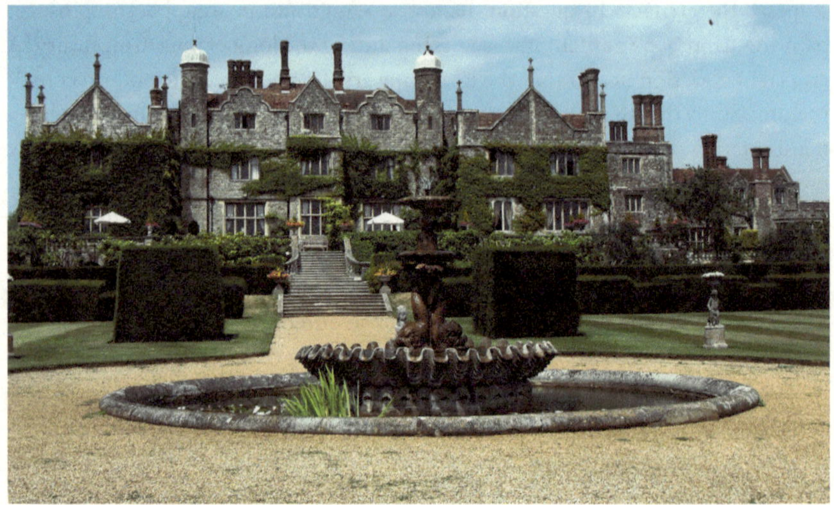

Figure 2.1. Eastwell in its current state, though considerably altered from its design when Finch lived there off and on, 1690–1720. Photo by author.

virtuous, landed patriarch to legitimize her own work while critiquing the London culture of publicity she engages from a distance."[15] The latter claim duly recognizes the importance of the landed patriarch in Finch's oeuvre while also revealing the need to interrogate why it matters—and indeed, what it means to say—that these patriarchs are "landed."

THE POLITICS OF LANDOWNERSHIP: STEWARDSHIP VERSUS AESTHETICS

Owning land serves as a cornerstone in Britain's social structure; it is the sine qua non for membership among the ruling classes, granting the owner access to not only material wealth but also political citizenship and its concomitant sociocultural authority. (How apt, then, that the term *establishment* describes both a dwelling and the elite who inhabit it.) Moreover, landownership governs British society insofar as it entails a set of social relations among the owner and his (or, rarely, her) dependents. Rural land, it almost goes without saying, serves as the foundation for this social and political arrangement. Tom Williamson and Liz Bellamy specify the late seventeenth century as a decisive juncture in the nation's fundamental dependence on landownership.

> [L]anded wealth was safer after the Revolution than it had ever been before. The arbitrary power of the Crown had been abolished, [. . .] and the country was under the control of men who had most interest in the

> protection of landed property. Following the Glorious Revolution of 1688, Parliament was finally established as the supreme governing body and it was dominated by large landowners. The stability of political administration was rooted in the stability of landholding. [. . .] Despite the development of an increasingly diverse economy, and the emergence of new forms of commercial and industrial wealth, land was still seen in many quarters as the basis of national prosperity.[16]

This emphatic explanation of landownership's dominant role in politics at the very time when the Finches needed access to a country estate indicates the many reasons why landscape acquired such cultural currency throughout the nation and in much of Finch's poetry.

Several country-house poetic conventions prove especially serviceable for Finch's artistic and political ends, and her deviation from convention manifests her poetic innovation. Her handling of these conventions signals the form's malleability, in turn exemplifying how literary form encodes sociohistorical circumstance. I am indebted to Heather Dubrow in this regard; she analyzes Ben Jonson's "To Penshurst" (1616) and its influence on Thomas Carew's "To Saxham" (1640) in order to argue that "the country house poem offers an ideal test case for studying the potentialities and problems of formalist criticism. [. . . I]ts indisputable embeddedness in contemporary political and social tensions clearly invites an exploration of the relationship between literary forms and social formations."[17] My own study of landscapes as social formations, and the generic norms of estate poetry, profits from Dubrow's historicization of formalism. One of the conventions that most appeals to Finch is the politicized rhetoric of retirement and retreat, embraced most spectacularly in her recent past by Andrew Marvell in *Upon Appleton House* (written in 1651). These twin pastoral discourses make a virtue out of rural habitation and the rejection of urban life that it entails. Together, they prove invaluable to Finch, providing her with a powerful rhetorical tradition that enables her to insinuate her Jacobite affinities even while ostensibly distancing herself from the intense political partisanship of Williamite London. In this way, she builds upon a classical literary tradition bequeathed by Theocritus, Horace, and Virgil that rejoices in a life of exile from court and city.

This exile is real for Finch: her husband lost a prominent position in the court of the Duke of York (the future James II), and Heneage's refusal to swear loyalty to the new monarchs barred him from public life thereafter.[18] In practical terms, being exiled from London meant that for many years the Finches did not have a home of their own and thus depended upon the hospitality of various friends and relatives. Here we encounter another crucial topos of country-house poetry, namely the rhetoric of hospitality. This convention serves as a ready-made device for navigating her situation because it enables her to express gratitude to her hosts while also cultivating a poetic voice that derives strength, virtue, and wisdom from her encounters with nature. More importantly, for my purposes, she deploys country-house rhetoric in the service of women's artistic agency. Yet such self-realization, as Gillian Wright has argued, is grounded in a form of Jacobitism that undercuts the political implications of her proto-feminist self-assertion; the poet enacts "a Jacobitism which, while underpinning Finch's creative agency, allows no place for political agency."[19] The cross-currents of conservatism and proto-feminism in Finch's oeuvre thus confront scholars with a question of emphasis; whether privileging the former or latter tendency, we are compelled to qualify our stance with regard to the countervailing current.

Country-house discourse authorizes Finch's writing even while endorsing the male authority that her estate poems honor. By venerating the patriarchs who encourage her to write, she circumvents the social forces that look askance at women's writing. As Keith has noted, the forces of censure and exclusion impacted Finch in more ways than many scholars recognize. In a unique reading of Finch's translations, Keith investigates how the poet's exclusion from the male preserve of classical learning compounded her trials as a Jacobite exile. Thus, she observes how Finch occupied a "doubled position as translator and socially displaced person, [and] used a range of translation practices to make these internally exiled cultures legible. [. . .] Finch uses translation to restore the truths of Jacobitism and feminism."[20] Such ideologically driven translations attest to both the turmoil Finch endured and the creativity that helped her cope with it. The "doubled position" that Keith identifies also manifests in Finch's location on the threshold between forward- and backward-facing landscapes. The translations from antiquity align her with the retrograde landscape of stewardship; meanwhile, her social displacement stems in part from the emergent landscape of absolute property that Williamite Britain helped establish and that occasioned her exile.

Though afflicted by exile, Finch nevertheless benefited from it insofar as the rural estates where she lived or visited, and the patriarchs presiding there, encouraged her poetic talent. In "The Preface" to the Folger Manuscript, she makes explicit the link between her poetic productivity and the rural estate where she resided while composing the manuscript. In an uncharacteristic blend of prose and verse, this text describes her anxiety over the scandal that could have arisen were she exposed as "a Versifying Maid of Honour" at the Stuart court (*Works,* 1:27, line 47). Living at Eastwell not only saves her from "the material losses, which I had lately sustain'd," but also averts disaster by providing both shelter and patriarchal sanction. The text's conflation of the two reveals the degree to which landed property is a male preserve.

> [W]hen I came to Eastwell, and cou'd fix my eyes only upon objects naturally inspiring soft and Poeticall immaginations, and found the owner of itt, so indulgent to that Art, so knowing in all the rules of itt, and at his pleasure, so capable of putting them in practice; and also most oblig-

> ingly favorable to some lines of mine, that had fall'n under his Lordship's perusal, I cou'd no longer keep within the limmits I had prescrib'd myself, nor be wisely reserv'd, in spite of inclination, and such powerful temptations to the Contrary. (*Works*, 1:28, lines 59–68)

Finch's deference to male authority almost obscures the estate behind the man whose superior knowledge provides the sanction—and, of course, the rural demesnes—that she lacked while living at Westminster Palace.

Shifting from prose to verse expresses in formal terms the inspiration that Eastwell offers:

> Whenever I contemplate all the several Beautys of this Park, allow'd to be (if not of the Universal yett) of our British World infinitely the finest,
>
> A pleasing wonder, throo' my fancy moves,
> Smooth as her lawnes, and lofty as her Groves.
> (*Works*, 1:28, lines 74–79)

This excerpt encapsulates the complex political valence of Finch's landscapes. Genuflecting to male authority, she fuses her femininity to a poetic fancy that in turn produces a landscape of stewardship of which she is the beneficiary. Thus, female artistry arises within a patriarchal landscape that nevertheless contains the kernel of woman's agency and in turn the germ of her independence. The gender paradox witnessed in "The Preface" manifests in a landscape of stewardship that also intimates a reliance on aesthetic pleasure, thus conjuring the landscape arts and their emergent landscape regime. For Finch to feminize Eastwell in verses that celebrate "her lawnes" and "her Groves" refracts the tension within a text that, on one hand, honors the partnership between patriarchy and stewardship, and on another, grounds the female poet's identity in her aesthetic expertise. The common femininity of poet and place coalesces in the scene, while its aesthetic components also glance toward an imminent transformation in landscape relations that privileges aesthetic pleasure while minimizing the expansive community that inhabits a landscape of stewardship.

In "The Preface" we witness an alchemical process whereby Eastwell's aesthetically pleasing aspects infuse Finch's poetic voice, meanwhile intimating their capacity to efface the obsolescent landscape's communal ethos. The transmission of desirable qualities from lord to estate to poet produces an aesthetic circuitry that transforms wise stewardship into a visual display of natural beauty. The woman at the center of this process may enact proto-feminist ideals, but her participation proves of dubious value when seen as contributing to the effacement of community. In this way, "The Preface" hovers on the threshold between the landscape of stewardship and the landscape arts, anticipating subsequent liminal landscapes in the Folger Manuscript.

"Upon My Lord Winchilsea's Converting the Mount in His Garden to a Terras" and "To the Honorable the Lady Worsley at Long-Leate" bring these liminal landscapes to life. As descriptions of country estates, and in keeping with country-house poetic convention, both poems honor the landowner and in turn conflate the wonders of the person with those of the estate to which they are linked.[21] Stewardship undergirds both poems, which treat the beauty and comfort of the estates as manifestations of their lords' virtue, wisdom, and taste (Lady Worsley serves as a proxy for her father, Lord Weymouth—a dynamic to be scrutinized hereafter). But the relative importance of each quality varies from one poem to the next—and herein lies the subtle yet significant distinction between the two poems. In "Upon My Lord Winchilsea," stewardship ultimately emerges as the lord's defining value, while in "To the Honorable the Lady Worsley," the presiding lord earns the speaker's admiration primarily for "The real Splendours of our fam'd Long-leate" (*Works* 1:367, line 46)—that is, for qualities that align it with the landscape arts.

As examples of country-house poetry, then, the poems serve as a study in contrasts. Whereas "To the Honorable the Lady Worsley" details the extravagant riches of Longleat, "Upon My Lord Winchilsea" honors the speaker's host at Eastwell by detailing his wise stewardship of an estate whose previous lord made grave errors in judgment. The emphasis in the latter poem falls on the current lord's stewardship of natural resources and concern for those who depend upon him; benevolence distinguishes this lord more than the finery of his estate. Moreover, the text's inclusion of a countervailing example of malevolent estate stewardship turns the poem into a moral lesson about the proper modes of stewardship. Ultimately, the poems animate the historical transformation of landscape and the shifting importance of stewardship, on the one hand, and aesthetics, on the other. The sense of community that emerges from Eastwell's landscape of stewardship diverges from the singularity of the presiding lord at Longleat, whose distinction inheres more in his elaborate estate improvements, the main effect of which is to dazzle onlookers rather than sustain a community.

"UPON MY LORD WINCHILSEA": PATRIARCHY, STEWARDSHIP, AND FEMALE LITERARY AGENCY

Finch's poem to her nephew Charles illustrates the convergence of her support for patriarchy and her assertion of female literary agency. That the poem identifies a specific act of stewardship in its very title underscores the importance of this principle; it is a fundamental component of a social structure based on male landownership. Finch abides by convention here insofar as she honors the landowner for performing his stewardly duties in such an exemplary fashion. At the same time, however, she deviates from convention by inserting a female voice into a genre that typically features male speakers and enlists female figures only when they embody ideal femininity. Jonson's "To Penshurst" offers a definitive example of the latter tendency with his multiple genuflections to "thy lady [. . .] named of Gamage," a reference to Barbara Sidney, née Gamage, wife of Sir Robert Sidney, the patron celebrated by the poem.[22] Jonson and the "sons of Ben" who continue the country-house poetic tradition (in addition to Marvell) speak as recipients of patronage and express gratitude to their patrons by celebrating their lords' idealized estates. Finch's deviation from convention is twofold in that she speaks as a woman and is the eponymous lord's relative rather than his client. Her transgression as a female speaker and fellow aristocrat reinforces the authoritative stance she assumes while celebrating and, crucially, judging his estate stewardship.

An imbalance of power obtains in both canonical country-house poetry and Finch's proto-feminist adaptation. In the first case the poet-speaker-client is subordinate to his patron-lord; in the second case the poet-speaker-woman is subordinate to her nephew-male host. But despite the inequality that Finch's speaker inhabits, she offsets it by exercising acute judgment with regard to the principles of stewardship. In the process of delivering an encomium to her nephew, she also establishes her cultural authority by demonstrating her astute insight into the governing values at Eastwell. She understands her lord's duty to be hospitable, just as she understands her own duty to express gratitude for his kindness and to do so specifically by praising his estate, understood as a physical manifestation of his wisdom and grace. Ironically, then, the female poet must share her lord's wisdom regarding stewardship in order to honor him and his property, for this situation equalizes her position, at least regarding matters of stewardship. By speaking as an authoritative judge thereof, Finch legitimates herself as a woman writer. This insight returns us to the paradoxical quality of her work: her proto-feminist self-assertion hinges upon her legitimation of patriarchy.

A detailed look at the poem's representation of Eastwell reveals how these complex dynamics play out. In the opening stanza of "Upon My Lord Winchilsea," the speaker announces her plan to assess her lord's stewardship in part through negative example; she will identify exemplary stewardship by describing how wise lords correct the errors of their unprincipled predecessors.

> If we those Gen'rous Sons, deserv'dly Praise
> Who o're their Predecessours Marble raise,
> And by Inscriptions, on their Deeds, and Name,
> To Late Posterity, convey their Fame,
> What, with more Admiration, shall we write,
> On Him, who takes their Errours from our sight?
> (*Works* 1:86, lines 1–6)

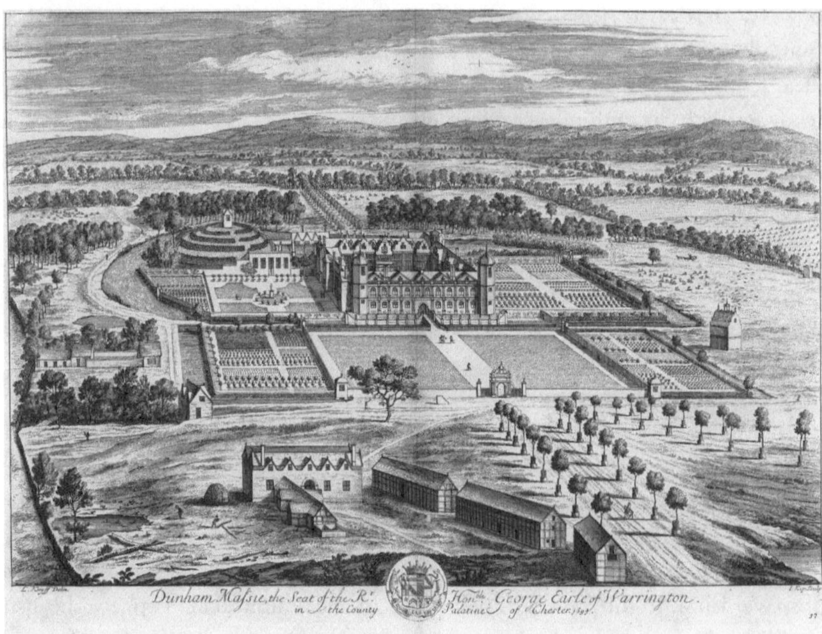

Figure 2.2. A mount at Dunham Massey; image engraved by Johannes Kip and Leendert Knyff, 1707. Antiqua Print Gallery/Alamy Stock Photo.

The speaker explains why it is appropriate to celebrate the removal of an error from the estate grounds; the lord's decision to remove the error exposes faulty stewardship by getting rid of it. By suggesting that the error's removal and the resulting benefit validate her lord's judgment (because they give cause for celebration), the speaker also implicitly validates her own judgment. It may be true that she merely copies Lord Winchilsea since his actions demonstrate his own understanding of erroneous stewardship—in this case, the building of a mount "Which long had stood, (though threat'n'd oft in vain) / Concealing all the beautys of the Plaine" (lines 9–10). (See figure 2.2 for an image of a mount that likely resembles the one Finch describes, though on a different estate.) But the speaker's next maneuver establishes her own expertise in the principles of stewardship, and this maneuver belongs to her alone.

The maneuver in question occurs in the long second stanza, devoted largely to an example of malevolent stewardship. Finch chooses to include a countervailing episode of stewardship in which the previous lord of Eastwell displays the very contrary of wisdom, in the form of a rash decision to fell a grove of trees. Her inclusion of this negative example signals her own sophisticated rhetoric, revealing an intellect that owes nothing (so far as we know) to Lord Winchilsea. Having announced her corrective strategy and briefly described the felled mount in stanza one (lines 1–16), she turns from the present to the past in stanza two (lines 17–45), when the objectionable destruction of the grove occurred. In sum, the first half of the poem initiates an encomium for Sir Charles in which the speaker dramatizes an episode from the past consisting of ill-judged stewardship. The poet's beloved Lord Winchilsea thus emerges as a benevolent patriarch who surpasses his predecessor in wisdom and foresight, and in turn Finch implements her own standard for distinguishing good patriarchs from bad ones.

The poet's reliance on negative example bolsters her own wisdom, but it also deviates from country-house poetic convention in ways that might complicate her integrity as a poet and a relative of Lord Winchilsea. The deviation involves the person whom Finch chooses to represent poor stewardship, for he turns out to be Sir Charles's grandfather and Finch's father-in-law Heneage, the third Earl of Winchilsea, who died ca. 1688. Sir Charles's father William Finch, Viscount Maidstone, died in a naval battle in 1672, before he could succeed to the Winchilsea title; this fact allows us to infer the identity of the predecessor in question.[23] In a genre characterized by veneration for an estate's noble lineage, it seems indiscreet if not downright offensive for Finch to treat her relative as a malevolent figure. Denigrating her father-in-law might induce negative emotions in her nephew, and likewise, she risks offending her husband by portraying his father in an unflattering light. The historical record reveals that the third Earl was a formidable character, but it offers no indication of animosity between him and his daughter-in-law, making it most likely that she uses the episode for dramatic effect.[24]

Given the effusive tone of "The Preface," it makes more sense to interpret Finch's unflattering depiction of her father-in-law as a strategic maneuver that amplifies her admiration for her nephew and host. The intricate tale she spins regarding the three generations of patriarchy in her marital family illuminates how she reveres these men in part because doing so enables her to pursue her artistic ambition. Claudia Kairoff and Jennifer Keith, the editors of *The Cambridge Edition of the Works of Anne Finch*, note that "c. 1685, Heneage Finch, third Earl of Winchilsea (1627/8-89) had alterations carried out by William Winde (d. 1722), one of the principal English country house architects of the late seventeenth century."[25] This information allows us to infer that the third Earl's act of poor stewardship occurred approximately eight years previously, when his grandson Charles was about thirteen years old. The editors also observe that because he reached his majority in 1693, that is the earliest date when he could have pursued the estate improvements detailed in the text. By that time, Finch would have known him for about nine years (having married his uncle Heneage in 1684). The mere fact of the marriage proves that she pleased her future father-in-law enough for him to approve it. We may also affirm that she knew Sir Charles better than she knew his grandfather, having known the elder man only five years but the younger man nine. Given the warmth she extends to her nephew in "The Preface," she seems to have pleased him at least as much as she had pleased his elder. Despite the risks of speculation, it is plausible and indeed likely that Finch showed the proper feminine deference to her male relatives. This behavior instantiates the bargain she has made with patriarchy, as "Upon My Lord Winchilsea" demonstrates.

In sum, the poem deviates from country-house poetic convention by featuring a female speaker who is the lord's relative and social equal and who for rhetorical purposes delivers an unfavorable portrait of one Finch patriarch (her deceased father-in-law). Such deviations exemplify why scholars tend to praise Finch for her originality and generic experimentation.[26] In addition to these strengths, she also cultivates her own cultural authority, introducing a subtext that questions the legitimacy of patriarchy or at least implies that worthy patriarchs sanction and encourage women writers. These matters impact the landscape of stewardship because they establish the appropriate conduct for legitimate stewards. In order for Sir Charles to fulfill the role of ideal patriarch, the speaker offers an example from the past that dramatizes the suffering endured when a cruel patriarch governed the estate. Chronology matters here as well; by locating the cruel steward—figured as an absolute patriarch—in the past, the poem suggests that patriarchy remains viable to the extent that it loosens its absolutist tendencies, especially in its expectations of women.

A nuanced assessment of the poem's idealized landscape of stewardship must also account for the text's model of masculinity, the very essence of patriarchy. Whereas the lord of the title possesses a refined masculinity, his predecessor stands out only for aggression against his dependents and carelessness with his natural resources. In the following lines, the speaker laments the missing trees and imagines the drama that culminated in their felling.

> To see a shelt'ring Grove the prospect bound,
> Just rising from the same prolifick ground,
> Where late itt stood, the Glory of the Seat,
> Repell'd the Winter blasts, and skreen'd the Sommer's heat;
> So prais'd, so lov'd, that when untimely Fate
> Sadly prescrib'd itt a too early Date,
> The heavy tidings, cause a gen'ral grief,
> And all combine, to bring a swift relief,
> Some Plead, some Pray, some Councel, some Dispute,
> Alas! in vain, where Pow'r is Absolute.
> Those, whom Paternal Awe, forbid to speak,
> Their sorrows, in their secret whispers break.
> Sigh as They passe, beneath the sentenc'd Trees,
> Which seem to answer in a mournfull Breeze.
> (*Works* 1:87, lines 23–36)

Identified with absolute power and "Paternal Awe," the man alluded to in this passage controverts the solicitous and judicious qualities of his heir. Finch's speaker thereby constructs opposing models of masculinity through the contrasting actions of hewing an obstructive mount, on one hand, and leveling a beautiful and protective stand of trees, on the other.

The passage's vilification of the former estate patriarch has several layers, for his aggression toward his dependents and apathy to their suffering also extend to his property. Given the scarcity of timber in England at the time—forests having been depleted during the Civil Wars—the former lord's conduct strikes readers as profoundly egregious.[27] By calling the grove "the Glory of the Seat," the speaker implies a widespread reverence for the trees, to which the presiding lord proves unaccountably indifferent. Such callousness results from two grave errors: first, he fails to grasp the trees' salubrious function—they "Repell'd the Winter blasts, and skreen'd the Sommer's heat"; second, he fails to see the extensive appreciation of the trees. By implication, the lord lacks the refinement that a suitable steward should have. The personification of trees that "seem to answer in a mournfull Breeze" further underscores his cruelty; he causes pain that both his dependents and the objects of their devotion must endure. The lines make an incontrovertible case that the ideal patriarch must, by contrast, prove worthy of his role by prioritizing the needs and comfort of his dependents.

When, in the subsequent lines, the speaker stages the ancestor's violent act, he becomes even more menacing.

> The very Clowns, (hir'd by his dayly Pay),
> Refuse to strike, nor will their Lord obey,
> 'Till to his speech, he adds a leading stroke,
> And by Example, does their Rage provoke.
> Then in a moment, ev'ry Arm is rear'd,
> And the robb'd Palace sees, what most she fear'd,
> Her lofty Grove, her ornamental Shield,
> Turn'd to a Desert, and forsaken Field.
> (*Works* 1:87, lines 37–44)

The image of an ax-wielding tyrant dominates the scene, justifying the timidity and fear he incites in his laborers. War imagery ("ev'ry Arm is rear'd,") mingles with crime imagery ("robb'd Palace"), impugning the reckless lord for turning what should be a domestic sanctuary into a battlefield and a crime scene. Finch's hyperbolic language dramatizes Eastwell's turbulent recent history, and the feminization of the estate ("what most she fear'd," "her ornamental Shield") intimates how the violation, though not named a rape, sounds alarmingly close to one. The subtext embedded in the tree-felling interlude leaves no doubt that such a volatile lord does not abide by sound governing principles and therefore deserves censure as an illegitimate patriarch.[28] In the context of Eastwell as Finch idealizes it, the mount that Sir Charles removes exemplifies the ostentation that a wise steward would avoid. Her endorsement of the useful, and her lamentation for the trees and their advocates, locate her in a communitarian landscape of stewardship.

The failed stewardship of which the third Earl of Winchilsea is guilty constitutes a violation of what Erin Drew theorizes as "the usufructuary ethos." This legal doctrine regarding landownership coincides to a remarkable degree with the values grounding the landscape of stewardship, for both value systems prioritize the landowner's obligation to his (and rarely, her) family and other dependents. Usufruct not only codifies the landlord's duties but also defines the land itself as something belonging to its owner only during his or her lifetime. "Deriving from Roman property law," Drew explains, "'usufruct' refers to 'the right of temporary possession, use, or enjoyment of the advantages of property belonging to another so far as may be had without causing damage or prejudice.'"[29] By identifying landed property as always "belonging to another," the doctrine renders landownership decidedly contingent, imposing limits on the owner's right to the land's use and fruits (the term derives from the Latin *usus* and *fructus*[30]). Responsible estate stewardship thus comprises a landowner's primary duty, which he owes not only to his dependents and heirs but also to the estate's natural resources. The doctrine is a moral and religious matter as well as a legal one, for Drew demonstrates that usufruct constitutes, first, "a moral relationship between humans and their environments in late seventeenth and early eighteenth-century England"; and second, a religious principle linking "humans, nonhumans, and God, as well as the social, political, and natural worlds."[31] Given the third Earl's dereliction of duty to both his "Clowns" and his trees, interpreting his failure as a violation of the usufructuary ethos reveals both the urgency and complexity of his ruinous stewardship.

Finch's "Upon My Lord Winchilsea" figures significantly in Drew's argument that generational continuity and respect for nonhuman nature constitute essential components of usufruct. Tree-felling therefore violates this law in several ways: "The fact that Heneage's destruction of the grove repudiates his environmental duties as landlord is evident not only in the fact that undoing his alterations is framed as a restoration of environmental and generational continuity but also in the fact that Finch calls pointed attention to the 'untimely Fate' of the trees, which were 'Sadly prescrib'd . . . a too early Date' (27–28). The problem is not just that they were cut down, but that they were cut down without consideration for the future repercussions of their absence." Sir Charles thus conforms to the usufructuary ethos by rectifying his grandfather's error, and Finch implies that he does so in part because he inherited "the future [and now present] repercussions of [the trees'] absence."[32] Considering "the interdependent Chain of Being" that governs a society based on usufruct, the third Earl's transgressions are an affront not only to his ancestors and heirs but also to God.[33]

Drew's insights into the generational, environmental, and ethical dimensions of "Upon My Lord Winchilsea" enrich our understanding of the landscape of stewardship while also registering its obsolescence during the eighteenth century. She identifies in "mid-century mercantile monocultural georgics" such as John Dyer's *The Fleece* (1757) and James Grainger's *The Sugar-Cane* (1764) an "increasing tendency [. . .] to understand the environment as wealth-generating, rather than sustaining."[34] An approach to land management that maximizes wealth corresponds, in Sullivan's taxonomy, to the landscape of absolute property, which displaces that of stewardship and custom. And the landscape arts, as we have seen, emerge as the aesthetic expression of the proto-capitalist landscape. By tracing the dwindling role of usufruct, Drew's study complicates and amplifies the history of landscape embedded in Finch's country-house poetry. In light of the fact that Finch and her husband were to inherit Eastwell when Sir Charles died in 1712, the poem unwittingly helps Finch prepare for her role as Countess of Winchilsea. Her accession to the title bolstered her status, in turn valorizing Eastwell's landscape of stewardship and the female agency she exerts while honoring the estate.

THE JACOBITE OAK

When "Upon My Lord Winchilsea" engages the politics of stewardship, it likewise insinuates the partisan conflict that wrought such havoc during the English Civil Wars and the Revolution of 1688. In the volatile context of the 1690s and throughout the reign of Queen Anne, the last Stuart monarch (1702–1714), stewardship serves as a crucial value to which both Parliamentarians and royalists, and later Whigs and Tories, lay claim. The same is true for the twin pastoral discourses of retirement and retreat. The poem fashions a retreat at Eastwell with maneuvers that amplify Finch's generic innovation. In addition to crafting a female voice who speaks as her host's relative and social equal, the poem violates convention by having the speaker, rather than the addressee, retreat from political turmoil. The Jacobite subtext emerges in the poem's depiction of violence and "Paternal Awe" (line 33), a likewise innovative strategy that might offend her audience by disparaging a deceased family member but mitigates the risk by situating his malevolent stewardship safely in the past. Delving into the political resonances of these maneuvers exposes the poem's Jacobite innuendo and in turn positions me to establish the poem's contribution to the evolution of landscape.

After digressing into an episode of sinister destruction, the text appeals for peace, thus crafting a trajectory that imbues the poem with a political subtext. In this way, "Upon My Lord Winchilsea" complicates Finch's country-house poem by deviating from the genre's original emphasis on social harmony and plenitude, resulting in greater variability of mood and tone. The violent tree-felling episode exemplifies this modulation, moving from commemoration to disorder and finally to peace, and in the process evoking the recent political upheaval that the Finches witnessed firsthand, which compelled them to flee London in the wake of their monarch's departure for France. As I have argued elsewhere, political instability and personal dislocation converge to a remarkable degree in Anne Finch's life, and this convergence puts into relief the role of country houses not only as precincts of the powerful but also resorts of the dispossessed in the aftermath of the Revolution of 1688.[35] She thus offers an intriguing qualification to Mark Girouard's thesis that country houses are monuments to power in a political situation where monarchical authority is receding before a tide of aristocratic land magnates.[36] Finch's estate poem modifies this narrative by expressing the experience of a woman whose social status, political orientation, and personal and artistic future are deeply entwined with the factional disputes of the post-Restoration era. By innovating on the royalist narrative of landed wealth, she provides further evidence of her strategic bargain with patriarchy, revealing an eagerness to celebrate the Stuart monarchy (which included four kings and one queen) so long as doing so would license her self-assertion as a woman writer.

The Jacobite subtext is much less explicit in Finch's "Upon My Lord Winchilsea" than in other poems, such as "The Petition for an Absolute Retreat," which have garnered more scholarly inquiry where her political investments are concerned.[37] Yet biographical details embedded in the former poem provide persuasive explanations for its modulation between violence and ease, a dynamic that serves as the basis for its Jacobite insinuations. Aside from the tree-felling episode, the poem's cheerful equanimity suggests Finch wrote it during a stable period, when she and Heneage had achieved a measure of security in a home that, though not their own, still welcomed them indefinitely. These circumstances make sense given the period during which she wrote the poem, 1693–ca.1701–1702. This broad chronological span makes it more than likely that over these years Finch would experience both "the spleen" and exhilaration, and it is this latter emotion that dominates by the poem's end. Drawing her encomium to a close, she calls upon the "gen'rous Arts" to bless the estate.

> Oh! May Eastwell, still with their aid encrease,
> Plenty surround her, and within be peace.
> (*Works* 1:88, lines 70, 72–73)

In light of such beatific appeals, the countervailing tone of the tree-felling episode becomes all the starker. Given the potential (and actual) violence that troubled the nation in the late 1680s, Finch's call for peace necessarily evokes the specters of war that haunt the seventeenth century, intimating the poem's Jacobite undertones. Furthermore, her strategic location of Sir Charles's predecessor in the past expresses her optimistic view of patriarchy: as the nation's aristocrats inherit their patrimony and become benevolent estate stewards, they will wisely use it in service to women writers. Such a pact between hierarchical and patriarchal rule underwrites the ideal landscape of stewardship as Finch envisions it.

Scholarly debate over the political nuances in Finch's poem demonstrates how arboreal figures, especially the oak—a standard Stuart emblem—are at the nexus of these issues.[38] A critical consensus has yet to emerge regarding the identity of the tree-felling lord or, for that matter, the trees themselves. Whereas the previous analysis treats the lord as a stand-in for Finch's father-in-law, Wes Hamrick reads the man as a Parliamentarian and perhaps even the most powerful partisan: Oliver Cromwell, Lord Protector. This reading in turn affirms the felled trees as oaks, leading Hamrick to argue that "in the context of Finch's Jacobite poetics of retreat, the oaks also function as a coded reference to the actual Stuarts, and therefore inject the memory of past conflict into her poetic rendering of rural retirement."[39] Assessing the poem almost twenty years after I first wrote about it, I still find that identifying the referent(s) for the tree-felling tyrant is not an either/or matter. It may be true that the third Earl of Winchilsea was a royalist whereas the figures to whom Hamrick refers were Parliamentarians and their heir William III. But this inconsistency does not mean that one reading discredits the other; rather, it amplifies the extent to which the ideology of stewardship—which uses tree-felling as anathema to its ideals—lends itself to appropriation by opposing political factions.

Drew's *Usufructuary Ethos* introduces an ecocritical perspective that renders moot the distinctions among Hamrick's reading, my own, and that of Finch's editors insofar as we all concur that "the Glory of the Seat" at Eastwell consisted of oak trees. Drew's bold though not decisive argument challenges our partisan readings of the grove as unnecessarily narrow and grounded in faulty logic: "[T]he explicitly partisan frames that have been used to interpret the poem's environmental ethos are political red herrings, creating the appearance of political incoherence by locating the confluence of politics and environmentalism in the wrong place." By treating the "political symbolism associated with the oak" as irrelevant, Drew instead foregrounds "other ways that trees signified for early modern writers, in particular how they functioned as a key literary trope of the usufructuary ethos through their embodiment of mediality and accountability to the public and posterity."[40] Drew's interest in how trees mediate humanity's obligation to nature and to God demonstrates, as previously seen, the convergence of usufruct and the landscape of stewardship. As with my rejoinder to Hamrick, so too I find that Drew's reading does not necessarily discredit the opposing views under scrutiny. Republican or royalist, oak or ash—we need not resolve these matters in order to appreciate Finch's commitment to a mode of landownership and stewardship long associated with the past and vulnerable to an environmentally, economically, and politically imperiled future.

Finch's royalist landscape of stewardship also reveals the ideological ambiguity of improvement rhetoric. The third Earl no doubt believed he improved his estate by building the mount, just as Sir Charles believes he improved the place by removing this "fault." Finch's subtitle locates her work in the discourse of improvement, noting her lord's "Converting the Mount in His Garden to a Terras, and Other Alterations, and *Improvements*, in His House, Park, and Gardens" [my emphasis]. As seen in chapter 1, Whigs such as Joseph Addison treated improvement as a practice that could encompass both the expansion of a landscape park and the "frequent Plantations [. . . and] Fields of Corn."[41] In light of the eighteenth-century ideological struggle over what exactly constitutes improvement, Finch's poem serves as a precursor to that debate. In the aftermath of the English Civil Wars, estate improvement and arboreal stewardship proved especially urgent concerns across the political spectrum. Parliamentarians marshaled the rhetoric of stewardship against their adversaries; to be sure, both royalist and Republican (i.e., Parliamentarian) administrations contributed to the laxity of forest regulation, for both partook in excessive deforestation and had politically expedient reasons for doing so.[42] Given the adaptability of the ideology of stewardship, and the way this principle maps onto landscape in significant ways, "Upon My Lord Winchilsea" illuminates the liminal quality of the landscape of stewardship, speaking to both backward-facing royalists and forward-facing Republicans. These historical and political resonances render the poem a powerful example of how a retrograde political program might acquire a progressive dimension when rendered in a female voice, investing woman with the wisdom and authority to adjudicate conflicts over matters of estate stewardship.

LADY WORSLEY AND HER FATHER, VISCOUNT WEYMOUTH

The second poem under consideration, "To the Honorable the Lady Worsley at Long-Leate" (hereafter "To Lady Worsley"), dramatizes the ascent of the landscape arts. Together, Finch's two estate poems layer the landscape of stewardship over the landscape arts (or vice versa), exposing their possible coexistence despite the tension between their regressive and progressive tendencies. By celebrating the estate lord's superior taste, "To Lady Worsley" ultimately valorizes the landscape arts over the landscape of stewardship. And by describing estate improvements remarkable for their extravagance rather than their solicitude for the lord's dependents, the poem redefines the ideal steward in terms of aesthetic and not moral sophistication. The title's reference to Longleat indicates that Finch addresses Frances Worsley (née Thynne), daughter of Heneage Finch's sister Frances Thynne (née Finch) and her husband Sir Thomas Thynne, the first Viscount Weymouth. The estate had been in the family since the sixteenth century; Sir Thomas inherited it in 1682 and presided over it until his death in 1714.[43] Lady Worsley, then, was raised at Longleat and may have celebrated the early months of her marriage there (see figure 2.3). These and other biographical details testify to Finch's affinity for an aristocratic (indeed, noble) milieu, but they also introduce compelling

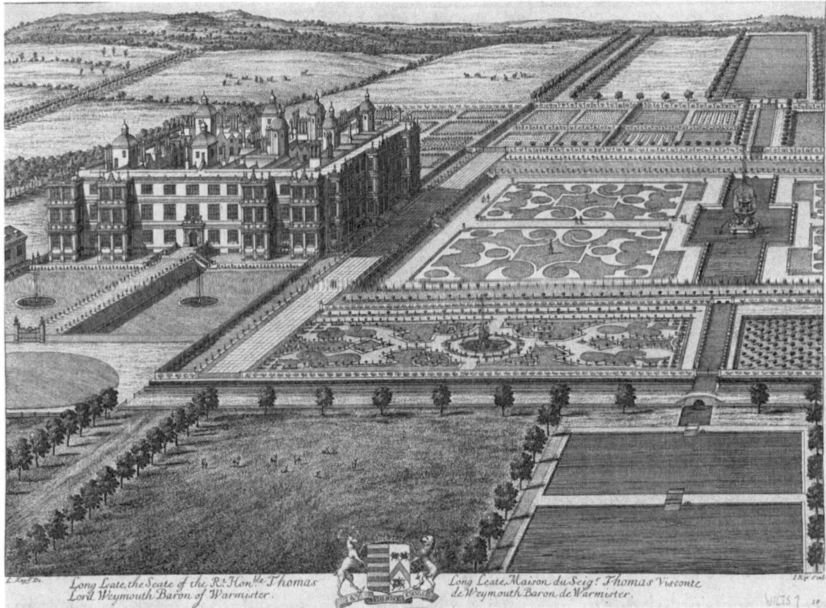

Figure 2.3. *Long Leate* in *Britannia Illustrata* engraved by Johannes Kip and Leendert Knyff, 1707. Royal Collection Trust/© His Majesty King Charles III 2023.

departures from literary convention that distinguish Finch's literary agency. Her example shows how artistic innovation may advance certain interests that appeal to today's feminist critics while also impeding what we would call progress (i.e., social and gender equality).

As several scholars have noted, following Finch biographer Barbara McGovern, the Thynnes extended considerable hospitality to the Finches in the wake of the Glorious Revolution.[44] Finch wrote numerous poems commemorating the friends and relatives with whom she spent time at Longleat. The rhetoric of hospitality that infuses estate poetry again appeals to Finch here; Eastwell and Longleat emerge in these texts as the first- and second-most important estates in her adult lifetime, respectively. Like "Upon My Lord Winchilsea," "To Lady Worsley" presents complex questions regarding its conformity to or deviation from literary convention. Both poems deserve consideration for their originality in adapting a somewhat formulaic genre to a new set of historical and personal circumstances. Indeed, the latter poem offers perhaps even stronger evidence that Finch is making a strategic bargain with patriarchy so that she may simultaneously advance her female artistic agency.

Finch probably wrote "To Lady Worsley" sometime in the second half of 1690, when Heneage was being held in London under charges of treason, after his failed attempt to join his exiled monarch in France. The speaker's initial expression of despair suggests that she wrote during a particularly trying time, "from some lonely and obscure recesse / The shunn'd retreat of solitary peace" (1:365, lines 1–2). Yet the poem's subtitle also expresses gratitude to her niece, "Who had most obligingly desired my Corresponding with her by Letters." Moreover, as Finch's editors note, her reference to Lady Worsley in line 25 as "With Joys incompass'd and new Joys to come" (1.366, line 25) suggests Finch may have composed the poem around the time of her niece's marriage to Sir Robert Worsley, in August 1690 (1.705). These details explain Finch's fragile state in her opening lines as well as her cheerful appreciation for Lady Worsley's solicitude. As with her encomium to Sir Charles Finch, this poem culminates in a sense of wonder, dispelling the gloom of a dissonant scene and thus regaining its composure as an estate poem.

"To Lady Worsley" features other qualities that place it in continuity with "Upon My Lord Winchilsea," not only in terms of generic innovation but also in a persistent genuflection to patriarchy. Although the gloom in the Worsley poem arises from the speaker's circumstances and not from the threat of a menacing patriarch, it is remarkable that even its joyful resolution depends on the extraordinary accomplishments of another, albeit more benevolent patriarch. Prior to his appearance, the poem departs from convention by featuring not only a female speaker but also a female addressee (whom the speaker pastoralizes as Utresia). Nevertheless, what begins as appreciation for a female relative morphs into a celebration of a famous estate and its improver, Viscount Weymouth. The displacement of Lady Worsley by her father in this poetic tribute results from the fact that though she is the source of solace, Lady Worsley does not occupy the position of owner or mistress and therefore cannot assume the responsibility or praise for the estate's provision of hospitality. The synecdoche that conventionally links estate and owner cannot operate in Lady Worsley's case, and so her father inadvertently usurps the glory meant for her.[45]

These aspects of the poem constitute another instance of the paradox traced in my discussion of "Upon My Lord Winchilsea": Finch's valorization of women's writing hinges upon her legitimation of patriarchy. Abiding by literary tradition necessitates that women be relegated to the margins, leaving us to ponder the other consequences—literary, material, or otherwise—that result from forms that encode male privilege. Thus far, then, the poems suggest that whether she conjures a landscape of stewardship or the landscape arts, both social formations necessitate a certain measure of female subordination.

The most significant dimension of Lord Weymouth's displacement of his daughter appears in the poem's lengthy description of the improvements undertaken at Longleat, which in turn necessitates a celebration of the man who initiated them. In the absence of praise for the estate's mistress (Frances Thynne, viscountess of Weymouth), then, Finch's estate poem demonstrates the ascendance of the landscape arts. One striking reason for this impact is that the passage describing the lord and his improvements surpasses in length the previous passage, which thanks and praises Lady Worsley. Another is that the second passage employs figurative language and allusions of such a hyperbolic nature that the beauty and wonder of the estate far exceed the beauty and wonder of Utresia. The passage describing Lady Worsley clearly amounts to no more than twenty-eight lines (13–40). By contrast, the speaker devotes lines 45–111 to depictions of Longleat and "His Genius who th'orginal improv'd" (72). Even if one discounts lines 99–111, which depict Paradise as a precursor for Longleat, it remains the case that over half the poem (fifty-four lines) refers to Lord Weymouth and/as his estate. McGovern, acknowledging the speaker's tribute to her niece, likewise notes, "the laudatory verses to [Lady Worsley's] father, the Viscount Weymouth, are the true nexus of the poem. Weymouth has laid out the gardens in the Dutch fashion, and the descriptive passages of the flowered labyrinths, terraced landscapes, and Italian-style fountains and cascades are a tribute to his genius."[46]

McGovern's reference to "terraced landscapes" reminds us of the term's capacious meaning. Her usage implements definition 1.a from *The Oxford English Dictionary*: "A view or prospect of natural inland scenery."[47] This deceptively simple definition obscures the historical process that has occluded the landscapes of stewardship and custom in order to institutionalize (according to Sullivan) the landscape arts and their corollary, the landscape of absolute property. Appreciating the distillation of meaning in the *OED* definition helps us grasp how visual aesthetics operate in the poem. Its accumulating details paint a vivid scene that derives its rhetorical power from a visual display, thus augmenting McGovern's implied reference to the actual hill-space with a broader reference to the poem's representation of natural scenery. Landscape might be a piece of land or a representation thereof. Finch's emphasis on aesthetic experience thus demonstrates how the poem participates in the landscape arts.

Closer scrutiny reveals the rich and allusive quality of her landscaping; after professing a desire to surpass the poets John Denham and Abraham Cowley, the speaker suggests that she faces an even greater challenge in the prospect of capturing Longleat's beauties in verse.

> Or shew (the harder Labour to compleat)
> The real Splendours of our fam'd Long-leate
> Which above Metaphor itts Structure reares
> Thô all Enchantment to our sight appears
> Magnificently Great the Eye to fill
> Minutly finish'd for our nicest skill
> Long-leate that justly has all Praise engross'd
> The Strangers wonder and our Nations boast
> Paint her Cascades that spread their sheets so wide

> And emulate th'Italian Water's pride
> Her Fountains which so high their streames extend
> Th'amazed Clouds now feel the Rains ascend.
> (*Works* 1:367, 46–56)

The references to *sight* in line 48 and *Eye* in line 49 signal the passage's reliance on visual rhetoric, producing an aesthetic emphasis that propels the rest of the poem. The speaker bolsters this technique with hyperbole that almost turns the scene into an international gardening contest; Longleat is the "Nations boast," a stature it can claim by appropriating Italian and Dutch styles. This assertion extends the synecdoche between lord and estate to encompass the nation too—an intimation of Britain's imperial ambitions. Evidence of this appears in the speaker's reference to "Th'Assyrian Rose" (line 66).[48] As Longleat historian David Burnett has documented, Lord Weymouth imported rare plants from the Indies; his gardeners also used advanced horticultural practices such as root selection, grafting, hot-houses, and forcing-frames.[49] The text's visual emphasis, alongside its embrace of botanic exotica, sustain the poem's enactment of the landscape arts, the subtext of which implies that the lord expends great wealth in order to display his stature. Thus, he inhabits a landscape of absolute property.

Lord Weymouth's displacement of his daughter animates a version of the country-house lord whose worthiness arises from his taste rather than his wise stewardship. His ownership of Longleat grounds the poem, just as detail about his estate improvements obfuscates the laborers and constructs the local community as a small coterie of fellow aristocrats. Finch's silence regarding the laborers at Longleat stands out not only against her Winchilsea poem but also against Jonson, her distant forerunner. The landscape arts encompass her Longleat poem in part by transforming the ideology of stewardship into a matter of personal taste rather than mutual support. Such a landscape occludes any notion of stewardship as a principle that serves the estate's dependents as well as their lord. The link between Weymouth's landscape and capitalism lurks in the subtext, wherein readers may infer the tremendous costs incurred for performing these improvements (see figure 2.4).[50] Together, the aesthetic and financial registers join forces to give the impression that the ideal landscape is one to be looked at, and one whose splendors require imperialist commerce. Global capitalism operates in the Assyrian, Italian, and Dutch garden features, insinuating a link between aesthetics and politics. Such a link serves as a powerful reminder of the ideological subtext embedded in aesthetic practices. Exposing the subtext in turn strengthens the historical dimension of my argument; the poem's reliance on the landscape arts, and its silence regarding the laborers who performed the estate improvements, signal the ascent of a landscape of absolute property. Landscape may superficially be a matter of aesthetics, but so much more lies underground, as it were.

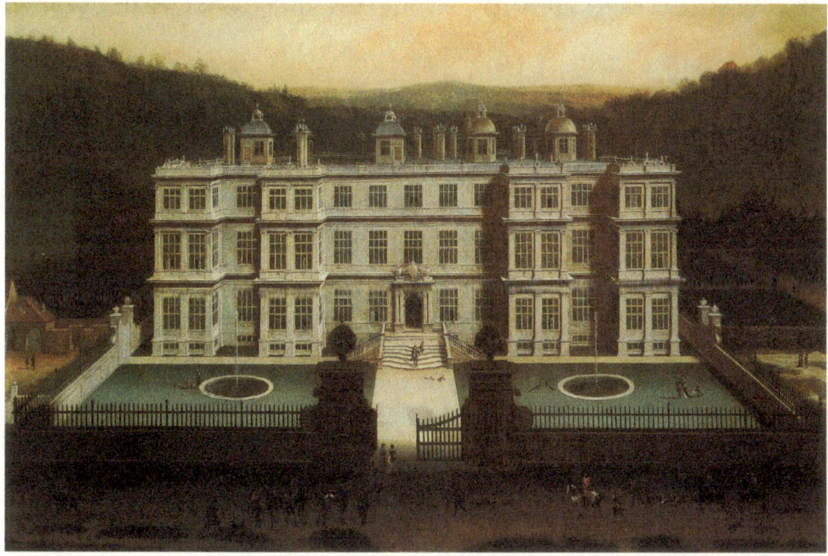

Figure 2.4. *View of Longleat* by Jan Siberechts, ca. 1678. Public domain image via Wikimedia Commons.

"To Lady Worsley" features other strategies that aggrandize Lord Weymouth and minimize most others. The sole mortal figures mentioned in the poem, besides Utresia and the speaker herself (who, like the lord, need not name herself), remain anonymous: "The Strangers" in line 52; "he" who walks through the "Lab'rinths into which, who fondly comes" in lines 62 and 64; and finally, "his great Offspring here" in line 85. The latter relatives would have included Lady Worsley's brothers Henry and James Thynne, both of whom predeceased their father, though most likely not before the poem's composition. By contrast, Jonson distinguishes Lord Robert Sidney by claiming, regarding his children,

> They are, and have been, taught religion; thence
> Their gentler spirits have sucked innocence.[51]

Jonson then adds four more lines in a similar vein. Even Marvell's iconoclastic *Upon Appleton House* culminates (in stanza 86) in a rhapsodic, ornate, and lengthy figuration of *Maria*, Sir Thomas Fairfax's daughter Mary. Thus, country-house poetic convention uses the lord's offspring as embodiments of his fertility, and that of the very estate's fertility. These precedents make Finch's deviation from convention—by not depicting child-rearing on the estate—all the more striking; they also underscore the poem's individualist ethos—a hallmark of the landscape arts.

VISUAL RHETORIC: SEEING AND BEING SEEN AT LONGLEAT

"To Lady Worsley" crafts a visual aesthetic that signals in multiple ways that seeing is never a neutral process; rather, ideology motivates sight and thus infiltrates a purportedly impartial realm with politics. Echoing the pattern of the stanza describing Longleat, the subsequent one professes the speaker's inability to find adequate language to describe the "Genius" of the place.

> No Syllables the most sublimely wrought
> Can reach the loftier Immage of his thought
> Whose Judgment plac'd in a superiour hight
> All things surveys with comprehensive sight
> Then pittying us below stoops to inform us right
> In Words which such convincing Reasons bear
> We silent wish that they engraven were.
> (*Works* 1:367–368, lines 76–82)

Given the hyperbole already witnessed in the poem, this passage verges on hagiography. So, too, the speaker sustains her previous emphasis on visuality ("comprehensive sight") and summons the rhetoric of the survey ("All things surveys"). As Mary Louise Pratt's landmark study *Imperial Eyes* argued, Western imperialism constructs the stance of Western man as "monarch of all I survey," a phrase popularized by William Cowper's poem "The Solitude of Alexander Selkirk" (1782).[52] The survey in line 79 resonates with the implied imperial ambitions of "our Nations boast." Similarly, "the loftier Immage of his thought" translates a nonvisual entity, thought, into visual form. A perplexing phrase, it refers perhaps to the landscape components itemized in the poem—the cascades, terraces, garden maze (*Lab'rinths* in line 62), and so forth, which render visible Lord Weymouth's brilliant thoughts. The riot of visual imagery in this passage (and throughout the text) constitutes a key means by which the poem steers the meaning of landscape into a specifically aesthetic realm. Longleat exists to be looked at more than lived in—and in any case, those who live or move through it appear to do nothing other than take pleasure in the experience.

The gender politics of the poem's visual rhetoric demands scrutiny here, especially in light of my argument that estate poetry convention demands that Lord Weymouth displace his daughter as the poem's hero. The male gaze does not necessarily operate in a poem with a female speaker; nevertheless, it is striking to witness the text's progression from observations about the sight of Utresia to ones referencing the sight of the estate. These lines occur prior to the passage featuring "The real Splendours of our fam'd Long-leate."

> Utresia [. . .]
> Who like the Sun in her Meridian shows

> Surrounded with the Lustre she bestows
> Her Self dispensing by her long'd for sight
> To every Place She visits full delight [. . .]
> Who when such Eyes so soft and bright we view
> Soften our Cares and grow enlighten'd too.
> (*Works* 1:366, lines 24, 26–29, 33–34)

To the extent that patriarchy thrives on female objectification—and the poem at several points feminizes Longleat ("Paint her Cascades" [line 53]; "Her Fountains" [line 55])—one could build a strong case for the text's conflation of Utresia and Longleat as female figures. Lord Weymouth, meanwhile, is the male "monarch" who surveys them. Such a reading reiterates previous instances where Finch aligns herself with patriarchy.

Nevertheless, Utresia exerts a visual force within the poem that invests her with agency and complicates the apparent objectification to which the text subjects her. The uncertainty regarding to whom the "sight" in line 28 belongs ("Her Self dispensing by her long'd for sight") is just one indication of how the passage collapses the subject and object of observation. The dominant meaning is that Utresia sheds light on those who long to catch sight of her, making "sight" an act that her observers perform. But the expression also implies that Utresia spreads "delight" (line 29) simply by looking upon others and their surroundings, in effect making her vision a conduit through which pleasure travels. The ambiguity expands the movement of light (code for pleasure and wit in the poem, also apparent in the use of "enlighten'd" in line 34) such that it flows both to and from Utresia. Furthermore, eyes figure prominently in the passage ("Who when such Eyes so soft and bright we view"), further refracting the poem's visual thematic; the key components of vision—light and the sensory organs that perceive it—come to define Utresia and determine her interactions with others. And by forecasting the way that Longleat will fill the visual field ("Magnificently Great the Eye to fill" in line 49), the reference to Utresia's eyes renders her as much an observer as an object of observation. The subtleties in Finch's manipulation of visual rhetoric exemplify her propensity to advance female agency even as she also endorses patriarchy.

The contrast between "Upon My Lord Winchilsea" and "To Lady Worsley" emerges in the types of landscape(s) that each poem enacts; in the former, we witness the landscapes of stewardship and custom while in the latter, we see the landscape arts, subtended by the landscape of absolute property. What makes the two poems so historically rich is their capacity to trace, together, a gradual and uneven transition from landscapes valuing community to those privileging the wealthy individual—usually a male individual. The stewardship ethos, especially, proves serviceable to Finch's Jacobite allegiances, though its adaptability across the political spectrum makes it likewise appealing to William of Orange and his Whig allies. Finally, gender is a crucial lens through which to interpret Finch's landscapes, as we have seen, because of her strategic engagement with patriarchy, which she cannily manages to harmonize with her performance of female independence. Her complicated political position seems to necessitate this poetical scheming of sorts. Her negotiation of visual rhetoric stands out as a particularly effective way to trouble the subordination of women who, as both objects and agents of the gaze, elude the frailty and passivity that social forces might otherwise impose upon them. In this way, we witness how Finch avails herself of the virtues and beauties associated with country life, and of the privileges available to the aristocracy, in order to forge a literary identity that paradoxically marries patriarchy and proto-feminism. In Sarah Scott, the focus of chapter 3, we encounter another writer who makes a calculated bargain with patriarchy when it advances the independence of landed women. As we will see, Scott embraces the discourse of the country estate and uses it to fashion a women's utopia, thus offering a story that echoes Finch's arboreal imagery.

> To see a shelt'ring Grove the Prospect bound,
> Just rising from the same prolifﬁck ground.
> (*Works* 1:87, 23–24)

3

"AND THE COUNTRY ADJACENT"

Sarah Scott's Literary Landscaping

SARAH SCOTT'S *A Description of Millenium Hall and the Country Adjacent* (1762, hereafter *Millenium Hall*) has a peculiar tendency to produce contradictory readings; while some critics celebrate the novel's putatively radical feminist utopianism, others implicate it in the symbolic violence that accompanies capitalist social relations, depending as they do on the misrecognition of exploitation as benevolence.[1] A related controversy involves the elitist subordination—sometimes termed a sacrifice—to which the Hall women subject their female social inferiors.[2] Likewise, spectatorship and its variants—voyeurism, visuality, surveillance, the gaze—also serve as key, though contested, vectors of the novel's agenda. Advocates for the novel's feminism point to how the Hall women perform as subjects rather than objects of the gaze.[3] Meanwhile, skeptics of a feminist reading of the work foreground how the unnamed male narrator treats these women as "aesthetic objects" or as visionaries who must be surveilled and contained while sympathetic gentlemen export the women's philanthropic methods into British society at large.[4] A germane investigation of the politics of vision, though not specifically in Scott's work, appears in Alison Conway's study of the eighteenth-century English novel's reliance on portraiture. According to Conway, "The portrait's frequent appearance in the novel renders the issue of visual agency—in relation to both display and beholding—an important means of assessing how the eighteenth century understood women's connection to the cultural power that was associated with those activities."[5]

It would not be an exaggeration to state that *Millenium Hall* is a veritable riot of "display and beholding." Not only does the narrator deliver blazons of several Hall women, but they themselves call attention to characters' physical appearances, both past and present. Consider, for instance, the narrator's early claim that "I shall endeavour to give you some idea of the persons of the ladies, whose minds I shall afterwards best describe by their actions."[6] Despite paying lip service to the principle that actions matter more than appearances, the narrator's habitual attention to each Hall lady's "countenance" reinforces his talent for female objectification. Two sentences later, he observes the woman who will become his native informant, who also turns out to be his cousin: "Mrs. Maynard is between forty and fifty years of age, a little woman, well made, with a lively and genteel air, her hair black, and her eyes of the same colour, bright and piercing, her features good, and complexion agreeable, though brown. Her countenance expresses all the vivacity of youth, tempered with a serenity which becomes her age" (59–60). In the process of describing Mrs. Maynard's face, the narrator also constructs her character: "piercing" eyes and "complexion agreeable" bespeak the woman's perceptiveness and good humor. As Lisa L. Moore and Katherine Nolan have noted, the novel interrogates gender inequality by scrutinizing the operations of the gaze.[7] Visual agency belongs to both the narrator and the women at various points in the story.

Although born in Yorkshire, Sarah Scott (née Robinson, 1720–1795) spent most of her formative years at the maternal estate of Mount Morris in Monks Horton, Kent (see figure 3.1). Her severe bout of smallpox in 1741 constitutes an

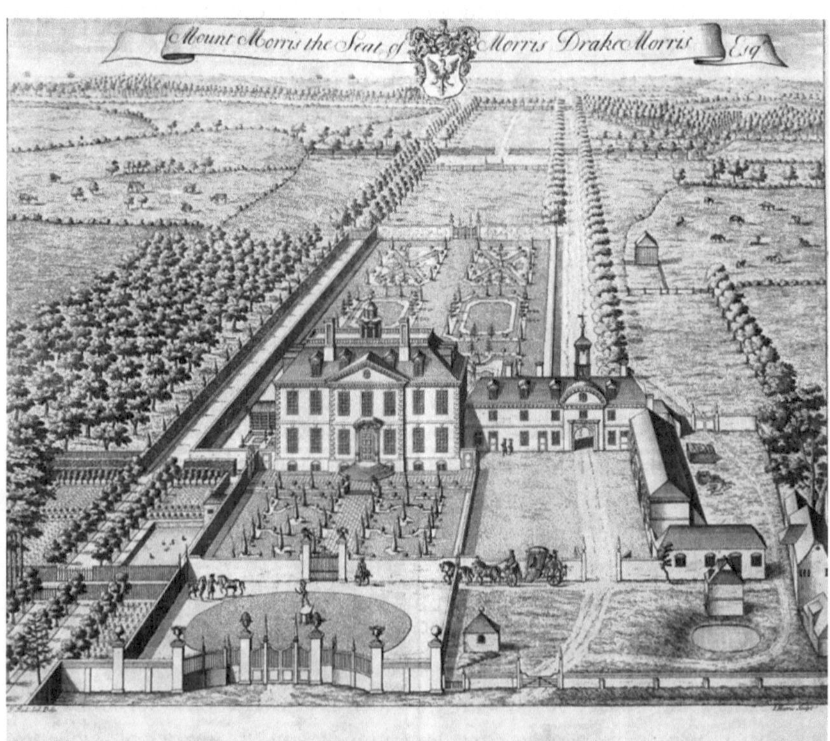

Figure 3.1. *Mount Morris*, near Hythe, engraved by Johannes Kip and Leendert Knyff, 1707. History and Art Collection/Alamy Stock Photo.

early milestone, especially in the present context, since the disease was "then regarded as ruining a woman's beauty and thus lowering her value on the marriage market."[8] Given British culture's obsession with female beauty, one might expect this episode to afflict her with a profound sense of loss. Yet scholars argue that Scott turned calamity into opportunity by immersing herself even further in the erudition that family life in the Robinson household had inculcated.[9] The illness separated her from her beloved elder sister, Elizabeth (later Montagu [1718–1800], featured in chapter 4), but they remained forever close despite occasional disagreements. Perhaps even more decisive was Scott's relationship with the invalid Lady Barbara ('Bab') Montagu (no relation). Sarah and Bab began living together in 1748 and continued to do so once Sarah married George Lewis Scott in June 1751 (an arrangement Gary Kelly calls "not uncommon"). Kelly also notes that "there is no unequivocal evidence that there was or was not a sexual dimension to [Sarah and Bab's] love."[10] In a startling intervention that scandalized contemporaries and still puzzles scholars, Scott's father and brothers removed her from the marital home in April 1752; the author's mandated and posthumous destruction of her papers perpetuates the mystery.

Prior to Scott's marriage, she and Lady Bab began pursuing charitable projects that prefigure those in *Millenium Hall*, which prioritize female learning, piety, and probity. As Nicole Pohl demonstrates, Scott embraced "Practical Christianity as a basis for social reform," and the Hall heroines' exemplary conduct enacts this distinctively Anglican commitment to benevolence.[11] A perpetual dearth of funds led her to begin writing novels and histories, and one translation, in order to supplement her income. From *The History of Cornelia* (1750) to *The Test of Filial Duty* (1772), she produced five novels and three histories, *Millenium Hall* being the most successful, with four editions by 1778. As if to bring the novel to life, and with the support of her sister and Sarah Fielding (among others), Scott planned a utopian community at Hitcham (Buckinghamshire) in 1766. Nevertheless, financial uncertainty, Scott's ill health, and quarrels about the scheme prevented its realization. Yet her signature exemplarity endured in another sense when she wrote a sequel to *Millenium Hall*, *The History of Sir George Ellison* (1766), which features the narrator emulating the Hall women's utopian scheme on his own estate.

This biographical sketch, in particular Scott's own disfigurement from smallpox (a trait she assigns to the character Mrs. Trentham in *Millenium Hall*), indicates the extent of her entanglement with questions of visuality. Yet, rather than seeking to identify whose gaze dominates or endures, this chapter analyzes the implications of the way that Scott's novel subjects both women and land to similar forms of objectification.[12] I then relate these insights on visuality to my broader focus on the historical transformation of landscape, deducing a connection between the Hall ladies' visual agency and their participation in what Garrett Sullivan identifies as the landscape arts. An example from the text's opening sequence demonstrates that even before introducing the women, Scott intimates how gazing upon the land engages a process that resembles that of encountering an attractive woman. During the buildup to the narrator's first encounter with the Hall and its owners, the text describes a beautiful avenue of oaks, "a mile and a half in length," that entices the travelers forward.[13] He and his companion, the young "coxcomb" Lamont, follow the avenue, wondering where it will lead (*Millenium Hall*, 55). After viewing further evidence of the estate's outstanding beauty, including a group of neatly dressed and cheerful haymakers, whose "rosy cheeks shewed the benefits of youthful labour," the narrator again asserts that the land around the avenue continues to intrigue him: "Curiosity is one of those insatiable passions that grow by gratification; it still prompted us to proceed, not unsatisfied with what we had seen, but desirous to see still more of this earthly paradise" (58). The eroticism of the narrator's language—"insatiable passions [. . .] gratification [. . .] desirous"—demonstrates how he casts a voyeuristic gaze on the land in a way that resembles a voyeur's view of a beautiful woman. Yet as Judith Broome observes, Scott neutralizes any trace of desire; in her ideal community, "all sexuality has been relegated to the land," the fertility of which I will scrutinize at the end of the chapter.[14]

An inspection of the novel's opening paragraphs reveals how Scott initiates an interest in spectatorship. After announcing a plan to publish the letter he is writing about his journey to Cornwall, the narrator disavows the imputation of vanity: "As I have no other share than that of a spectator, and auditor, in what I purpose to relate, I presume no apology can be required" (*Millenium Hall*, 54). Thus, spectatorship drives the text from the very beginning. The fact that readers meet this spectator even before reaching the exposition intimates how fundamental this visual device will prove throughout the text. Readers next encounter that exposition: A carriage accident leads two gentlemen travelers to stumble upon a remote Cornish estate while touring the countryside, where they enjoy a dazzling encounter with the six gentlewomen who have pooled their resources in order to preside there.[15] Over the course of two days, the visitors alternately marvel at the beautiful property and listen to the tales of tribulation and parental or spousal turpitude that compelled the ladies' rural retirement. In the process, the men learn that one of the Hall's original founders, Mrs. Morgan, inherited the estate from her deceased husband, and that the ladies have since devoted themselves in part to improving their property.

Once attuned to the remarkable similarity of the visual pleasure provided by the women and their land, one comes to suspect that a common force initiates these forms of objectification. The novel thus exposes two crucial manifestations of the visual apparatus of patriarchy. Looking at comely women and looking at a scenic estate prove to serve similar functions in a society governed by male landownership. A comparison of the novel's voyeuristic treatment of its heroines and their landed property reveals the novel's distinctive reliance on scopophilia. Thus, by interpreting the novel's complex visual dynamics specifically through the lens of the land, this chapter seeks to illuminate the relationship between visual agency, landownership, and female independence in *Millenium Hall.*

GAZING AT WOMEN AND THEIR LAND

Given the aggressively chaste character of the Hall women and the narrator himself, readers infer that voyeurism operates here as a way to sustain the patriarchy; though not the landowner, the narrator nevertheless controls the ladies and their land to the extent that he keeps them under his gaze. He practices a proprietary form of the gaze, which Elizabeth Bohls has theorized in relation to "the period's conceptualizations of gardening, painting, and merely contemplating a natural scene. [. . .] Looking at landscape becomes a paradigmatic mental exercise in ownership."[16] Bohls identifies a visual practice that corresponds to the narrator's in the foregoing scene, revealing in turn how Scott follows a well-trodden path in her double-objectification strategy. As Carole Fabricant argued decades ago, "Since a walk through a well-designed garden was viewed as a 'journey [. . .] through a succession of pictures,' the grounds of an estate were in effect a natural extension of the picture galleries constructed indoors, in the great halls and salons, where both landscapes and women were commonly framed and placed on display."[17] We may glean two key insights from this passage: First, Fabricant's use of the term *landscape* aligns with the landscape arts—a commonplace usage that reifies the standard definition from *OED* definition 1.a: "A picture representing natural inland scenery."[18] (I adopt this usage accordingly, with the proviso that the history of landscape renders it problematic.) Second, she notices the parallel between how eighteenth-century British culture looks at landscape and how it looks at women. Together, Bohls and Fabricant help us grasp how profoundly British culture's power structure depends on the twin objectification of women and land.

The male travelers in *Millenium Hall* follow in a long line of landscape voyeurs. Critics disagree as to whether Scott censures or perpetuates this conflation of landscape and women through their objectification. The fact that she is of course the creator of these male voyeurs heightens the complexity of the novel's visual conceits. Does her status as creator undermine male authority as it objectifies women and/or the land? Similarly, does the fact that the ladies direct the male gaze away from exploited women and instead onto the land suggest that ultimately, the text vests decisive visual agency in its heroines? Regardless of one's stance on these issues, what matters most is the equivocation embedded in the novel's reliance on these forms of objectification. Compounding this equivocation is the fact that objectifying both women and land functions in the text as a form of mystification. The ladies' calculated grooming of their property uses vision to seduce the male travelers while at the same time blinding them to the reality of the estate's exploitative treatment of socially subordinate women. And whether we attribute this mystification to the ladies, the narrative, and/or Scott, the ambiguous agency behind the obscurity surely contributes to its significance.

These insights on the politics of visuality reinforce my assertion that Scott's novel plays an important role in the historical transformation of landscape. Thus far, we have witnessed her ambiguous use of objectification and her reliance on landscape description as a means to entice the travelers and thus the reader further toward the estate and into the story. For the opening of the novel to dwell at such length on the landscape suggests that it is not incidental or merely decorative. Rather, it is an initial glimpse of the purposeful attention the text pays to the landscape arts. Though he doesn't realize it at the time, the narrator identifies crucial evidence of the ladies' excellence in estate management. Noting "the remarkable verdure and neatness of the fields" (*Millenium Hall*, 56), and the dazzling color of the flowers, he demonstrates an awareness that such carefully manicured grounds leading up to the mansion must signal the wisdom of those who preside over the place. In short, he glimpses what Sullivan labels a "landscape of stewardship" and thus adds another layer to our key term's meaning. In the first two pages of *Millenium Hall*, then, readers encounter what we now recognize as an obsolescent landscape of stewardship—that is, one operating according to principles of reciprocity. The novel intertwines this landscape with multiple evocations of the landscape arts, the corollary for the emergent landscape of absolute property. But as Sullivan has demonstrated, the latter landscape accompanies the early phases of capitalism, thus exposing a chronological error and perhaps even a deception embedded in Scott's "Historical Anecdotes and Reflections," as her subtitle reads.

By troubling the chronology of landscape's history—treating as *new* a mode of reciprocal relations that in fact pre-dates the capitalist social arrangements governing the Hall estate—Scott mystifies the true nature of her utopia. Consequently, *Millenium Hall* tactically but deceptively embraces the landscape of stewardship while in fact mobilizing a landscape of absolute property, thus obscuring the exploitation on which her utopian experiment depends. The novel enables us to identify how, like Anne Finch, Scott conspires with patriarchy, though her method differs from Finch's insofar as the novelist appropriates British patriarchy's most essential institution, landownership, and confers it upon genteel women. This maneuver ultimately disables the text's feminist commitments by prioritizing the ladies' social superiority over gender equality and by enabling them to reap the rewards of the capitalist system they serve while purporting not to. These observations expose further resonance between Scott's novel and Finch's poem "To the Honorable the Lady Worsley at Long-Leate," wherein Utresia (a sobriquet for Lady Worsley) both exercises visual agency and undergoes objectification. Both texts demonstrate the complex dynamics of visuality and their entanglement with the gender inequality embedded in male landownership. In their several ways, they reveal how this institution governs social relations and in turn how consequential it is for women rather than men to be landowners.

Narrator and character interactions with land help us understand the significance of Scott's decision to make female independence hinge upon landownership, and more specifically a form of landownership that embeds this mandate within agrarian and proto-industrial capitalism, or what Gary Kelly calls "gentry capitalism."[19] A material substance, land undergoes a kind of alchemical process when it encodes social relations, conferring social status on landowners and dependents alike. This process distills the land into an intangible but formidable product—a landscape. Because Millenium Hall constitutes landed property that the women own and steward collectively, and because the narrative details the extent, contours, and (wo)man-made structures of the estate, the novel effectively transforms the Hall land into a landscape. By constructing both female bodies and rural land as objects of the gaze, the novel sensitizes readers to British society's degradation of women as a kind of property. As David Oakleaf asserts, "At the heart of *Millenium Hall* lies the radical assumption that those whose lot in life often made them little more than property themselves can in fact be proprietors."[20] Building on Oakleaf's observation, this chapter investigates how the Hall landscape encodes female agency and confers independence upon those with sufficient virtue, status, and wealth to qualify them to preside over an estate. Tempering this feminist reading (qualified though it may be), the chapter also evaluates the inner workings of the ladies' stewardship and reveals it to be dubious, based as it is on deception and perhaps hypocrisy. Yet I undertake this interpretation while also appreciating that Scott's decision to make women's self-determination hinge upon landownership constitutes a milestone in eighteenth-century British fiction. Balancing the censorious and celebratory dimensions of my argument demonstrates how this didactic novel transmits lessons well beyond those that Scott could recognize.

With these insights in mind, the chapter enters the debate over the novel's representation of social and gender relations by situating these within the discourse of landscape. There is no question that *Millenium Hall* endorses the social hierarchy; more open to debate are the causes and consequences of this social rigidity. Emma Major emphasizes Scott's Anglicanism as an important source of her views on class. This perspective introduces religion as a significant though ancillary explanation for the novel's treatment of landownership, insofar as the Church of England itself codifies the social hierarchy. In so doing, the Church reinforces other institutional valorizations of landownership, such as primogeniture (the principle allocating the rights of inheritance to the firstborn son), the entail ("the rule of descent settled for any estate; the fixed or prescribed line of devolution"[21]), and other legal mechanisms for controlling the transmission of landed property in order to preserve the social status quo. As Major argues, "The practical piety of Scott's novel is rooted in an understanding of class and the duties appropriate to its different levels, for [. . . she] sees Christianity as operating through the preservation of those orders." These insights offer compelling religious context for what Major calls "the providential social order in *Millenium Hall*," enabling us to see how social inequality was built into the very architecture of the Protestant state.[22]

Linking the novel's intertwined social and religious agenda to its investment in landownership is a matter of identifying the material and ideological substrate of this women's country-house utopia. While Scott's conservative views ground the novel in tradition, it is no less noteworthy that she identifies within that tradition the possibility for female independence, albeit for the few with access to landownership. More important, for my purposes, is how the novel illuminates both the historical transformation of landscape and women writers' participation therein. The previous chapters on Jane Barker and Anne Finch demonstrated the historical forces that, in Sullivan's terminology, put complementary landscapes of stewardship and custom into competition with the emergent landscape of absolute property and its aesthetic corollary, the landscape arts—the latter two of which express capitalism's privileging of the individual over the collective. Moving forward a half century in time but returning to the genre last encountered in Barker's novelistic *Galesia Trilogy*, I have chosen Scott's novel for its unique capacity to demonstrate the interdependence of gender, capitalism, and the landscape arts.

In *Millenium Hall* we witness the ascendance of these arts, understood in Sullivan's terms as a suppression or co-optation of the experiences of those who do not own the land. As we will see, the novel frequently depicts gentlewomen overseeing charitable projects that provide employment to peasants who might otherwise go hungry. Scott performs a certain legerdemain by rendering the labors of the poor as spectacles, occasions of aesthetic pleasure for their superiors. For instance, near the novel's very end, the narrator visits a carpet and rug factory founded and managed by the Hall women: "Here we found several hundreds of people of all ages, from six years old to four score, employed in the various parts of the manufacture, some spinning, some weaving, others dying the worsted, and in short all busy, singing and whistling, with the appearance of general cheerfulness, and their neat dress shewed them in a condition of proper plenty."[23] In addition to straining the limits of plausibility, the laborers' merriment and tidiness expose the scene's idealism, which proves to be a product of the ladies' self-righteousness rather than an authentic portrait of a messy and no doubt toilsome industry. Scott thus assimilates the poor within the purview of the landscape arts, meanwhile obscuring the fact that the poor at one time occupied a customary landscape, wherein their well-being operated as a matter of right rather than charity.

Sullivan helps us understand the obsolescent landscape of custom, which Scott has rendered invisible, by tracing in early modern literature a perspective founded on reciprocal relations or what he calls "customary landscapes."[24] She depicts a world wherein the principle of reciprocity, which at one time invested the poor with agency and rights comparable to those of their stewards, has morphed into a principle of compulsory gratitude for the privilege of being able to labor. To explain the material and ideological processes by which this transformation occurs, I turn to a more recent study of custom by landscape historian Nicola Whyte. She argues for a more nuanced scholarship on the customary landscape, finding that some fellow historians oversimplify it in efforts to attribute its obsolescence to parliamentary enclosure of common land. Contending that enclosure does not operate as "an underlying structural force," but rather varies by regional history, topography, market structure, etc., she complicates the terms of an ongoing debate about England's entwined agricultural and ideological history.

Whyte questions, for example, whether certain scholars are right to claim that enclosure contributes to the gradual emergence of individualism and capitalist ideology. According to them, "enclosure, as well as being the physical manifestation of these social and cultural changes, also had a major impact on the physical and cognitive experiences of landscape, as local communities were effectively disconnected from their ancient customs and traditions, their systems of knowledge and memories."[25] One need not take a stand on the vast and intricate debate over enclosure in order to appreciate the complexity of scholarly efforts to understand the relationship between ideological and agricultural history. Scott's novel depicts what appears to be a customary landscape embedded in the rare but revealing speech of a low-born woman inhabiting the Hall estate; her "cognitive experiences of landscape"—her disconnection from ancient tradition—flickers in a narrative otherwise devoted to her benefactors' experiences.

By marginalizing the experiences of poor women, Scott valorizes the philanthropy of the Hall saviors over and above the virtuous gratitude of their beneficiaries. This valorization operates, according to Karen Gevirtz, as a significant pattern in the eighteenth-century English novel, most particularly in depictions of poor widows. Regarding *Millenium Hall*, she observes that "benevolence requires a needy object, and the best needy objects are passive, not diluting the benevolence of the benefactor by making any effort on their own behalf. [. . .] Benevolence may rescue the helpless, but the focus of the action is the rescue itself."[26] By way of example, Gevirtz observes the recently widowed clergyman's wife for whom the Hall women provide a house, an income, and household assistance (among other aids). Such provision renders the widow needy, helpless, and thus worthy of a place among "the best needy objects." A telling corollary to this diminution of poor widows appears in Scott's reluctance to imagine how low-born women might speak for themselves, thus rendering their experience nearly mute. By contrast, she gives abundant speech to the Hall benefactors. Mrs. Maynard's narrative, though implausibly quoted by the narrator, constitutes over half the novel so that, combined with the reported speech of other Hall inhabitants, the female philanthropists' monologues dominate the text as a whole. By studying the novel's celebration of the Hall gentlewomen's philanthropy alongside the text's intertwining of women's landownership, benevolent stewardship, and independence, then, we may better understand the historical transition from landscapes of stewardship and custom to a landscape of absolute property driven by emergent capitalism and manifested in the landscape arts.

BENEVOLENT STEWARDSHIP OF THE LAND AND THE POOR

While landownership serves as the foundation for what Felicity Nussbaum (borrowing from Mary Louise Pratt) calls Scott's "feminotopia," the principles by which the Hall women inhabit their property is at the crux of her feminist experiment.[27] These principles include the benevolent stewardship, aesthetic cultivation, and industrious productivity of rural land, which I have previously identified as "the landscape ethos."[28] This concept enabled me to analyze the relationship between form and content in the novel, thus foregrounding its reliance on a landscape aesthetic that inculcates sensitivity to the arrangement of objects in a vista, which in turn informs the very structure of the novel. In this prior reading, landscape transcends the status of a visible object or even a way of seeing and becomes a carefully wrought textual system that harmonizes the content (landscape) and form (framed narratives) of the novel. The primacy of aesthetics in this formulation of the novel's composition locates it in the realm of the landscape arts. That is, the landscape ethos prioritizes visual experience and presupposes that the term's fundamental meaning involves the visual perception and/or depiction of rural scenery.

The premise of *Prolific Ground*, however, rests on the notion that aesthetic conceptions of landscape do not tell its full story; indeed, they disguise the historical processes that led to the obsolescence of experiential conceptions of landscape—i.e., the landscapes of custom and stewardship—in tandem with the rise of visual ones. The prehistory for the processes in question involves a transformation in modes of landownership, which arises in turn from the commodification of land. Sullivan emphasizes the transformative nature of this process, observing that "land formed the basis for a social world; to identify it first and foremost as a commodity was to expose the fragility of that world, or, at least, to dislocate land from the moral economy that was supposed to be inseparable from it."[29] The historical transformation in question, then, displaces social conceptions of land with economic ones. At the heart of the obsolescent moral economy lies the notion that all members of a community, whether landowner or laborer, have certain rights and responsibilities that issue from the land. Reciprocity governs these relations insofar as all inhabitants of an estate have a duty to others as well as certain rights guaranteed by custom. The mutual dependence of all who inhabit the land produces an ineffable bond that transcends the market value of the land in question.

These insights demand in turn that we interrogate the moral economy inhering in the social relations governing Millenium Hall. Reciprocity appears explicitly and repeatedly in the text and for this reason demands scrutiny. The extent to which the novel dwells on this principle suggests that Scott considers it the ethical foundation for her country-house utopia. But the valence of reciprocity, like so much else in the novel, is up for debate. April London recognizes the text's "tactic of equivocation [which is] confirmed in the novel's final uneasy accommodation of critique with affirmation of 'things as they are.'" I will have occasion to amplify the question of equivocation hereafter, but here I would note that London draws a more sympathetic conclusion regarding the ladies' use of their property than I do. Observing how "a series of deaths had left the founders free to pool their resources," she asserts that "this interruption of patrilineal inheritance [. . .] allows the women to recover an older notion of community in which social relations are defined by collective responsibility rather than individual emulativeness or aspiration."[30] The "patrilineal inheritance" here refers to the bequest inherited by Mrs. Morgan, whose husband died after a life of dissipation that her patient virtue inspired him to regret on his deathbed. London and I concur that women's collective property ownership constitutes a crucial aspect of the utopia, and that this retrograde arrangement aims to recuperate "an older notion of community." But by taking the novel's dedication to community at face value, she underestimates the significance of its socially exclusive quality. Our divergent interpretations emerge in part from her emphasis on the salutary effects of conversation versus my own concern with landscape, and her attention to wealth in general versus my own focus on landed wealth. As we will see, privileging land and landscape as my categories of analysis exposes contradictions that undermine the Hall's ethical coherence.

Because the historical transformation of landscape is my primary interest, I would also argue that Scott belabors the community's commitment to reciprocity because it offers her project the veneer of ethical integrity while also disguising the exploitation that necessarily operates in a landscape of absolute property. The novel endeavors to depict as a landscape of stewardship what is in fact this other kind, in effect prioritizing the landowners' values and prerogatives. The vagaries of capitalism, the substrate for a landscape of absolute property, make themselves felt on the numerous occasions when the text describes various financial hardships afflicting many members of the ladies' community. These moments occasion the charitable work—in the form of services or cash—that imbues the Hall gentlewomen with the aura of benevolent stewards and thus obfuscates the exploitative system that preserves the economic inequality necessitated by capitalism.

There are several manifestations of this obfuscation, which in turn expose an insidious deception at the Hall's core. First, the narrative structure introduces reciprocity in a purposeful way. Second, the scene showcasing reciprocity as the estate's governing principle instead casts doubt on its alleged accessibility to the entire female gentility residing on the estate. Likewise dubious is the underlying assumption that in embracing reciprocity as the condition of their residence, the genteel inhabitants possess equal access to self-determination. (To be clear, the novel never questions the subordination of the working poor.) Having received four ladies to tea who "likewise lived in a large society," the Hall women propose walking "part of the way home with them." This proposal initiates the scenario enacting the value of reciprocity and inadvertently exposing its flaw. During their walk the narrator observes that such a bucolic idyll would likely lead one "to disclaim all commerce with mankind, since he could not be benefitted by them."[31] Thus ensues a debate over the nuances of reciprocity. Lamont voices the callow views of a coxcomb, prompting the Hall's other original founder, Mrs. Louisa Mancel, to hold forth on their Christian ethos, and to counter his objections by insisting that reciprocity could resolve all discord if only everyone would embrace it: "What I understand by society is a state of mutual confidence, reciprocal services, and correspondent affections. [. . .] I would wish [people] to have leisure to consider by whom they were sent into this world, and for what purpose, and to learn, that their happiness consists in fulfilling the design of their Maker, in providing their own greatest felicity, and contributing all that is in their power to the convenience of others. [. . .] This reciprocal communication of benefits should be universal, and then we might with reason be fond of this world" (*Millenium Hall*, 111, 112). The validity of these claims comes under scrutiny during the subsequent discussion of the home where the lady visitors reside, to which the walk has brought the party in close proximity.

By constructing a scene in which reciprocity dominates the diegesis and then animates the set piece that follows, the novel presents an artful display of its key principle. "Reciprocal services" constitute the "universal" ideal that the Hall ladies strive for by founding a kind of satellite Millenium Hall. As we now learn, the mansion is a home for "indigent gentlewomen," created for "those women, who from scantiness of fortune, and pride of family, are reduced to become dependent" (115). Having previously noted that "the strangers seemed to look on the ladies of the house with such gratitude and veneration," the narrator here encounters the source for these sentiments. The minutely detailed description of the foundation and operation of this home for so-called "toad-eaters" extends over the next six pages (109, 115). Mrs. Maynard enumerates eleven rules that she and her fellow Hall residents devised for "this sisterhood," among them the pooling of financial resources, a clothing allowance, and a prohibition on "imprudence," the violation of which results in expulsion (117). For all the beneficence behind the creation of a secondary Millenium Hall, the female self-determination that would seem to motivate such an endeavor proves to be one value that the originators will not confer upon their acolytes.

MYSTIFICATION AND (NON)RECIPROCAL SERVICES

A further indication of the Hall's ethical inconsistency is that the founders do not enumerate their own governing principles but instead produce an explicit social contract in the process of constructing a "sisterhood" home nearby. Whether the rules therein correspond to those followed at the Hall is to some extent immaterial. We do not know, for example, whether the stipulation regarding expulsion also applies to the Hall, but the more significant fact remains that the Hall residents decide how to discipline their neighbors. The founders' attention to minutia, down to their provision of resources whenever one of these neighbors falls ill, signals a system of governance that operates outside the circuit of reciprocity. The satellite community cannot reciprocate by stipulating the terms of the Hall's governance—an ethically incoherent proposition. A parenthetical remark betrays Mrs. Maynard's anxiety that the Hall's nonreciprocal authority might provoke resistance in their dependents: "By [the Hall ladies'] example and suggestions, (for it is difficult to give unreserved advice where you may be suspected of a design to dictate) by their examples and suggestions therefore, they led them to industry" (118). The denial of any "design to dictate" exposes the truth that the Hall is built on this very design. Mrs. Maynard's potent aside offers the glimpse of a certain misprision in the estate operations, evident in her and her fellow designers' need to manipulate their neighbors into a form of behavior they might resist were the expectation made explicit. The satellite sisterhood has in effect exchanged one form of dependency for another.

Mrs. Maynard's remark exemplifies the text's tendency to invoke a landscape of stewardship in conditions that actually constitute a landscape of absolute property, also made manifest in its instrumentalization of the landscape arts. The Hall ladies' perspective and needs are paramount, and as we will see hereafter, this principle becomes visible in the aestheticized land that seems incidental but in fact expressly serves their interests. Nor is it clear to what extent the ladies realize their act of deception. In the process of conflating their own perspective with that of their genteel neighbors, they also deceive themselves. Furthermore, they violate a more fundamental principle of their enterprise—namely, gentlewomen's self-determination. The back-stories that proliferate and sometime blur together in the multiple inset narratives provide variations on the theme of gentlewomen's enslavement to circumstance when they lack the wealth to be independent. Flickering between an ideal community governed by reciprocity and a compromised retreat beholden to the dictates of capitalism, *Millenium Hall* exposes the historical contingency of landscape.

What is most striking, then, about the estate is its fusion of various landscapes that are in flux. *Millenium Hall* demonstrates the dynamism of the three landscapes in question; stewardship dominates the discussion whenever the ladies themselves explain how their project operates, but their insistence on the principle of reciprocity belies the one-way nature of their authority. A landscape of absolute property actually governs the Hall estate, even as its owners imagine themselves partaking in a landscape of stewardship sustaining and sustained by a landscape of custom. The tension among competing landscapes, evident in characters' exertions to perceive an idealized landscape of stewardship in the face of conditions that controvert it, echoes a dynamic encountered in the two previous chapters. Jane Barker's heroine Galesia almost deceives herself that she can turn her view of the London rooftops into a bucolic spectacle that is safe from financial instability. An obdurate landscape of absolute property thwarts her access to the landscape of stewardship she so desperately wants to inhabit. Meanwhile, two of Anne Finch's estate poems locate her on the threshold between contrary historical models of landscape. While one poem celebrates the male stewardship of her host and thus animates that mode of landscape, the other one exposes the capacity for the landscape of absolute property to co-opt the values of its precursor and competitor. In their several ways, these three authors illustrate the double consciousness that arises when women writers of their era pursue female independence via social relations embedded in the land.

The Hall ladies' dominance also manifests in the reported speech that the narrative grants to the landowners but denies to their subordinates. With two exceptions, discussed hereafter, only the ladies and their male guests participate in the dialogue about the estate's ethical and material operations. The inhabitants of the satellite Hall never speak. The narrator registers this silence by observing that "not chusing to be present while their actions were the subject of discourse, they had gradually strayed from us" (120). His interpretation signals that he has adopted the Hall's privileged perspective and assumes that the other women's silence expresses their modesty rather than, for example, resentment of their subordinate position. The novel's utopianism may explain the contented cooperation of the Hall's genteel neighbors. Yet when Lamont mentions "petulancy of temper" as likely to result in quick turnover at the residence, Mrs. Maynard demurs, noting "there has been but one expelled" (119). Their exchange demonstrates Scott's imputation of discord—though rare—within the ranks of the sisterhood but not on the part of the sisters toward their benefactors. Subtle details such as these indicate the Hall's subordination of their genteel neighbors and thus the limitations of "reciprocal services."

The novel's treatment of the working poor conjures a different type of landscape than the one inhabited by the indigent gentlewomen, whose location in a landscape of stewardship, however problematic, hinges on their genteel status. Some of the workers evoke the landscape of custom that in Sullivan's taxonomy accompanies that of stewardship, together producing a holistic social hierarchy. The tenantry form the core of a landscape of custom, deriving their well-being from social relations inhering in the land. But the novel does not imagine the lower ranks as a unified tenantry of the sort that Sullivan's model features. As a result, the landscape of custom has limited applicability to the text. This limitation exposes the deceptiveness of the novel's nostalgic representation of a quasi-feudal community; despite the evocation of an idealized rural order, the text betrays evidence of the shifting economic and ideological conditions that accompany emergent capitalism. The haymakers glimpsed in the novel's opening scene offer the closest approximation to a landscape of custom; they derive their identity from their agricultural labor, and their implicit relationship with the landowners ensures that the estate fulfills the needs of these dependents. From a certain vantage, Scott's representation of the tenantry captures the social harmony of the interdependent landscapes in question. This reading endorses the novel's deceptive tendency to portray the utopia as consisting in retrograde social relations despite the evidence of capitalist exploitation. The chronological implausibility of the backward-facing landscapes becomes apparent in other ways as well. For instance, a landscape of custom entails the tenants' *rightful* access to the benefits of the estate, but Scott does not vest these workers with the dignity belonging to customary laborers. Instead, she transforms the lower orders into recipients of charity, thus signaling not the endurance of a quasi-feudal system but rather its erosion. The haymakers' "happy amiable innocence" renders their well-being a reflection of their benefactors' generosity rather than the standard state of affairs in a feudalistic order (57).

The presence of nonagricultural workers among the lower ranks provides further evidence of the novel's distance from a landscape of custom and in turn its accommodation—albeit uneasy—of an emergent market economy. Twelve female cottagers live near the Hall and participate in its philanthropic enterprise of taking in poor children so as to provide relief for their large families nearby. The narrator's only conversations with members of the lower ranks include one encounter with an old woman representing the cottagers and another with the Hall's housekeeper. Unlike the silence of the indigent gentlewomen, the substantial reported speech of these laboring women is striking. Yet the apparent integrity implied by granting such women their own voice does not amount to a portrayal of dignified inhabitants in a landscape of custom. Rather, the dialogue in question provides further evidence of the text's need to promote charity as the panacea for the social ills occasioned by emergent capitalism. In this light, the women's effusive comments on their benefactors serve to normalize the exploitation of the poor and their vulnerability to contingency in a social order that does not guarantee their well-being as a built-in part of estate operations.

The working women's speech reads as a kind of rhapsody for their patrons that belies the exploitative economic system that is actually in place. Deprived of agency, they glorify their landladies for doing what would have been ordinary estate stewardship in a former time. As the cottager explains: "I was almost starved when they put me into this house, and no shame of mine, for so were my neighbours too; [. . .] but that was not our fault, you know, as we had not things to work with, nor any body to set us to work, poor folks cannot know every thing as these good ladies do" (65). At once a denial and an admission of responsibility, the woman's comment treats her poverty as both "no shame of mine" and yet something she could have tried harder to forfend. The housekeeper expresses a similar helplessness, adding to the impression that the sole purpose for granting the women speech is to amplify the praise of their mistresses.

The moral incoherence of the self-blaming yet defensive cottager expresses on an individual level a narrative ambiguity over how to assign responsibility for the poor. The scene engenders both an individualist reading, making poverty her own fault, and a communitarian one, making her condition a systemic concern. The addition of a backstory complicates the issue, for we go on to learn about two parish squires who occasioned her poverty in the first place. Their role makes the scene legible as a matter of both (or either) derelict stewardship and/or rapacious capitalism; in a traditional society, the squires would take responsibility for their dependents, while emergent capitalism would leave them vulnerable to exploitation. The ambiguity exemplifies how the novel captures several landscapes that are in flux; both negligent stewards and exploitative capitalists produce poverty. Thus, the text captures a community on the threshold between an obsolescent landscape of stewardship and an emergent landscape of absolute property. Despite the remnants of stewardship, though, significant details render the latter landscape the more plausible one to explain the woman's plight. As she explains, "Few of us had rags to cover us, or a morsel of bread to eat except the two Squires; they indeed grew rich, because they had our work, and paid us not enough to keep life and soul together" (65). The damning reference to wages paid by the squires, stingy though they may be, implies that the woman expects nothing else from her employers. Such an arrangement involves purely transactional rather than social or moral relations; the exchange of labor for wages constitutes the entirety of her relationship with the squires.[32] These landlords and their female dependents inhabit a landscape of absolute property. The old woman's words suggest in turn that capitalism is displacing most remnants of an earlier system wherein cohabiting the same estate would have brought the lord (or lady) and tenants into closer and more complex contact.

A PARADOXICAL PARTNERSHIP: THE GIFT ECONOMY AND EMERGENT CAPITALISM

At this juncture we have sufficient evidence to contemplate the various ways in which Scott's utopia serves a paradoxical purpose. We have witnessed the chronological manifestation of this paradox: it accommodates the Hall ladies and their dependents to a new economic and social reality while altogether mystifying and, in some sense, eliding that reality. By presenting the appearance of a regenerated state of affairs, of having breathed life into an obsolescing system—that is, the landscape of stewardship—the narrative portrays as *new* a scenario that actually harkens back to the past. Of course, it is not necessarily paradoxical to envision a utopia that idealizes a bygone era; the golden age witnessed in the pastoral and georgic traditions from antiquity makes such nostalgia conventional. But not only does this troubled chronology mystify the true, socially exploitative nature of Scott's ideal world; it also instrumentalizes a comparably novel version of landscape, the landscape arts, in its construction of utopia. In effect, mobilizing an emergent form of landscape (the arts) in order to revive an obsolescent one (stewardship) exposes Millenium Hall as a historical impossibility. The estate thus becomes a literal utopia, a "no place" (in the term's Greek derivation). The chronological and ethical dissonance between the two landscapes at play manifests the sleight of hand at work in the Hall operations. My point is not to incriminate Scott for any ethical dishonesty on her part but rather to interrogate why a certain self-deception seems necessary in order for her and her proxies (the ladies of Millenium Hall) to achieve the equitable social and gender relations to which they lay claim.[33]

Why, then, is the novel compelled to embrace a form of social equality—in the form of "reciprocal services"—that belies the social hierarchy that remains secure throughout the text? Julie McGonegal has wrestled with this perplexity in terms that resonate with my own, though in reference to both *Millenium Hall* and its 1766 sequel. Regarding the text's economic system and its preservation of social distinctions, she observes, "Scott neutralizes the harsher effects of the reproduction of capitalism through its feminization, which promotes misrecognition of the brutal consequences of mercantilism for labourers. Charity and benevolence [. . .] were 'powerfully reasserted' in this period as part of the mystification of the violence of agrarian capitalism."[34] McGonegal's title, "The Tyranny of Gift Giving," reveals her focus on gift circulation in the novel rather than the discourse of landscape. But it cannot be coincidental that two distinctive frameworks for evaluating the novel's economic and social orientation reach such similar conclusions. Focusing on "the relations of dependence" that gift-giving entails when the recipient cannot reciprocate the gift, McGonegal concludes that a purportedly generous arrangement in fact oppresses the ladies' subordinates. Whether the mystification arises from the gift economy or from the landscape of absolute property disguised as a landscape of stewardship, both of our interpretations identify a misrepresentation in the novel's utopian scheme. By foregrounding landscape as an essential category of analysis, my argument enables us to connect the economic drivers of the utopia—both land and mobile property—to the landscape arts.

This approach both complements and complicates McGonegal's reading, and it does so by expanding both the scope of the novel's misrepresentations and the source of the ladies' agency. Whereas she locates agency in their role as donors (Scott "present[s] the woman as a powerful agent in the gift economy"), I locate it in their landownership.[35] This institution thus becomes legible as the condition of possibility for the authority the ladies acquire as gift givers. Moreover, the novel's abundant landscape descriptions exert a significant force on the narrative by emphasizing visual agency, especially the visualization of land. These forces contribute to the mystifications in question and reinforce landownership as an essential component of self-determination. With these caveats in mind, we may better appreciate how the text makes the landscape arts an essential mechanism in its treatment of capitalism and, crucially, how it uses aesthetics—primarily visual aesthetics—to disguise exploitation as generosity.

Like McGonegal, Jennie Batchelor also scrutinizes the gift economy that governs relations at the Hall, providing a sanctuary for women otherwise exploited in the marriage market. She, too, identifies a damning inconsistency in the utopia's gift economy, observing the insidious indebtedness that Miss Mancel endures when her surrogate father, Mr. Hintman, uses his generous gift-giving since her childhood as a means to coerce her reciprocal duty to become his mistress.[36] Batchelor asserts, "In an argument that counters the novel's claims for the necessity and value of women's work, Mrs. Mancel implies that community members can return the obligations owed to their deliverers without active service: their thankfulness is gift enough. At this key moment in the text, the logic of the gift falters, becoming indistinguishable from the exploitative logic of obligation the novel seeks to overwrite."[37] Batchelor thus uncovers a misrepresentation in the logic of the gift that resembles my argument about the fallacious landscape of stewardship. She suggests that by critiquing obligation as a kind of exploitation, only to then impose obligation upon others, the ladies commit a kind of hypocrisy that resonates with my own interpretation regarding their putative landscape of stewardship.

In our several ways, then, McGonegal, Batchelor, and I attribute the Hall's unstable value system to its unwitting (or unacknowledged) debt to capitalism and its ancillary ideologies. According to Batchelor, "Mrs. Mancel's account of the benefits conferred by the community's members fails to counter [Lamont] the rake's suspicion that the gift is a convenient fiction crafted to mask cultural, social, and economic ideologies."[38] As Batchelor's essay elsewhere demonstrates, those ideologies intersect with capitalism—for instance, via its "ethos of equitable exchange."[39] Meanwhile, McGonegal identifies a different manifestation of capitalism in domesticity, whose entanglement with capitalism has been well documented.[40] She observes tension between the novel's commitment to wealth and lineage, on the one hand, and its endorsement of "the emergent ideology of domesticity," on the other.

This ideology emphasizes the "importance [of] female education and virtue since these impart the attributes of female frugality, self-sufficiency, and order that imply an ability to practice capitalism effectively."[41] McGonegal considers the novel's ideal femininity—which in addition to the traits she names also includes Christian piety and industry—as an instrument for capitalism despite the text's misrepresentation of its socioeconomic orientation.

From their various perspectives, then, both scholars recognize how the novel operates within a broader economic context in which capitalist forces are driving social change. Regardless of its specific operation in and/or beyond the Hall, capitalism necessarily figures into my own analysis because it designates the necessary conditions for the emergence of a landscape of absolute property. Here, the prerogatives of private property supersede other social arrangements that granted rights in the land to dependents as well as landowners (i.e., a landscape of custom). Because both critics perceive the novel's commitment to female independence (however delusional or compromised that condition may be), their critical framework of the gift also corroborates my own argument that the landscape arts play an essential role in the text's fabrication of that ideal. We all concur that Scott advances her capitalist-feminist agenda through various forms of ideologically driven misprision; what sets my argument apart is that I ground this misprision in the novel's reliance on aesthetics—primarily visual aesthetics.

Further explanation for the obfuscated landscape of absolute property is necessary if we are to grasp how it operates through the aesthetics that manifest in the landscape arts. Closer scrutiny of the women's philanthropic projects reveals that their fixation on reciprocity disguises the landscape of absolute property that actually prevails at the Hall. Their keen interest in owning their obligation to the needy belies the fact that the moral imperative driving their behavior does not compensate for the exploitation on which their economy depends. When the narrator expresses "astonishment" at the ladies' selfless charity, he fails to notice how it necessitates but elides their dependents' exploitation (*Millenium Hall*, 76). His capacity to discern reciprocity does not extend to the subtextual assumption that the low-born members of the community will embrace compulsory gratitude and asymmetrical indebtedness as the bedrock of their position. Given the various forms of misrepresentation previously discussed, the narrator's wonder insinuates a certain subterfuge on the part of the ladies, and his dumbfounded credulity affirms the success of their strategy. These conditions expose a similar misprision regarding the Hall customs. Despite the ladies' valiant effort to make reciprocity the foremost custom of their community, they cannot sustain their utopia outside the confines of absolute property; in effect, the circulation of capital has become more customary than the reciprocity that once codified the interdependence of landowners and their tenantry.

THE CASH NEXUS AND THE MYTHICAL LANDSCAPE OF STEWARDSHIP

I am now positioned to return to my contention that the novel's repeated claims about the women's commitment to the "reciprocal communication of benefits" is symptomatic of their anxiety that a more inhumane landscape might prevail at the Hall. When we consider how often the women's projects involve the distribution of money, it becomes more apparent that a cash economy has displaced one in which reciprocal services governed the community. Beyond various educational and vocational projects, the women also donate money to a striking number of people, establishing themselves as a reliable financial resource for every exigency. For instance, we learn that soon after Mrs. Morgan, Mrs. Mancel, and their fellow Hall resident Lady Mary Jones settle into their estate, they undertake a range of charitable activities including donating money for newlyweds in addition to emergency support for those who fall ill.

> The next expense they undertook, after this establishment of schools and almshouses, was that of furnishing a house for every young couple that married in their neighbourhood, and providing them with some sort of stock, which by industry would prove very conducive towards their living in a comfortable degree of plenty. They have always paid nurses for the sick, sent them every proper refreshment, and allow the same sum weekly which the sick person could have gained, that the rest of the family may not lose any part of their support by the incapacity of one. (159)

As such instances of monetary support accumulate, it grows ever clearer that the women's financial assistance provides the safety net for those who would otherwise face penury. The systemic sponsorship upon which the community depends exposes an underlying acceptance of not only inequality but also persistent poverty. Reciprocity supposedly mitigates the worst of these conditions, but it does not provide the panacea that the Hall ladies assume it does.

Similarly, after the narrator attends a wedding celebration for one of the young women raised at the Hall, he explains, "My cousin told me that Miss Mancel gave the young bride a fortune, and that she might have her share of employment and contribute to the provision for her family had stocked her dairy and furnished her with poultry" (163). Though he doesn't specify the amount of the "fortune," Miss Mancel clearly provides a monetary gift. The morning after the wedding, the narrator speaks with the housekeeper and learns further details about the Hall women's monetary charity.

> From her I learnt that since the ladies had been established in [Millenium Hall] they had given fortunes from twenty to an hundred pounds, as merit and occasion directed, to above thirty young women, and that they had

> seldom celebrated fewer than two marriages in a year, sometimes more. Nor does their bounty cease on the wedding-day, for they are always ready to assist them on any emergency; and watch with so careful an eye over the conduct of these young people as proves of much greater service to them than the money they bestow. (167)

As stewards of the community's economic, social, and moral welfare, the women sponsor newlyweds and step in with emergency funds whenever necessary. The passage recalls the income that the Hall women settle upon the clergyman's widow, as previously mentioned. The claim that the women's surveillance of their needy social inferiors benefits the recipients of their charity more than money does operates as further evidence of the novel's ethical misprision.

The multiple occasions for distributing money, necessitated by the lack of employment for the poor and the greed of squires who ought to steward the community, demonstrate that the women's charity salvages a situation that would otherwise leave the poor indefinitely destitute. Evidence of impending destitution appears in the narrator's explanation for how the women manage the rug factory: "But as they feared an enterprising undertaker might ruin their plan, they themselves undertook to be stewards; they stood the first expense, allowed a considerable profit to the directors, but kept the distribution of the money entirely in their own hands: thus they prevent the poor from being oppressed by their superiors" (243). The concern about an "enterprising undertaker" indicates the women's awareness of the risk that an unscrupulous industrialist would pose to the community. For the women to step in to protect the poor from exploitation exposes the reality of a capitalist economy that oppresses the poor—unless they are fortunate enough to have benefactors to protect them. Scott's use of the word *stewards* in reference to the ladies reinforces my interpretation of the notional landscape of stewardship, suggesting her own credulity regarding her utopian creation.

In devoting themselves to reciprocity, the Hall ladies cultivate the belief that everyone can contribute to the community's success, regardless of wealth or stature. By investing their estate management with moral integrity, they imagine themselves to inhabit a landscape of stewardship, wherein landowners pursue the best interests of their dependents and have the wisdom to achieve results that benefit everyone involved. But given my earlier assessment of the cash economy in which the ladies participate, the benevolence of their stewardship proves to be an affective posture that leads their dependents to accept the status quo; the ladies do not engage in a transformative mode of conduct that could mitigate the reality of their dependents' ongoing exploitation. The extent of kindness, generosity, and selflessness practiced by the ladies suggests an awareness that the ideology of stewardship could, if co-opted effectively, enable them to soften the subordination and lack of agency required of the lower orders in what is actually a landscape of absolute property.

As McGonegal and Batchelor, among others, have argued, the Hall ladies' putative generosity disguises a more nefarious dimension of their philanthropy. The former critic identifies an "ideology of benevolence" that operates in the eighteenth century as philanthropic endeavors work to mask the subtle violence of emergent capitalism.[42] Her portrayal of the social transformations depicted in Scott's two novels resonates with my own study of these changes through the discourse of landscape.

> While appealing strongly and nostalgically to a dwindling, precapitalist land economy, that is, to an older ideal of the autonomous English state where classes were fully interdependent and labour was exchanged for more than wages (in a gift economy that was also prone to brutal manipulation), *Millenium Hall* and *Sir George Ellison* are also shaped by the early, precarious stages of capitalism during which the pacification of labourers through philanthropic activities was an essential method of counteracting, or more accurately, concealing, the violence enacted by the enclosure of land and other practices of direct domination.[43]

As one of the few scholars to identify land as an important (and not self-evident) critical category in *Millenium Hall*, McGonegal assesses the estate in a way that evokes both the landscape of stewardship and its transformation into a landscape of absolute property.

In identifying an economic transition underway in Scott's novel, this critic notices, crucially, that the emergent capitalist system by no means protects the lower orders from exploitation. Yet, she also captures the importance of social relations under the quasi-feudal regime, wherein the classes "were fully interdependent and labour was exchanged for more than wages." Her subsequent observation that women were especially well equipped to ease the transition to capitalism makes a persuasive case with regard to the Hall women's provision of virtuous sympathy; "the pacification of labourers" and "the labour of nurturance and conciliation" together suggest that the women's gentleness and maternal care contribute to the transition by tempering its brutal tendencies.[44] In light of these issues, it becomes possible to see the stewardship the ladies perform, marked by consummate kindness, as merely an affective posture that belies the economic hardship compelling the poor to revere their patrons. As I argue in the next section, an essential feature of this misrepresentation of exploitation as selfless care is that it operates through not only affect but also aesthetics. The ladies' affective posture traffics in pleasant emotions that amplify the pleasures that the estate's landscape arts provide.

Building on McGonegal's interpretation of the texts' compromised utopianism, and her recognition that land plays a fundamental role in the historical processes to which the novels bear witness, I focus on a topic that lies beyond McGonegal's (and most other critics') purview: namely, the landscape arts. Understanding their contribution to the ladies' chaste seduction of their visitors enables us to investigate a crucial connection between politics (landownership) and aesthetics (the landscape arts) that I consider one of the novel's most important features. Thus, the political project of benevolent capitalism succeeds through the aesthetics that mask it. Once we grasp the importance of the landscape arts, then, we will be positioned to assess the implications of Scott's strategic negotiation of patriarchy—that is, her willingness to perpetuate the subordination of many women in order to achieve a modicum of independence for the novel's few financially independent and virtuous gentlewomen.

THE ALCHEMY OF THE LANDSCAPE ARTS

When landscape is conceived as an aestheticized view of rural land, as Sullivan suggests, a complex social process—in short, the emergence of private property—has operated to render that view as definitive rather than specific to the property owner: "That the landowner's view has been taken as the only one attests less to the power of his vision or the splendor of his prospect than it does to the fact that, by now, the only other available views are obstructed ones. More precisely, insofar as the word evokes the perspective, they are not 'views' at all."[45] The triumph of the landowner's view constitutes, for Sullivan, the landscape of absolute property. It is not coincidental that prospect painting emerged in the late seventeenth century, for such aesthetic renderings of land legitimated and institutionalized private property. Moreover, the emergence of landscape gardening in the eighteenth century functions in a similar way; like prospect painting, it creates views of the land that treat the landowner's view as the only one that matters and erases the possibility of other views—that is, other landscapes.

If, as Sullivan's history suggests, the landscape arts are the aesthetic expression of the triumphant landscape of absolute property, then we may appreciate how aestheticized land consolidates landed property and strengthens a political system that enfranchises only the landed. The political function of aestheticized land is readily apparent in *Millenium Hall*, wherein Scott mobilizes the landscape garden to express the ladies' qualification to oversee the entire operation of their community. Thus, the novel demonstrates not only the eighteenth-century fashion for landscape gardening but also the tendency to use such gardening as a synecdoche for wise governance on a broader scale. By making landscaping skills an essential dimension of their management of the community, the novel proposes that women with the appropriate values, knowledge, and experience deserve to determine the course of their own lives—that is, they deserve their independence. Because such independence arises from landownership, the text legitimates female authority within the community and proposes that society at large would benefit from the women's philanthropic approach to estate management.

The literary precedents for Scott's work deserve attention here insofar as she builds upon an ancient literary tradition that had been adapted in seventeenth-century British poetry and laid the foundation for texts that treat the country estate as a microcosm of the state. In his survey of seventeenth-century country-house poetry, Alistair Fowler explains: "As a unit of rural organization, the estate easily serves as a sample of the country at large—a manageable example of national issues [. . .]. Britain is conceived of as itself a large estate."[46] Scott imagines Millenium Hall as a "political and moral microcosm" of the sort that Fowler describes.[47] Following a poetic legacy that identifies the rural estate as the proving ground for a landowner's integrity, her novel acquires a conservative quality in that it looks backward for its values and literary precedents, seeking, paradoxically, to fashion something new—a women's utopia—by modeling it on something old. Anne Finch's iterations of country-house poetry, as seen in chapter 2, conflate the landowner's virtue with his wise stewardship, and Scott builds upon this time-tested model by integrating female philanthropy as a key expression of the landladies' stewardship.

The rich literary history embedded in Scott's novel, with precedents going back to antiquity, also obliges us to consider how this nostalgia illuminates the historical transformation of landscape. The incursions of early capitalism previously discussed demonstrate that advances in gender equality prove more viable when they accommodate and even perpetuate the hegemony of the market. At the same time, Scott's tactical appropriation of quasi-feudal values such as reciprocity suggests the advantage to be gained by moderating the market's brutal forces with a legerdemain that disguises those forces as benevolence. Aesthetics constitute a crucial dimension of this legerdemain. The "natural" beauty of the country estate testifies to the fitness of its lord and/or lady to govern there, implying that the qualities exhibited by the landowners would serve the nation well if applied more broadly. As Tom Williamson and Liz Bellamy observe:

> Only the owner of a great estate could assess the needs of the country. Only he could recognize what would be for the benefit of all. The great landowner was mythologized as a wise and powerful figure, who embodied the aspirations of the community which he served. His benevolent omniscience was a result of his landed status, for as an owner of part of the nation he was seen to be able to understand its needs. Moreover, the fact that his wealth was rooted in land was thought to convey an impartiality denied to those more closely tied to the means of production. Merchants, financiers and industrialists were seen as biased by self-interest, but the landowner's wealth was in the nation, and his interest was thus the national good.[48]

These insights into the superior political stature of the landowner help us appreciate Scott's discernment in choosing landownership as the basis of her program for women's independence. By giving her heroines a stake in the national estate, she signals an awareness that landownership may be the most effective way to imbue them with sufficient gravitas to qualify them as both local and national stewards.

Signaling her debt to the country-house poetic tradition, Scott advances the principle that a well-landscaped estate demonstrates the landowners' aesthetic sophistication. On multiple occasions the narrator and other characters view the land surrounding the mansion and savor its beauty. Such moments reveal how the novel establishes a character's refinement in part by valorizing her capacity to appreciate the landscape. Furthermore, the novel does not confine its valorization of the landscape arts to outdoor scenes. In the narrator's detailed description of the large room he enters upon first being invited indoors, we encounter a woman and a girl who are both "drawing a landscape" (*Millenium Hall*, 59). The tableau of artistic activity serves as a set piece wherein the text animates in a single scene a whole range of values and activities that the narrator will spend the rest of the novel understanding (or in some cases failing to understand).

The novel's opening scene illustrates the ladies' commitment to aesthetic sophistication, productivity, and women's education. For we later learn, near the conclusion of "Miss Mancel and Mrs. Morgan's History continued" (123), that the girls in the opening tableau receive a free education from these charitable women. Mrs. Maynard explains that worthy young members of the community "are educated in such a manner as will render them acceptable where accomplished women of a humble rank and behaviour are wanted, either for the care of a house or children" (160). Here we encounter one of the many examples of the philanthropy to which the Hall women dedicate their lives and expendable income. It may seem like an insignificant detail that one of the Hall ladies and one of the girls under their tutelage are drawing landscapes in the opening tableau. Yet, when placed in a broader assessment of the novel's multiple and sometimes intricate landscape depictions, the snapshot of the production of the landscape arts proves all the more laden with meaning. An incidental detail in the first depiction of the Hall's interior, the two figures "drawing a landscape" suggest that the women not only value the landscape arts but also believe that artistic production constitutes an important part of every girl's education. In light of my argument that the ladies adopt what we might call crypto-capitalism, it becomes all the more significant that they indoctrinate their young charges in the landscape arts so as to obscure the nonaesthetic nature of their exploitation.

The novel also dramatizes the integration of the landscape arts as an essential component of the ladies' estate stewardship. It is necessary to recall here my previous analysis of the text's objectification of both women and land, for the aesthetic seduction appeals to the travelers and the reader alike. Even before the narrator learns anything about the talented landscapers who live on the estate, he first expresses interest in it after a glimpse of its remarkable beauty. As noted at the beginning of this chapter, a beautiful avenue of oaks entices him to walk farther, and in turn he and his companion undergo a kind of arboreal and botanical seduction: "The thick shade [the oaks] afforded us, the fragrance wafted from the woodbines with which they were encircled, was so delightful, and the beauty of the grounds so very attracting, that we strolled on, desirous of approaching the house to which this avenue led. It is a mile and a half in length, but the eye is so charmed with the remarkable verdure and neatness of the fields, with the beauty of the flowers which are planted all around them and seem to mix with the quickset hedges, that time steals away insensibly" (56). The travelers' first intimation of the Hall, then, features a sensuous and beautifully composed space that charms viewers and draws them closer to the house. The narrator's language implies how the land so impresses him that it propels his movement: "The beauty of the grounds [was] so very attracting, that we strolled on." A depiction of the land charming the travelers foreshadows subsequent scenes in which the land bears features that catch the visitors' attention and make them "desirous" to know the source of such beauty. In hindsight, the passage seems less fortuitous than cunning, once we recognize it as an instance of the ladies' calculated design of the landscape; they instrumentalize the grounds so as to prettify what might otherwise unsettle the viewer. Finally, the narrator's evocation of the utopia's ambiguous temporality, his claim "that time steals away insensibly," adds to the scene's uncanny quality, its intimation that the Hall might bring visitors backward in time even while steering them to the literal utopia that is "no place."

It is worth pausing here to consider a different expression of the uncanny, this time arising from the oddly familiar scenario in which novelistic characters endure a carriage accident that serendipitously steers them to a transformative encounter with a country estate. (We must recall here that a coach accident occasions the gentlemen's visit to the Hall.) Scott's opening scene echoes a similar episode in Jane Barker's *A Patch-Work Screen for the Ladies* (1723), wherein the heroine Galesia's coach is overturned, compelling her to walk through the estate where she finds herself to search for aid. As seen in chapter 1, she happens upon the lady of the estate, who had "resolv[ed] to walk home over the Park, it being a fine smooth Walk betwixt two Rows of Lime trees, planted and grown in exact Form."[49] Not only do the coach accidents mirror one another, but so, too, do the chance encounters with an avenue of trees. Both novels thus enact landscapes of stewardship wherein the characters have fortuitous encounters with benevolent gentlewomen who come to their rescue and afford them access to a fine country estate. Likewise, both women writers embrace such retrograde landscapes while rejecting or misconstruing the proto-capitalist landscape of absolute property that their characters actually inhabit. Together, these similarities amount to striking evidence of the power derived from locating a woman's utopia in a country estate that is both geographically and chronologically remote.

With her narrator ensconced in the Hall but still only partially informed of its extent and organization, Scott builds upon the arboreal enticement of the previous day to increase the visitors' curiosity. She intensifies her visual rhetoric, dazzling both viewer and reader with copious detail, concocting a kind of blazon of the land itself. By itemizing its component parts, fixing the narrator's gaze on the scene, and having him observe the harmonious beauty of the whole, she objectifies the land in order to exploit his inclination to read the landscape as a manifestation of the ladies' wise stewardship. After the narrator has spent the night at the Hall, he rises early and ventures outdoors.

> I first went into the gayest flower garden I ever beheld. The rainbow exhibits not half the variety of tints, and they are so artfully mingled, and ranged to make such a harmony of colours, as taught me how much the most beautiful objects may be improved by a judicious disposition of them. Beyond these beds of flowers rises a shrubbery, where every thing sweet and pleasing is collected. As these ladies have no taste but what is directed by good sense, nothing found a place here from being only uncommon, for they think few things are very rare but because they are little desirable; and indeed it is plain they are free from that littleness of mind, which makes people value a thing the more for its being possessed by no one but themselves. Behind the shrubbery is a little wood, which affords a gloom, rendered more agreeable by its contrast with the dazzling beauty of that part of the garden that leads to it. (*Millenium Hall*, 64)

We hear echoes in this passage of the *utile dulci* ideal, propounded for example in Alexander Pope's "Epistle to Burlington" (1731; "'Tis use alone that sanctifies expense").[50] Observing the ladies' "good sense," the narrator believes they have banished extravagance from the estate grounds. Noting their disdain for that "littleness of mind" that seeks exotic plants as a way to distinguish oneself, he infers their wisdom from their choice of flowers.

The ladies' supercilious attitude toward modish gardening tastes demands to be read as effecting a convergence of the landscape arts and the landscape of absolute property. The narrator insinuates that the ladies' landscaping talent is an artful distraction from the fact that this estate *is* their absolute property. On a subsequent tour of the estate, the ladies point out attractive prospects that privilege their perspective as landowners. The foregoing passage thus also serves as a means to prepare the narrator and readers for subsequent evidence of the ladies' tasteful estate design. Likewise, his attention to the layout of the plantings ("they are so artfully mingled") and a similar contrast between the flowers' "dazzling beauty" and the gloomy wood next to them suggests that only "judicious" gardeners could have created such an impressive display. The way the landscape elicits admiration, which in turn redounds upon the ladies, operates in the same way that fine estates across the nation proclaim the power and prestige of their owners. In sum, Scott participates in a well-established tendency to treat an estate's landscaping as a measure of the landowner's taste, wealth, and stature. The narrator's credulity in the ladies' selfless philanthropy shows that treating an estate as a physical manifestation of its owner now occurs as a matter of course.

The political subtext of the scene also requires further scrutiny, for the narrator does not merely savor the beautiful scenery and in turn admire "the genius of the place."[51] The text's reliance on a trope analogizing the estate and its owner demonstrates how Scott captures a historical pattern that some scholars have identified as an expression of capitalism. Although the ladies pride themselves on being indifferent to the fashion of their times, the text is nevertheless implicated in a historical process that shores up the cultural and political power of landownership, effectively subsuming the age-old reverence for landed wealth within the ambit of capitalism. Landscape scholars have demonstrated that as the fashion for distinctively landscaped estates came increasingly to serve as opportunities for conspicuous consumption, and as the consolidation of wealth and power continued apace among the landed, the landscape park emerged as the ideal method by which the gentry and aristocracy could assert their superiority over the burgeoning middle classes. As Williamson explains, "Landscapes [. . .] were important markers of social status. The crucial feature of the park in this context was not merely that it was a form of landscape which could be shared by great landowners and lesser gentry. It was also one which was completely unavailable to the broad mass of the middle class. Parks could only be created by those who owned land in abundance."[52] Not only does the novel describe the luxuriant flowerbeds adorning various parts of the estate, but it also devotes considerable narrative time and attention to its park. Given the novel's publication in 1762, when the landscaping style of Capability Brown, with its sweeping lawns and carefully planted clumps of trees, was the height of fashion, it is likely that this form of landscape design influenced Scott's depiction of the Hall grounds.

In light of my previous discussion of the Hall's paradoxical value system, which scholars have linked to an array of ideological concerns, it becomes possible to discern how the ladies' engineering of their estate serves a contradictory purpose. On the one hand, they adapt to and advance themselves within a new, proto-capitalist world, while on the other hand they maintain (under the cover of restoring) obsolescent values such as reciprocity and solidarity with the collective. The Hall brings social stability to the community insofar as the estate grants stature, security, and rural tranquility to formerly disadvantaged members of society; gentlewomen without sufficient wealth to live independently now do so at the Hall, thanks to their shrewd ability to disguise as philanthropy an estate economy that accommodates the market's hegemony. Benevolent capitalism serves as the bargain the novel makes with patriarchy in order to give worthy, i.e., charitable, women access to emergent capitalism's vastly expanding wealth.

The landscape arts thus prove an invaluable tool for Scott's project because they translate her economic project into a different register—an aesthetic one.

Thus far, the text's depictions of landscape serve primarily as a means for the narrator to make inferences about the landowners before meeting them and, once he does meet them, to read their gardens as an index of their character. But when the ladies invite their guests to tour the park, a conversation about landscape design brings the topic into the diegesis, making it an explicit concern among the characters. Their treatment of the topic in turn testifies to a shared understanding of its importance and timeliness. During their walk, the narrator explains:

> They conducted us to a very fine wood which is laid out with so much taste that Lamont observed the artist's hand was never more distinguishable, and perceived in various spots the direction of the person at present most famous for that sort of improvement. [. . .] The ladies smiled, and one of them answered, "He did their wood great honour, in thinking art had lent her assistance to nature, but that there was little in that place for which they were not solely obliged to the latter." Mrs. Trentham interrupted her who was speaking and told us, that, "As she had no share in the improvements which had been made, she might with the better grace assure Mr. Lamont, that lady Mary Jones, Mrs. Mancel, and Mrs. Morgan, were the only persons who had laid out that wood, and the commonest labourers in the country had executed their orders." (*Millenium Hall*, 68)

Lamont's assumption that a famous landscape architect—no doubt Capability Brown—designed the wood raises two important issues. One, it situates the text within the century's pervasive and sometimes controversial discourse of landscape, dramatizing divergent views about the wisdom of hiring experts. Two, framing the design as a product of both nature and art ("in thinking art had lent her assistance to nature") signals the ladies' recognition of landscape design as a realm for artistic practice. Yet Mrs. Trentham's insistence that the ladies are "solely obliged to [nature]" for the wood's beauty implies that they may hold landscape architecture in some suspicion—perhaps seeing it as a form of artifice that would degrade the quality of their more natural work. Stephen Bending makes a similar claim, also observing the scene's ideological subtext: "In rejecting Brown and his ilk, Scott sought to reassert the moral responsibility of the landowner and to resist the increasing commodification of land as landscape, signaled by the decision to buy a product from a professional designer."[53] Ironically, Scott still contributes to the commodification of land to the extent that her novel marshals the landscape arts in ways that obfuscate and yet legitimate the landscape of absolute property.

The passage's treatment of manual labor further supports a reading of the scene as a landscape of absolute property. Whether art or nature makes for the superior guide in landscape design, it is remarkable that "the commonest labourers

[who] had executed their orders" barely register as agents in the design process. Given her commitment to the social hierarchy, we cannot expect Scott's text to consider how the presumably male laborers might benefit from the land where they work. Thus, the scene exposes the assumption that these laborers' sole purpose is to "execute [the ladies'] orders." Such treatment of the common folk exemplifies the text's stance on the lower orders, who never take on individual form but instead serve as an anonymous mass, worthy of interest only as recipients of charity or provisioners of labor. The conversation thus illustrates on several levels that the landscape arts are the purview of the landed elite. Although the novel appropriates the rhetoric of stewardship to mitigate the Hall's exploitative tendencies, ultimately the elevation of characters for their distinctive landscape tastes affirms the novel's reliance on a cultural marker that correlates with the ascendance of capitalism.

As Williamson and Bellamy suggest in their claim about the "mythologized" great landowner, the principle of constructing a prospect specifically in order to create an impression of vast, unobstructed space exemplifies one of many methods that designers used to privilege the landowners' view and thus to naturalize their ownership of the prospect. *Millenium Hall*'s park-tour scene, which extends over multiple inset narratives, reveals the degree to which Scott has assimilated the contemporary fashion for landscape design, appropriating certain trends and putting them in service of the women's agenda. When the narrator and his hostesses first set out on their tour, the narrative offers lengthy descriptions of the wood, temple, canal, and grotto—all signature features of the era's landscaping tastes. The prospect view, a hallmark of the landowner who savors the expansiveness of his property, appears in modified form as the narrator appreciates the solitude provided by one highlight of his tour: "On an eminence, 'bosomed high in tufted trees,' is a temple dedicated to solitude. The structure is an exquisite piece of architecture, the prospect from it noble and extensive, and the windows so placed, that one sees no house but at so considerable a distance, as not to take off from the solitary air" (*Millenium Hall*, 69). Dedicating their temple to solitude may give the ladies' choice of landscape ornamentation a virtuous cast, but they clearly designed the temple and its prospect for themselves and their guests. Only owners and their proxies, not their subordinates, qualify for access to the prospect.

Just as featuring a landscape park on their property signals the ladies' wealth and taste, so too does their well-concealed grotto. The secrecy and quiet of this space resonate with the tranquility of the temple, while the grotto's tastefulness echoes Mrs. Trentham's denial that the ladies hired a professional to design their park. Following a lengthy paragraph about the wood, we encounter another extended description: "At the verge of this wood [. . .] we found ourselves in a most beautiful grotto, made of fossils, spars, coral, and such shells as are at once both fine and rustic; all of the glaring, tawdry kind are excluded, and by the gloom and simplicity preserved, one would imagine it the habitation of some devout anchoret" (70). The ladies' solemn character emerges from a landscape design that rejects "glaring, tawdry" seashells and instead cultivates solitude and "gloom and simplicity." Such qualities reinforce the Christian piety that informs the entire Hall project. Despite the severity that some observers (including Lamont) perceive in an encounter with such women in such a place, we cannot ignore the economic implications of this seemingly virtuous enactment of the landscape arts. Critics have interpreted the grotto as a symbol for female sexuality, what with its dark and moist, womb-like space, but in the present instance what matters most is the simultaneous display and obfuscation of wealth.[54]

Owning such an extensive plot of land, with little of it devoted to agriculture or husbandry, exposes how the ladies deploy the landscape arts to achieve less than virtuous aims. Williamson and Bellamy offer further evidence of the ideological function of extensive parkland: "The landed elite surrounded themselves with landscapes ostentatiously divorced from productive agriculture, but which still emphasized the nature of their power and status. The layout of trees and lawns was usually contrived so that the house appeared to blend into a supposedly natural landscape and to be in complete harmony with the surrounding environment. In this way the landed elite appeared to be a natural part of the rural order, but their dominance of that order was reinforced by the contrast between the park and the landscape of labour."[55] Such an effort to contrive a view of vast, unobstructed land operates in the ladies' temple to solitude, in which "the windows [are] so placed, that one sees no house but at so considerable a distance, as not to take off from the solitary air" (*Millenium Hall*, 69). When we recall the opening scene in which the narrator rhapsodizes about the haymakers, whose "rosy cheeks shewed the benefits of youthful labour," we detect the very contrast to which these scholars refer. Scott takes care to include depictions of agricultural labor, but she sanitizes them by treating the physical exertion of working the land as pleasurable and healthy rather than toilsome.

The happy haymakers turn out to be a rare instance of agricultural labor on the estate, for the next phase of the estate tour, following the first part of "The History of Miss Mancel and Mrs. Morgan" (78), features no visible sign of human toil. Rather, we learn the women have embraced the aesthetic appeal of the landscape park but altered it with invisible sites of productivity. Whereas the vast acreage devoted to unobstructed views typically signaled the vastness of a landowner's fortune, the Hall women instead embed useful features within a landscape that the untrained eye might overlook. Although such land use registers as virtuous in one respect, it also exemplifies the subterfuge that operates in a landscape of absolute property that passes itself off as a landscape of stewardship. After devoting nearly forty-five pages to the past tribulations of the Hall founders, Scott stages a visit from their neighbors, a group of formerly "indigent gentlewomen." After dinner, "Lady Mary observed, that after having shewn us the beauties of the place, they ought to exhibit the riches of it"(*Millenium Hall*, 109). The group then embark on another tour of the estate, and the text delivers its perhaps most explicit description of the landscape park.

> It is not quite three miles round; the inequality of the ground much increases its beauty, and the timber is remarkably fine. We could plainly perceive it had been many years in the possession of good economists, who unprompted by necessity, did not think the profit that might arise from the sale a sufficient inducement to deprive it of some fine trees, which are now decaying, but so happily placed, that they are made more venerable and not less beautiful by their declining age. This park is much ornamented by two or three fine pieces of water; one of them is a very noble canal, so artfully terminated by an elegant bridge, beyond which is a wood, that it there appears like a fine river vanishing from the eye. (*Millenium Hall*, 109–110)

The dimensions of the park—"not quite three miles round"—along with the uneven terrain, fine timber, and water features give the impression of the vast acreage that typifies the landscape park. The "artful" placement of the scene's diverse features and the ladies' wise preference for arboreal beauty over profit from timber together demonstrate that they know how to use their resources wisely. After delivering his impressions, the narrator learns that the park features other structures that escaped his notice. As Mrs. Morgan informs him, "that building (pointing to what we thought a pretty temple) which perhaps you imagine designed only for ornament or pleasure, is a very large pidgeon house, that affords a sufficient supply to our family, and many of our neighbours" (110). Making similar observations about a hill housing a rabbit warren and waters teeming with fish, the narrator's hostess averts any hint of luxury by establishing the utility of seemingly ornamental landscape features.

This clever method of making the beautiful landscape park equally serviceable coheres with the Hall women's commitment to productivity. Their property provides them with beautiful scenery while at the same time provisioning them with almost all they need to sustain themselves and their dependents. The coupling of natural beauty and productivity enables Scott to subsume the ladies' landscape park within the broader project of benevolent estate management. Such a harmonious arrangement legitimates their authority and suggests that this exemplary model of stewardship deserves to be adapted—as indeed it will be, in the *George Ellison* sequel featuring the narrator's execution of these very principles. Nevertheless, we also witness in this lengthy description a tour de force in landscaped deception. The ladies' landscape design begs the question, why is it necessary to hide the sources of sustenance that the land provides? Presumably the ladies worry that allowing viewers to see the land's comestible bounty might compromise its beauty. In this way, the text contains within itself the seed for suspicion that the landowners' piety and philanthropy are likewise dubious.

Millenium Hall offers a unique example of eighteenth-century fiction that uses landscape to marry what James Thompson (among others) calls aristocratic ideology to gender equality. Land, he explains, is the fundamental guarantor of value in this institution: "On the simplest level, aristocratic ideology is necessarily conservative, for it maintains the present disposition of power and of property; those families which now control land, wealth, and power will be the same families controlling land, wealth, and power in the future."[56] Scott's novel perpetuates this conservatism insofar as it builds a proto-feminist agenda on the foundational institution of landownership. Although the inset narratives critique the dissipation of court culture often associated with aristocratic ideology, the text never questions the validity and utility of this fundamental institution. The text's unique provocation, I maintain, is its objectification of both women and land, manifesting Scott's canny appropriation of the visual apparatus of patriarchy in the interest of gentlewomen. She may strike us as having made a devil's bargain when she adapted such conservative values for her women's utopia. Yet, making gentility a precondition for female uplift is a regrettable but not surprising position for her historical moment. The deception embedded in her treatment of the lesser gentility exposes the ethical compromise that accompanies her paternalistic political agenda. The inconsistencies and hypocrisies in her novel function, then, as symptoms of this moral instability. By reading her novel as a decisive example of eighteenth-century British feminism's bargain with early capitalism, I propose that the singularity of land is what animates her story and gives it staying power. As Thompson continues, "Unlike land, which is stable and inert, unchanging over time, immutable and transhistorical, money is associated with alchemy, with changeability per se."[57] Scott reveals that land, too, involves a kind of alchemy when social relations turn it into landscape. That the heroines in her novel prove adept at both kinds of alchemy surely produces a powerful form of female agency.

4

ELIZABETH MONTAGU, BLUESTOCKING LANDSCAPER

ELIZABETH MONTAGU, NÉE ROBINSON (1718–1800), presided over a certain sector of the literary public sphere as one of the most celebrated salon hostesses in London. Samuel Johnson christened her "Queen of the Bluestockings," a position she embraced through devotion to patronage and other forms of charity that grounded her reputation in virtue and benevolence. As Betty Schellenberg has demonstrated, Montagu participated in one of Britain's most prominent literary coteries of the century's second half, circulating private letters and manuscripts among an exclusive and carefully controlled inner circle.[1] Seemingly inhabiting the private sphere, she was also a remarkably successful businesswoman—a coal magnate—and thus presents a challenge for scholars seeking to encapsulate the impact of such a formidable figure in eighteenth-century women's literary history. Ultimately, she belongs neither to the public nor the private sphere. (Indeed, Schellenberg elsewhere notes that "Montagu's letters circulated among admirers beyond the coterie."[2]) The sheer size of her epistolary corpus (ca. four thousand letters) provides perhaps a more detailed record of quotidian existence than exists for any other British woman of her era.[3] As Elizabeth Eger observes, "Montagu combined attention to detail and daily pragmatism with a longer view of the social purpose and responsibilities of wealth, ploughing her coal money directly into her ambitious cultural projects."[4] The image of Montagu "ploughing coal" provides an apt metaphor for a woman who harvested vast wealth from the farms and coal mines comprising her numerous estates. This chapter scrutinizes her landed property and its implications for her form of female independence.

Montagu also resists firm classification because of her dual socioeconomic status as both an agrarian and industrial capitalist. As the wife and then heir to the wealthy coal mine and landowner Edward Montagu, she worked as his business partner and later assumed full responsibility for the multiple rural estates and London townhouse that he bequeathed to her upon his death in 1775. Because she devoted significant time, effort, and money to improving her property, she illuminates the arduous discursive process of assimilating industrial activity within the social profile of Britain's elite. Insofar as the ruling classes distinguished themselves through ownership of agricultural land, Montagu serves as a fascinating case study of how industry complicates social relations that inhere in the land—that is, in landscapes. Meanwhile, managing her agricultural property demanded comparable effort of a different sort in order to sustain the ideal landscape—and the ideal self—that she cultivated on her preferred country estate at Sandleford Priory in Berkshire. In carefully modulated engagement with her agricultural and industrial properties, Montagu emerges as an astute landowner of consummate propriety whose epistolary self-construction nevertheless exposes both the costs and the benefits for a woman thus staking her identity in the rural landscape (see figure 4.1).

The Montagu letters attest, in important new ways, to the crucial relationship between landscape and women's independence in this period. Industrial and agricultural lands require her steady and sometimes strenuous attention, especially once she is widowed; yet they also amount to a vast estate that instills in her a sense of purpose, accomplishment, and authority. Her own self-description, in a 1767 letter to her sister, Sarah Scott, hinges her identity on landownership: "I am a Critick, a Coal Owner, a Land Steward, a sociable creature."[5] Unlike the other women featured in this study, she was not known primarily for her writing. Nevertheless, her voluminous correspondence has made her a valuable source for historians across a range of topics, from patronage, politics, sociability, and politeness to Shakespeare (the subject of her sole single-author publication), material culture, patriotism, and national and Anglican identity. Nicole Pohl emphasizes the breadth of Montagu's involvement in eighteenth-century European culture: "She was a businesswoman and landowner, literary critic, patron of architecture and the arts, interior designer, and center of a range of overlapping social circles, including patronage alliances and kinship ties that also provided the basis for some of the voluntary transnational networks that Montagu enjoyed and nurtured."[6] With landownership so deeply embedded in her identity, one would expect her letters to manifest the multifaceted, at times rewarding and at times troubling aspects of her landed position. Evidence for this claim appears not only in her descriptions of her various properties but also in the records of her engagement with the people affiliated with these places. The social relations inhering in the land—the landscapes—come to life in Montagu's letters. In this way they animate the final phase in Garrett Sullivan's historical model of landscape, when proto-capitalist social relations have displaced the quasi-feudal model—the interdependent landscapes of stewardship and custom—that obsolesced over the course of the long eighteenth century.

Building on Sullivan's model, then, this chapter foregrounds Montagu's status as a landowner whose agricultural and industrial properties instantiate the two iterations of landscape that together signify the commodification of land: the landscape of absolute property and the landscape arts. Grounded in a capitalist

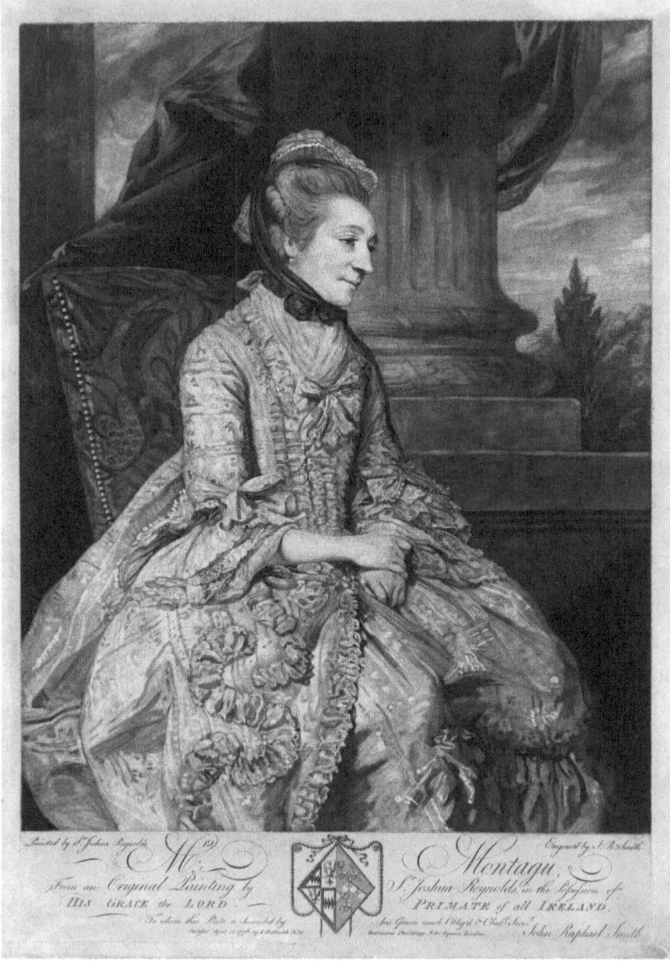

Figure 4.1. *Elizabeth Montagu*, mezzotint engraving by John Raphael Smith after portrait by Sir Joshua Reynolds, 1776. © National Portrait Gallery, London.

economy, these two forms of landscape operate together to produce social relations in the land that are no longer governed by reciprocity but instead by wage labor. In both cases, the landowner's prerogative prevails while those who work the land have lost the customary rights that it once gave them. The landscape of absolute property designates the landowner's explicit, undisputed, and thoroughgoing economic interest in his property, most literally in the profits generated by his estate—or in this case, *her* estate. Conversely, the landscape arts constitute an aesthetic expression of the landowner's wealth. Though conceived as the corollary to the landscape of absolute property, the landscape arts also serve as a kind of cover for the stark manifestation of the landowner's wealth; they translate this wealth into an aesthetically pleasing form.

With a financial portfolio such as Montagu's, beautifying estate improvement in one locale could offset the challenges—social and otherwise—of owning coal mines in another. Her employment of Capability Brown, the century's foremost landscape designer, to remodel the Sandleford grounds testifies to her interest in rendering the property an ideal landscape according to the standards of her time. Her vast holdings—from Northumberland, on the border with Scotland, to Berkshire, one of the home counties—demonstrate how aestheticized land compensates for the industrial land that resists assimilation into the landscape arts. The north–south polarization of her properties maps onto the divergent personae she assumes in each place, whether the industrious businesswoman or the leisured gentlewoman. Yet this simplistic geography is a fiction, albeit one that Montagu herself relies on when the occasion suits her. Sandleford provides the consummate example of her landscaped art, but it is also an agricultural property that demands her stewardship and thus complicates her self-image as a woman of leisure.

The first half of this chapter studies the social anxieties arising from Montagu's role as a coal magnate in a society still attached to its agrarian identity. The second half then turns to the contradictory depictions of Sandleford, including those of her bailiff of nearly twenty years, James Woodhouse, the "shoemaker poet." A figure for the landscape of absolute property at Sandleford who unsettles her idealized construction of it, Woodhouse is a formidable foil for Montagu, bearing the brunt of her obsession with social distinction. Because both parties derive their identity, to some extent, from their relation to Sandleford, they animate the tension between the landscape of absolute property and the landscape arts. Building on this tension while also considering the two landscapes' interdependence, the chapter observes how Sandleford entangles Montagu in vexing social relations that challenge her adept self-construction as a benevolent female landowner. In turn, I examine this complex form of landownership in terms of its implications for female independence. As a landowner concerned with her social status at least as much as her gender, Montagu presents a provocative illustration of female landownership that complicates scholarship celebrating her as a proto-feminist. She exemplifies the struggle faced by eighteenth-century British women who pursued independence via landownership and encountered conflict when their class and gender interests did not coincide. These insights expose capitalism as an extremely effective but also problematic enterprise through which to pursue female independence.

FEMALE LANDOWNERSHIP: FARMS VERSUS COLLIERIES

Montagu's letters contain various kinds of discord between agriculture and industry, and it is instructive to read such tension in relation to the two landscapes operating under capitalism. Agriculture lends itself to aesthetic representation and thus the landscape arts, but such is not the case for industry. Consider the following excerpt, which she wrote from her collieries in Denton, Northumberland, to her dear friend and (aside from her sister) most frequent correspondent, Elizabeth Carter, a fellow Bluestocking and woman of letters. The passage illustrates how Montagu strains—not always successfully—to bring the collieries within the purview of the landscape arts.

> I went last night for the first time to ye colliery, it lies on the edge of the Tyne; ye meadows by the River are most beautiful & have a charming opposite shore & fine prospect; I never saw a sweeter spot for a garden, but *li ornamenti* are, a Fire engine, Staiths, Pitts, a brick Kiln, & a Lime Kiln, all profitable, & therefore pleasant objects to the Owner, but as a woman of taste, I sigh'd to see so lovely a place so dress'd. From the top of the Engine arises a vast column of black smoak, & a cloud of steam at ye bottom issues out, this engine pours into the Tyne about 1400 hogsheads of ill scented water in an hour, to the great disgust of the River God and water nymphs no doubt.[7]

The initial impression of bucolic serenity—charming meadows, fine prospect—locates Montagu in the realm of the landscape arts, ordering items in a scene, imbuing it with beauty and harmony. But then incongruous elements from the coal industry intrude on the scene and mar its serenity. Such an intrusion is of course Montagu's own doing, for she orchestrates the scene to enchant her reader, only then to disrupt the reverie with items that violate the conventions of the landscape arts. She seems even mildly amused at the incongruity of an Italianate vocabulary (*li ornamenti*) alongside discordant industrial terms like *Staiths, Pitts*, *Kiln*, and so forth.

Yet this is a minor pleasure, for nothing alleviates the distaste caused by the image of industrial waste, "1400 hogsheads of ill scented water." Returning to the pastoral mode with reference to a classical deity and nymphs, Montagu implies that industry may finally be incommensurable with her rural idyll. Her subsequent turn to more pragmatic matters—"We hope a few days will bring us to the coal when our profits will begin"—indicates her willingness to tolerate such dissonance for the sake of economic gain. But the dissonance disrupts her own sense of self; the colliery contraptions are "all profitable, & therefore pleasant objects to the Owner, but as a woman of taste," she does not enjoy them. A sense of alienation emerges in her third-person reference to "the Owner" who does not share the perspective of the tasteful woman. Ultimately, Montagu's knowing attempt to synthesize her coal-mining efforts with her tasteful sensibilities operates at once on ironic and serious levels. She knows that industrial machinery strains the bounds of agrarian beauty and feminine tastefulness and is both amused and unsettled by the fact.

The excerpt serves as a concise summation of the evolving history of British landscape, whose course has been the focus of this book. The numerous epistolary depictions of Montagu's property enact a competition of sorts between landscapes of absolute property and the landscape arts. The competition attests to the efficacy of putting landscape in the service of capitalism, a process that obfuscates the negative impact of the social inequality that this landscape produces. Thus constituted, the Montagu lands manifest a mature phase in the history of landscape in Britain, when absolute property is more entrenched, and the landscape arts naturalize this arrangement. The proto-capitalist landscape of absolute property underlies and enables the landscape arts that qualify her as a woman of taste. As one of the wealthiest women of her era, Montagu forges a path to female independence by mobilizing the landscape of absolute property primarily through her coal mines, which in turn fund her investment in the landscape arts. The crucial fact undergirding this interpretation is that her coal mines were extremely profitable. As Les Turnbull argues, "It was not the farms in Berkshire and Yorkshire, nor those in Durham and Northumberland, that provided the finances to refurbish the old family home at Sandleford or build the new London town house in Portland Place, but the colliery at East Denton."[8] Consequently, her rhetorical skill proves an essential means for her to translate industrial labor and profit into aesthetic appreciation for the land.

The vastness of Montagu's epistolary corpus in a certain sense matches the vastness of her properties. She inherited enormous wealth when Edward died in 1775, leaving her country estates in Yorkshire (Allerthorpe Hall and Eryholme), Berkshire (Sandleford Priory), and Northumberland (Denton Hall and collieries, near Newcastle); and a townhouse on Hill Street in London.[9] Once widowed, she pursued more ambitious building projects than she and Edward had ever undertaken, of which the Brownian transformation of Sandleford is a prime example. Thus partaking in the quintessential form of authority in Britain—property ownership in land—she demonstrates how the prerogatives of landownership are accessible to women, and how they require her to finesse her feminine identity so as not to encroach on terrain traditionally understood as masculine.

Montagu's distinction as a woman of fabulous wealth and a writer of voluminous letters makes her significance in *Prolific Ground* hinge to a greater extent on her landownership than was the case in the previous three chapters. The remarkable extent of her properties, and the pride she took in stewarding them, lead historical geographer Briony McDonagh to consider her exceptional. She is struck by Montagu's boasts about her estate improvements, of which the landowner notes that "few Gentlemen in ye Neighbourhood have done more." McDonagh goes on to observe that "Montagu of course was a leading Bluestocking and it is unclear whether other propertied women saw their estate management and landscaping projects as transgressing the boundaries of appropriate feminine action in quite the same way."[10] These observations support an interpretation of Montagu as a proto-feminist figure, though her pride has led other critics to identify her instead as a self-serving egotist.[11] McDonagh also suggests that although Montagu's landowning persona may have been extraordinary, female landownership at the time was more widespread than most scholars realize. McDonagh's study of Parliamentary enclosure awards from 1700 to 1830 finds that "10.3 per cent of land in the sample was owned by a woman, either alone or jointly with one or more other parties. Female landowners were, moreover, a relative commonplace within rural communities up and down the country."[12] In light of this data, the extent of Montagu's self-regard, grounded as it is in landownership, becomes an even more compelling reason to treat her as an illustration of the importance of such ownership to female independence. As McDonagh indicates, Montagu may be exceptional, but less so than previously thought. Paradoxically exceptional and exemplary, Montagu presents a thorny yet fruitful encounter with female self-construction through landownership.

Scholars have long interpreted Montagu in relation to landscape as it is traditionally construed to mean rural land or a representation thereof. Mid-twentieth century critics mined the Huntington Library's Elizabeth Robinson Montagu Papers, a trove of nearly 7,000 letters (over half her own) and identified therein her penchant for robust and suggestive depictions of the natural world, applying such categories as the Romantic, the sublime, and the picturesque.[13] Twenty-first-century scholarship has tended to address the more complex social and political implications of her engagement with rural land. For instance, Emma Major investigates Montagu's depictions of her 1776 journey to France, which prompted her to compare the happiness of French women to that of their British counterparts. Noting how "the condition of women is imbricated [in Montagu's letters] with notions of liberty, landscape, religion, and progress," Major reckons with Montagu's depictions of land as political statements in their own right.[14] Finally, Stephen Bending focuses on her landscape improvements at Sandleford and her manipulation of various pastoral personae to fashion herself a virtuous woman in retirement there.[15] He observes contradictions in Montagu's self-conception that also manifest in my study of her landowning practices as crucial components of her identity. By expanding the scope of her landownership to encompass both coal mines and farms—occasions for both labor and luxury—I seek a broader assessment of her landed identity. Such an endeavor accounts for the vexed condition of the female landowner, who transgresses the bounds of proper femininity and in so doing, confronts suspicion and censure in a culture that sometimes treats her as an anomaly.

INDUSTRIAL LANDSCAPING AND THE FEMALE SELF

The most recent scholarship on Montagu's experience as a coal magnate exposes the difficulty of assessing her industrial expertise in its appropriate historical context. On the one hand, there is evidence that the uniqueness of her involvement in the coal industry has been overstated; on the other, this point does not discredit the many indications of her struggle to align her coal-owning endeavors with her self-conception as fashionable lady. One could survey the available scholarship and conclude that she thrived in her industrial pursuits and thus navigated a challenging but not entirely hostile realm and emerged a stronger woman—perhaps even an avatar for future businesswomen. This reading would suggest that the anxiety over her industrial interest pales in comparison to her triumphant depictions of her mastery of this domain. In the face of these considerations, one must weigh Montagu's variously enthusiastic and beleaguered depictions of her coal mining interests and draw conclusions about their significance for her landowning persona.

It is plausible to interpret her industrial affairs as an energizing endeavor that in turn nourished her estate improvements and other cultural projects. McDonagh and others take this approach, treating Montagu's business interests more as a source of energy than anxiety. Surveying her many business contacts, diversified properties, and sound reputation as a businesswoman, McDonagh observes that "she maintained a regular correspondence with her agents and managers and had an excellent knowledge of matters relating to the coal trade in the north, as her letters on the subject attest."[16] Similarly, Elizabeth Child argues that Montagu's self-confidence soars in her work as an industrialist in ways that elude her as a woman of letters: "The epistolary persona of Montagu the businesswoman is in general confident—even triumphant. [. . .] The epistolary persona of Montagu the author and critic is more vexed."[17] In drawing positive conclusions about her coal mine–owning experience, these scholars broach the businesswoman from a sympathetic angle that aligns with their feminist interpretations.

Assessing Montagu within the history of coal mining, however, leads to the conclusion that feminist critics risk exaggerating her impact if they minimize the complexity of the coal trade or misconstrue the extent of her holdings. Turnbull blazed this trail by immersing himself in the archives of northern England, primarily the North of England Institute of Mining and Mechanical Engineers in Newcastle upon Tyne. Evaluating these records alongside the Huntington Library holdings, he models a comprehensive approach to Montagu the industrialist. For example, he weighs her manifest business success against the exploitative practices of the trade, which she herself criticized but did not entirely avoid. He seeks to balance her impressive expertise and profits with a robust understanding of the coal industry that controverts claims for her singularity as a female coal magnate. Observing that she "grasped the general principles but not the precise details of coal mining," he persuasively argues for a measured approach to Montagu's self-construction as "the Countess of the Coalpits."[18] This strategy involves situating her alongside not only her crafty male business associates but also her fellow female coal magnates. He concludes that "although she was an important coal owner, Elizabeth Montagu was not in the same league as these three [women] in terms of the size of her collieries, but she was their match in business acumen."[19] Turnbull's study produces a socially and geographically nuanced portrait of Montagu that rings true as a realistic assessment of her significant but not unparalleled accomplishment as a female coal owner: "Montagu was doubtless a match for John Blackett, Henry Liddell, Thomas Clavering, and their ilk; but she was neither the first nor the only woman to confront the captains of Newcastle's coal trade. [. . .] The drawing rooms of Hill Street and Portman Square, where Montagu could entertain her business associates Mary Bowes, Alice Windsor, and Mary Stewart, were more influential than Denton Hall."[20] Turnbull maintains the geographic diffusion and gender inclusivity of the coal industry, thus overriding notions of the trade's north–south polarity with an awareness of its broad, intranational operations and its mixed-gender composition. He thus challenges women's literary historians to take a likewise balanced approach that incorporates a reliable assessment of Montagu's accomplishments as an industrialist.

How does one take the full measure of a woman whose nearly four-thousand-letter archive is dispersed across two continents and remains to be published or digitized in an optimal, user-friendly format?[21] My approach favors rhetorical analysis of select Montagu letters that demonstrate her effective landowning practices while also exposing a capacity to deceive herself and others in order to construct her ideal self. This method seeks neither to inflate nor denigrate a woman writer who necessarily expresses the values of her time but also defies them in significant ways. Her letters present epistolary puzzles that deserve careful consideration as instances of exemplary womanhood as conceived by eighteenth-century Britain. From this perspective, her occasional ambivalence toward the coal trade seems apt for a woman whose letters establish that she considers literature a higher calling than business. She may have thrived as a colliery owner, but she also bridled against its demands and regretted the shadow it cast on her self-image as a refined and accomplished woman of letters.

Montagu's ambivalence about her industrial endeavors manifests not only in her embellishments of the trade but also in her recognition that such rhetoric has its limitations. In a subsequent letter to Carter, written in late July 1766, Montagu wrestles with the tension between the coal mines' economic value, on the one hand, and the aesthetic and ethical goods that it produces, on the other. She sets the scene by describing her Denton lodgings and their obstructed prospect.

> Imagine an old Gothick house in the worst style of Gothick, gloomy without sublimity, the prospect much confined by trees & buildings. My best object the mouth of a coal mine, round which a horse is continually pacing in order to draw up the coals, the said coals look to the common eye as very ugly black objects, but my imagination sees them taking

> various shapes: the hand of bounty may bestow them in seasonable assistance to distress, the hand of taste transform them to beautiful forms, they may purchase sometimes pleasure sometimes ease, & indeed will procure many vulgar comforts, but health, friendship, cheerefulness, content . . . & the nobler joys are not to be dispensed but by the more immediate communication of the great Giver of good gifts, who imparts them as rewards for what has been well done. These courser things are only opportunities to do well.[22]

Framing her comments on the coal mine with a description of "the prospect much confined by trees & buildings," Montagu artfully employs a landscape device—a frame—to signal her own confinement within the material strictures of the coal trade. She constructs a literal coal-mine landscape with the "very ugly black objects" at its center, at which point her imagination sets to work transmuting the raw material into superior, immaterial form. Her tortuous thought process as she moves from the lower to the higher realm betrays the anxiety that her entanglement in the mining industry produces.

The passage only partially succeeds in navigating the tension between the economic, aesthetic, and ethical realms. Child offers a generous reading when she observes that Montagu "is unable to dispense the 'nobler gifts' of health and happiness, but as a benefactor, an enlightened employer can certainly provide 'coarser' material benefits even as she educates the recipients about those greater rewards yet to come from the 'great Giver.' Thereby she also earns herself those nobler gifts, by using her own material gifts well."[23] This seemingly neutral paraphrase of Montagu's narrative of self-legitimation passes over its rhetorical excess. The dense figuration of the passage—the double metonymy of "the hand of bounty" and "the hand of taste," the catalog of the good ("assistance to distress," pleasure, ease, health, friendship, cheerfulness, etc.), the periphrasis of "the great Giver of good gifts"—all display a verbal opulence that either escapes Child's notice or perhaps brings it up short. A turn of phrase in her next sentence implies but does not develop the notion that Montagu's musings are so many "flights of spiritual fancy," tolerable because offset by the concrete actions she takes to improve her workers' lives. Fanciful meditation on her divinely sanctioned wealth, Child suggests, might be merely self-serving if Montagu's actions did not make good on her words.

The defensive note in Child's interpretation betrays an awareness that Montagu might deserve gentle censure for congratulating herself on her good works. The final sentence in the passage, when quoted in full, adds to the impression that Montagu is groping for a way to justify her ambivalence toward her coal mines: "These courser things are only opportunities to do well, and if assistance to make a good use of them was not promised to those who seek it, they would be rather to be received as tryals and temptations than as blessings." Here Montagu reasons that divine assistance in doing good is what keeps her from experiencing her inordinate wealth as a burden rather than a blessing. Such a denial of ingratitude nevertheless introduces its possibility. The passage's complex rhetoric leaves good reason to argue, at the very least, that Montagu's stylistic excess betrays anxiety as she struggles but does not entirely succeed in harmonizing "vulgar comforts" and "the nobler joys."

Despite the discord, the passage also features Montagu's sheer joy in the imagination, revealing how the very tools that ease her conscience also expose her capacity for self-deception. Imagining the good that her wealth performs runs the risk of self-flattery, and it is worth emphasizing here the literary landscaping that she undertakes in the process of converting her ugly coal mine into a tableau of spiritual plenty. The conceit echoes similar gestures in her previous letter ("I never saw a sweeter spot for a garden, but *li ornamenti* [. . .]"), reminding us that in adapting an agricultural idiom for her coal mines, she exploits landscape's potential to straddle worlds she sees as distinct, and to aestheticize and thus elevate a seemingly sublunary realm. Her oeuvre is teeming with letters displaying a deep investment in the literary imagination, and the preponderance of evidence in the archive suggests that this creative realm matters the most to her.

Such is the image of Montagu encountered in *The Elizabeth Montagu Correspondence Online*, which asserts that "alongside her role as a socialite and 'Queen of the Bluestockings,' Elizabeth Montagu is best remembered for her contributions to literary history, as a literary critic, promoter of Shakespeare, and patron of poets, philosophers, and intellectuals."[24] From this perspective, her translation of coal into the stuff of literary criticism demonstrates the significant impact of a writer whose imaginative reckoning with wealth produces an ethical artistry worthy of careful scrutiny. It may be unremarkable to portray her agricultural property through the rhetoric of landscape. Yet applying that rhetoric to her collieries represents an innovative maneuver, revealing the transformative potential of the landscape arts, especially when these work in concert with the literary imagination. Her literary landscaping thus seeks to harmonize the discordant aspects of her social, professional, and gender identity, leaving us to puzzle over the partnership she enacts between aesthetics and ethics. Is Montagu's artful justification of her wealth merely a distraction from its excess or a valid resolution for the quandary she faces?

Regardless of our answer to the question, the more significant point in this context is that Montagu conducts her ethical struggle using the idiom of landscape, thus fusing a moral problem to an aesthetic one. Situating her struggle within landscape's historical transformation, we are now better positioned to appreciate how her rhetorical flourishes, and their particular manifestation through the apparatus of landscape, reveal the historically specific nature of her response to the problem of the right use of wealth. Such flourishes resemble the arboreal and floral enticements that enchant the narrator of Scott's *Millenium Hall*, persuading him that its owners use their wealth to the best advantage by harmonizing their aesthetic and ethical commitments. Aestheticized land offers both sisters a justification for their material privilege, such that adornment obscures the deception underway in the very premise that ethical problems have aesthetic solutions. Writing in the second half of the eighteenth century, Scott and Montagu enact a common strategy for accommodating the injustices of capitalism by concocting beautiful distractions and insisting on beauty as sufficient evidence of worth.

ETHICS AND AESTHETICS: THE POLITICS OF THE LANDSCAPE ARTS

The partnership between ethics and aesthetics that both women embrace echoes Sullivan's two-part schema as previously discussed: the landscape of absolute property and the landscape arts. The two forms coalesce as a larger landscape under capitalism, though at times the arrangement produces a certain dissonance, as witnessed in Montagu's strained effort to aestheticize a landscape consisting of a "Fire engine, Staiths, Pitts," etc. In that example, her landscape art resists the components of her landscape of absolute property. Her conceit's simultaneously entertaining and unnerving effects cast doubt upon her implicit goal of harmonizing two seemingly incommensurable domains. They also expose how the landscape arts tend to be at odds with nonagrarian uses of land. If at first we identify the incongruity as a matter of aesthetics versus economics, it must also be said that the very distinction depends upon her moral judgment. She perceives the potential injustice of inordinate wealth, and the vice of being ungrateful for it, and devises elegant distractions from these wrongs. In thus cleansing her wealth, her stylistic legerdemain obfuscates the possible deception at work in such a technique.

The era's landscape discourse typically contains a moral dimension, something little noted until now in order to first situate Montagu within the historical transformation of landscape. In his overview of "Literature and Landscape in the Eighteenth Century," Bending offers a useful gloss on landscape's moral dimension, which merges with questions of aesthetics. In reference to two male literary landscapers, he observes that "what both writers shared was a sense that point of view enables the viewer to construct landscape from physical terrain but also allows the viewer to see beyond the physical limits of that terrain. They insist, that is, that landscape is moral and political quite as much as it is visual and 'aesthetic.'"[25] By integrating morality into an assessment of Montagu's industrial landscape, we discern the moral framework within which she herself distinguishes that landscape from an agrarian one. While gazing upon her colliery along the riverbank, she insinuates that the utilitarian objects before her offer only financial but not moral rewards. So, too, does the reference to her womanhood suggest that her morality is likewise caught up in her femininity.

Montagu confronts us with the question of whether to accept the redemptive capacity of her moral–industrial imagination. Further evidence exposes the limitations in this form of redemption, which treats the production of economic value as beneficial because of its magical operation. In the following passage we again witness Montagu marveling over the transformative processes that her coal mines generate. But here the transformation has to do with both the redemption of base materials and their sublimation into currency. As she writes from Denton in a 1758 letter to fellow Bluestocking Benjamin Stillingfleet, "Coals that now lye 80 fathom below the surface of the earth by next summer may be carried in a gentleman's pocket to Arthurs & what has employ'd many strong hands to dig it filld many a waggon, & freighted a ship, shall lye in a silken purse & pass from one owner to another by ye speedy decision of a toss up."[26] It would be difficult to surpass this dazzling picture of romanticized capitalism, one that uses agricultural language to valorize the mining industry. The imagery of a coal harvest—hands digging in earth, the extraction of produce from the soil—all create an amalgamation of agricultural and industrial processes.

The metaphorical richness of the passage animates this letter, just as the coal industry animates Montagu. A prosaic subject, coal mining here becomes the stuff of poetic language. The commodification of coal is rendered as raw material that moves—by invisible hands—from deep within the earth to the seaside and the city. The process brings to mind the partnership of "the hand of bounty" and "the hand of taste," figurations that treat exploitative operations as innocuous, seemingly automatic, and barely human. The image of coal sublimated into a more precious form, lying "in a silken purse," confers a magical, even alchemical mystery on the process. Crucially, the material conversion of coal into cash also involves the transformation of avarice into pure wealth; the alchemy of coal production washes away greed by converting vice into a productive rather than degenerative quality. Such processes recall similar instances of alchemy in the previous chapters, for example in Sarah Scott's transformation of land into landscape in constructing her utopian community for female uplift at Millenium Hall. Whether delivering its precious subterranean resources or displaying its terrestrial bounty, the land lends itself to productive transmogrifications that function for the benefit of women. The alchemical dimension of the process signals something dubious about conversions that make such significant compromises as to who is permitted to partake in them.

Exposing the deceptions embedded in various aesthetic processes reveals how they only partially succeed, and how landscapes of absolute property do not entirely harmonize with the landscape arts. Montagu's literary legerdemain may enrich the coal trade with aesthetic appeal and seemingly moral heft, planting it in the realm of the landscape arts. But her strategy does not fully cleanse the trade of its commercial taint. The ambiguity bespeaks her anxious need to establish a moral justification for her life as an industrialist. As someone perennially concerned with the state of the soul, who rationalized her ever-increasing fortune in terms of the good it would do others, she needed a moralized way of seeing the external world. Such ambiguity and anxiety expose a certain futility in Montagu's efforts to assimilate industry within the landscape arts.

The troubled partnership between the landscape of absolute property and the landscape arts also exposes how the larger capitalist landscape that contains them produces instances of resistance or strain. As symptoms of the system's damaging consequence, these instances sometimes appear as mere discord or incidental but not total failure. The depiction of a coal harvest exemplifies this seemingly incidental trouble that in fact discloses a larger problem. The agricultural substrate in Montagu's tableau of industry implies that growing grain and mining coal are equally natural and noble endeavors, but this is a pretense she cannot sustain, and she shifts her attention accordingly. After contemplating the magical extraction of monetary value from the bowels of the earth, she settles her gaze upon a visually attractive scene, observing: "[W]e hired a house on the banks of the Tyne for the occasion [of our visit here], it is a very pretty house extreamly well furnished & most agreably situated, ships & other vessels from Newcastle are sailing by every hour, the River here is broad & of a good colour, & we have a large reach of it."[27] In the wake of "great burthens of Coals" barreling out of the earth, the image of Montagu gazing at ships sailing past her lodging on the riverbank, presumably carrying that very coal as its cargo, returns her to the logic of the landscape arts. Stepping back, as it were, to reconstruct the panoramic view provided by her hired house, she finds visual pleasure in a tableau evacuated of its subterranean blemishes—a spectacle, then, of temporary or provisional beauty.

The Montagu letters contain a fascinating record of the discursive process that disaggregates and reaggregates aesthetic and functional aspects of the land. The dubious alchemy of industrial wealth also has implications for her social anxiety, which after all originates in her suspicion that this form of wealth debases her social status. As we saw in her depiction of a coal harvest, the coexistence of seemingly incommensurable kinds of landscape exemplifies the process by which the landscape arts subsume or obfuscate nonaestheticized (or commodified) valuations of the land. A shuffling of social and economic values is underway in depictions that strive and yet fail to confer beauty upon industrial scenery. In this sense, Montagu's anxious and often futile efforts to landscape her coal mines are symptomatic of an anxiety to assimilate colliery ownership within her genteel identity—and certainly, too, of the turbulent transition to capitalism.

INDUSTRY, LANDOWNERSHIP, AND THE SOCIAL HIERARCHY

It is instructive to consider both the personal and more broadly political explanations for Montagu's fixation with social distinction, for familial status and societal expectations converge to make her coal interests a potential cause for her concern. Though her parents were well born, highly educated, and had a fine estate in Kent, her lineage did not include aristocratic titles of the sort that punctuate the pedigree of her husband, the grandson of the Earl of Sandwich. Emma Major suggests that Montagu's liminal status within the upper tiers of the social hierarchy contributed to her extreme sensitivity to such matters. Major also identifies a persistent concern for propriety across a lifetime of correspondence between Montagu and her sister, traceable to their liminal social position: "Discussions about humility permeate the letters, and the inability of servants, friends, and family, to recognize proper boundaries is repeatedly lamented, criticized, and satirized. [. . .]. As the sisters of a baronet, Scott and Montagu's social status, like that of the women in Millenium Hall, hovers around the lower regions of the aristocracy, and in the upper regions of the gentry. They are not quite in a position to treat social niceties with scorn."[28] Montagu's particular personal circumstances seem likely to compel her acute sensitivity to the culture's intricate system for establishing social worth.

The complexities of the social hierarchy have likewise complex political dimensions that require elaboration. The synthesis of nonagrarian enterprise within the precincts of the gentility and aristocracy was a protracted and socially fraught process. Montagu's anxiety, I would argue, inheres in the fact that her immersion in the coal mining business is decidedly nonagrarian, her whimsical efforts to render it so notwithstanding. The striking recurrence of this anxiety, and its absence in similar efforts to harmonize agriculture and industry—for instance, the rug factory in *Millenium Hall*—suggest that the facticity of her example heightens the nature of the challenge. Unlike Scott, Montagu cannot use fiction to compel the market to satisfy a utopian desire for a harmoniously diversified economy.

When we situate coal mining within the broader political economy, we improve our grasp of her experience of elite society as it expanded its agrarian roots to include other forms of economic activity. Landownership was of course the sine qua non for membership in the ruling classes, and inheritance of landed wealth continued to be the most unassailable mark of high status. Historical scholarship affirms these basic facts, regardless of ongoing debate about the relative status among the upper tiers of the social hierarchy. Lawrence and Jeanne Stone's study of the English aristocracy places landownership front and center, showing how country seats were effectively the coin of the realm for the nation's elite.[29] Paul Langford nuances this arrangement, arguing that the narrative of entrenched division between landed versus non-landed—monied—interests has been both overstated and reductive with reference to an increasingly complex economy.

> The portability of some forms of property was a favourite argument of earlier generations, giving rise to a variety of metaphors. [. . .] Riches could take wing and fly away; land was encumbered with a "tail" in order to

> prevent its flight. In this residual sense that land was a unique and irreplaceable form of stake in one's country, the old conviction that it must be granted a special place in whatever constitutional arrangements sustained the State remained defensible. [. . .] Yet the civic superiority of land was by no means a satisfactory premiss [*sic*] on which to take a stand. Land was part of a complex economic structure. Individual landowners needed little reminding of their dependence on the market for agricultural produce created by a commercially diverse and growing nation. Many, too, derived profits, either directly or indirectly, from mining, manufacturing, or government securities. The concern of men who had made their money in something other than land to sink the proceeds of their enterprise in a landed estate is an enduring feature of English history. It showed no signs of letting up with industrial growth.[30]

Montagu's career as a "Coal Owner" and estate improver makes her a particularly compelling illustration of Langford's case for a diversified economy that nevertheless continues to treat land as the primary means to distinction. Descriptions of her evolving affairs at Denton Estates indicate the interdependence of agriculture and industry within the confines of her own property. Writing in 1783 to her fellow Bluestocking hostess Elizabeth Vesey, she details her business ventures there.

> I have now above 500 men at work below ground in the pits and above sixty in a wheatfield reaping [. . .]. My late purchased colliery is now working very successfully. [. . .] I have the satisfaction of finding all my affairs in great order and prosperity, [. . .] but for the pleasures of the imagination and the delights of rural life I cannot enjoy them here. [. . .] A new purchased estate which cost me £36,000 adjoining to Denton Estates will, now as belonging to the same proprietor, be as it were incorporated, and some farms will be enlarged, and many alterations of that kind present themselves.[31]

Referring to mining and reaping—the pits and the wheatfield—in one breath, Montagu demonstrates that in the north at least, agriculture and industry are mutually reinforcing enterprises, neither one favored over the other. Yet the beleaguerment in her voice suggests that her northern enterprises inhibit her access to the life of the gentlewoman. Such weariness appears primarily in reference to Denton, whereas Sandleford occasions more copious passages of landscape description.[32] In light of her thwarted effort to pastoralize her collieries, and her disdainful reference to the "very ugly black objects" that dominate the Denton scene, Montagu leaves no doubt that her work there is necessary but burdensome.

Noteworthy as well is the passage's compression of the social and economic value contained in her land; though not a source of rural "delights," the property instead signifies its monetary value—£36,000. Denton thus constitutes a landscape of absolute property whose import to its mistress inheres in the authority it gives her over more than "500 men" and in the wealth it will continue to generate. The social relations governing the estate derive from the landowner's payment of workers' wages. As we will see, Montagu occasionally adopts the rhetoric of stewardship when circumstances prompt her to engage in moral calculus regarding her vast wealth, but a comprehensive assessment of her landholding practices renders such rhetoric more self-serving than authentic. She concludes this portion of her letter by detailing the various meetings with stewards she will have in order to finalize the latest expansion and improvement of her land. Summing up her remaining business obligations, she betrays a sense of urgency in her desire to return south: "After I have considered [the stewards' scheme] and got all the information I can, the chief part of my business here will be settled, and I shall know when I may leave this place. I imagine I shall be at liberty in less than 3 weeks." The preponderance of economic and social detail accruing to Denton demonstrates how Montagu conceives of this property as the locus of pragmatic concerns that collectively constitute a significant proportion of her landed holdings. The absence of aesthetic detail in this letter, and the strain occasioned by her efforts to ascribe such detail in other letters, reveal how land given over primarily to industry resists assimilation within the purview of the landscape arts. At the same time, her decision to oversee—and indeed, expand—her industrial holdings suggests that the sacrifice is worth it because it sustains her independence and capacity for philanthropy. Still, the sense of affliction lingers, as if she faces a loss of some kind, and is paying a price.

In a letter written nearly two decades prior to the one in question, there is a similar note of barely suppressed affliction with regard to Montagu's career in the north, arising from her effort to prove herself grateful for and worthy of the fortune that enables her robust devotion to charity. As she writes from Denton to another close friend, the statesman and fellow patron George, Lord Lyttelton, "My manner of life [here] is unpleasant enough; however I never think myself unhappy when I can contribute to the happiness of others, and having made myself acquainted with the Distresses of the poor in my neighborhood, I have the pleasure of mitigating their suffering very often, as the people here are in a very rude state, they have the virtues as well as the vices of savages, they are extremely grateful for benefits, as well as resentful of injustices. I am wonderfully popular already amongst them."[33] Taking comfort in the moral purpose of her labors, Montagu nevertheless betrays ambivalence regarding what she describes as dismal and trying circumstances. It would be outré for her to admire the landscape in this context, when "the Distresses of the poor" and not the pleasures of their mistress should concern her.

NOSTALGIA FOR THE LANDSCAPE OF STEWARDSHIP

Montagu's engagement with her northern properties demonstrates the appeal and the inadequacy of the rhetoric of stewardship that she adopts in efforts to fashion herself a benevolent landowner. She evokes a landscape of stewardship even as she betrays an awareness of the nostalgic quality of such a fanciful self-image. As Major observes, "The 'Country Gentlewoman of ye last century' is one of Montagu's favorite characters in her letters," a claim that affirms the complex and purposeful quality of her epistolary self-construction.[34] After 1775, imagining herself in the last century could provide a way for her to approach her newly widowed condition with a fitting sense of responsibility and good will. Thus, playing the benevolent steward transports her to a distant time when her identity as a landowner would have been bound up in the customary care for her dependents. The appurtenances of landownership that Montagu encountered in her widowhood suggest that circumstances were ripe for her to assume a retrograde role. Her sense of living among the less civilized prompts her to approach her northern estates as remote in both geographical and chronological senses. The landscape of stewardship operates, then, as an advantageous fiction that she contrives in order to cultivate the social relations most suitable for her circumstances. Of course, the authority that accompanies landownership demands responsible conduct on her part. Montagu and her impoverished neighbors do, after all, occupy a working landscape; they inhabit land that she owns and, together, they all derive their livelihood from it. Their interdependence in this landscape produces the mistress's condescending benevolence, redolent of the aloof demeanor among the *Millenium Hall* ladies. Her civilizing rhetoric is of a piece with the moralized discourse of improvement, expressing her presumed superiority to her dependents and a dehumanizing attitude that offends modern sensibilities ("the vices of savages"). The combination of chagrin and submission to duty in her accounts of Denton reveals, then, the psychological process of assimilating industry to gentility, as well as her Whiggish conviction that virtue inheres in a productivity that in turn enables philanthropy.

The multiple roles at play when assessing Montagu's landowning persona expose the divergent historical forces that pull her forward and backward in time. This dynamic recalls the situation that vexed Jane Barker's heroine in *The Galesia Trilogy*, as seen in chapter 1. Though the heroine and her author had much less wealth than Montagu and predate her by several generations, all three women share the experience of navigating social relations governed by the land. For Montagu, this process is more complex as agrarian capitalism, greatly expanded commerce, and a more robust consumer culture complicate the social scene as the century progresses. She is of course an outlier in the extent of her riches, but this position also makes her a prominent figure in cultural debates about the social value of luxury.[35] It has become possible for women to inhabit a public role based on their tasteful consumption, and this development complicates earlier forms of identity formation inhering in the land. Though her northern properties conjure the image of the "Country Gentlewoman of ye last century," they also figure in a much-expanded consumer marketplace where desirable country estates and townhouses are not the only markers of status, nor do they circumscribe a woman's life to the same extent they would have earlier in the century. In this context, Montagu's thriving coal mines, and her entanglement in multiple market forces, render her evocation of a landscape of stewardship more a matter of whimsy—an imaginary place in which to play an archaic version of herself when it suits the occasion.

Further scrutiny of Montagu's persona as a benevolent coal magnate exposes her self-serving reliance on moralized notions of reciprocity. The scenario echoes the dubious ethical foundation for Scott's *Millenium Hall*, wherein reciprocal social relations purportedly constitute just ones. Montagu imagines that a dynamic of benevolence and gratitude between herself and her colliers can dispel the brutal reality of waged labor that sustains her estates. Inhabiting, then, a landscape of absolute property like the Hall ladies, she appropriates the landscape of stewardship in order to become worthy of her vast wealth. Her involvement in this process proves all the more striking in that it contributes to her lived experience; it is not a fictional or poetic fantasy but a record of actual events. Without belittling the value of these literary forms, I would reiterate that the facticity of Montagu's letters gives them additional heft and amplifies this book's argument about the crucial link between landownership and female independence in Britain. Finally, the fact that the landscape of absolute property arises alongside (and through) capitalism justifies my effort to situate Montagu within narratives of possessive individualism. Her epistolary corpus leaves the decisive impression that her prerogative prevails over others because she owns such vast landed property.

THE MORAL GEOGRAPHY OF NORTH AND SOUTH

One Denton description in particular demonstrates Montagu's fixation with the gradations of the social hierarchy, further underscoring her sense of affliction when compelled to associate with her social inferiors. Braiding together her assumptions about social and female propriety, the letter reveals how her business affairs in the north prompt her minute scrutiny of the ranks beneath her, whose negative example elevates her own refinement. As northerners, these subordinates prove all the more offensive in their extreme deviation from her standards of decency. Figurations of femininity dominate the passage, suggesting that her industrial affairs occasion especially acute sensitivity to her gender identity. The passage in question appears later in the June 1766 letter to Elizabeth Carter with which I began this chapter ("I went last night for the first time to ye colliery"). Having mentioned the distracting and costly impact of the local races, she then offers a more comprehensive description of the region's people.

> I should have much more hope of civilizing my barbarians if a good example was given by the middling sort, but we have a strange set of people

> here in the middle rank of life. The coalmines bring a great deal of money into this Country, many enjoy plenty, & not understanding ye delicate luxuries, they eat & drink like Hogs. [. . .] The Women guzzle & are half drunk all day. I mean those who are between the common people and the gentry. [. . .]. As to the men here, they are abominably drunken and profligate. [. . .] What a strange animal is man! One should think running out of the temptations of ambition and the allurements of pleasure should be virtuous, but the siren sloth, with her hair uncombed, her face unwashed, allures more souls into her filthy sty than her sisters bring to their Palace or their garden. I am confirm'd here in an opinion I have long entertain'd, that next to those people who earn their daily bread by daily labour, those in high rank are the best. I do not mean those who have titles or fortunes, but such as have had good education & have lived in polite company, for there the mind grows refined, and rises above brutal sloth or brutal pleasure.[36]

Montagu's assessment of Northumberland's social hierarchy offers a striking exposition of her own self-serving perception of the relative vices and virtues distinguishing each rank. Because they occupy the shared working landscape of the Northumberland coal mines, she is obliged to interact with people she considers distasteful. Her letter reinscribes social distinctions that the shared landscape threatens to erase. It comes as no surprise that "the best" consist of people, like herself, whose "education and [. . .] polite company"—rather than titles or fortunes—qualify them for distinction. Thus separating herself from those who possess riches without the refinement of gentility, she further exemplifies how elite culture identifies itself through certain ineffable—and presumably nonfungible—qualities. That she does so in the wake of an effort to aestheticize and legitimate her coal mining endeavors ("I never saw a sweeter spot for a garden") is, I think, significant. Her involvement in that enterprise seems to have rattled her self-image as a gentlewoman, and as we will see, one way to stabilize it involves returning to the refined realm of the landscape arts.

Most importantly in this context, the anxiety induced by business prompts Montagu to articulate her values in the conjoined languages of landscape and femininity. Writing to a dear female friend whose learning she reveres and whose lack of stature she discreetly honors, Montagu enacts the tasteful and modest femininity that she and her friend negotiate over a lifetime of letters. In the previous passage ("I should have much more hope . . ."), we see Montagu delineating the genteel position from which she can sustain her friendship with a famously retiring scholar; she polishes the rough edges of her industrial life so that her friend may more easily appreciate it. The letter testifies to her own qualification, for her striking use of figurative language performs the refined education she valorizes. The unkempt "siren sloth" works by negative example to illustrate her notion of proper femininity. Doing so compels her to construct a spectrum of improper forms of femininity;

thus, she opposes sloth to her "sisters" who, presumably, cannot resist "the temptations of ambition and the allurements of pleasure." And as she seeks to animate these competing vices—ambition and pleasure—she expresses them through the language of the landscape arts: "Their Palace or their garden." She may not adorn this garden with detailed description; yet, as the resort of excessive pleasure, the garden still operates in the realm of the landscape arts because it epitomizes a form of land use given over to aesthetic (and other) pleasures. In this context "their garden" serves as shorthand for the privilege of seeing and inhabiting the land as landscape, and as a result the letter locates Montagu in the realm of the landscape arts.

The tableau of sloth and her sisters also conjures an aestheticized geography that is not only feminized but also moral and physical. Though ambiguous, the reference to "running out of the temptations of ambition and the allurements of pleasure" may refer to departure from London, ground zero for such dubious pursuits. In this sense, Montagu marvels at people—especially women—who avoid urban vice and yet still wallow in rural forms of degeneracy. Perhaps less extravagantly corrupt, the north still produces its own version of vice. Setting aside the moral valence of the garden, more noteworthy here is its implicitly southern location. Writing in the midst of the foreign terrain that affronts her, Montagu conceives a polarized map of England in which the northern pole of rural sloth contrasts the southern pole of urban decadence. The garden, a conceivably urban space in this context, roots the landscape arts in the south. In the wake of her futile attempt to landscape her collieries earlier in the letter, Montagu betrays an affinity for this visual, aesthetic orientation even as she distances herself from immoderate expressions thereof.

It is worth returning here to the factual dimension of Montagu's epistolary depictions of Denton; as representations they are of course constructed, but not through fictional or poetic practices. In chapter 2 we observed Anne Finch cannily accepting patriarchy in her country- house poetry because doing so helped her gain access to the patriarchal estates where her poetry could thrive. Similarly in chapter 3, Scott's method of conspiring with patriarchy took the form of assigning landownership—typically a male preserve—to deserving gentlewomen. Thus, she modified the gender hierarchy by leveling the status of men and women who are social equals but otherwise accepted female subordination among the nonelite. Both the poet and the novelist used their literary resources to navigate the landscape as it suited their purposes; both succeeded, that is, in constructing their ideal landscapes. But Montagu leaves the impression that she cannot force the landscape to submit to her desire—in the present instance, the desire to see palaces and gardens, and their inhabitants, display the moderation and productivity proper to the gentility. Her failure suggests that perhaps gender inequality belongs to the factual landscape of the long eighteenth century, while verse and fiction express ideals that compensate for the intransigence of the real.

The refinements that distinguish the elite in Montagu's eyes assume especially significant form when she combines the landscape arts with what we might identify in this context as the feminine arts. Part of reality as Montagu conceives it in the north involves an array of scandalous femininity. Though accruing to both northern and southern modes of excess, the feminized corruption embodied in "siren sloth" and her sisters insinuates a scenario of seduction wherein women constitute the threat to the "strange animal" that is man. A conventional conception of sin, this Eve-inspired tableau unveils a certain misogyny in Montagu's perception of Northumberland's middle-class women, whose drunken and slatternly ways offend her delicate sensibilities even more than their husbands' vices do. In light of these insinuations, the garden assumes part of the burden for woman's fall, in the sense that its pleasures may corrupt those who enjoy them without the proper restraint.

The spatial polarization of female vice also occurs in terms of landscape, for "the siren sloth [. . .] allures more souls into her filthy sty than her sisters bring to their Palace or their garden." Montagu adds a layer of moral geography on top of the social geography separating lazy middle-class women from their overindulgent and socially superior sisters. As a landscape of sin, the garden of sloth's sisters may induce some to stray from the path of virtue, but this negative example implicitly recognizes its opposite—the landscape of virtue, which Montagu cultivates with equally dazzling artistry. Ultimately, the north emerges in her letters as the landscape of absolute property in that her construction of the coal mining milieu prioritizes its wealth-producing function; the failed attempts to aestheticize the mines in turn suggest that the landscape arts ought to inhabit the south. When representing her southern property, Montagu demonstrates how the landscape arts are especially suited to enact the subtle complexities, and the integration, of her social and gender identities specifically in relation to the aesthetic.

SANDLEFORD AND THE LANDSCAPE ARTS

Turning to Montagu's depictions of Sandleford, where she undertook elaborate improvement projects in the 1780s, we see little of the drudgery or distaste that appear in regard to her northern endeavors. Though she is more often associated with polite society in London, Montagu has generated considerable scholarship that integrates rural life into the current understanding of her richly varied experience.[37] Thanks to the insights of Stephen Bending, William Christmas, and Peter Denney, among others, it is no longer plausible to peg Montagu as a doyenne of fashionable society without acknowledging the significance of the countryside in her aesthetic, social, and economic profile. In taking stock of how she forges her identity in relation to various types of physical space, Bending and Eger offer complementary analyses, though with varying emphases on her rural and urban habitations, respectively.

Eger investigates the artistic and architectural projects that came to define Montagu's urban identity, "first at Hill Street, scene of the original, more intimate Bluestocking parties, and later in Portman Square, a grander and arguably more impersonal stage for social intercourse."[38] Noting the grandeur of Montagu's urban dwelling, Eger considers how her subject participates in a complex and ongoing debate about the civilizing effects of luxury. The critic's theatrical metaphor is apt given the extent to which Montagu epitomizes how identity emerges through rituals of display.[39]

Bending is likewise attentive to Montagu's self-conscious prominence on the public stage of eighteenth-century polite society. By focusing on her pastoral rather than metropolitan persona, he has done the most to expand critical understanding of Montagu so that her significance is not confined to the realms of sociability, the public sphere, and tasteful consumption. These latter discourses prevail in discussions of her Bluestocking salons and her pursuit of spectacular urban domestic interiors. It is in the countryside, Bending argues, that Montagu most effectively forges her relation to virtue, for here she could disavow urban culture with all its links to vanity, luxury, and corruption. As we see in her depictions of Sandleford, a country estate offers unique opportunities to cultivate her refinement as a gentlewoman with acute sensitivity to the ennobling aspects of nature. The landscape arts come alive in Montagu's Sandleford letters, revealing how aestheticized rural land, and the social relations it enacts, stabilize and even enhance the social and gender identities that were rattled on her journeys north.

While Bending focuses on the modulations of "pleasure and loss, tranquillity and loneliness" in Montagu's pastoral self-conceptions, I would like to trace how Montagu navigates the social relations inhering in the Sandleford land in particular.[40] Unlike her northern properties and their resistance to aestheticization, the Berkshire estate provides ideal materials for her to describe in terms of the landscape arts. When writing from here, she is unencumbered by the social quandary posed by her coal mine holdings. The extensive treatment of Sandleford in her letters, and its presence therein nearly from the beginning of this corpus, present an evolving perception of her rural property. The shift in her depiction, and especially in her deployment of landscape rhetoric with regard to Sandleford, offers a rich example of the link between landed property and personality—in Montagu's case, landownership and social and cultural authority. Moral judgment almost aways accompanies her aesthetic sensibility, suggesting an awareness of aesthetics and morality as inextricably linked. Early in her marriage, she betrays a sense of unworthiness for her great fortune and thus a heightened effort to prove herself of sufficient moral fiber to deserve it. Numerous passages describing her new home, and later, the improvements on what came to be her favorite abode, demonstrate how aestheticized representations of her estate serve as tools for social distinction and moral edification—as are the landscape arts themselves. Whether displaying her eye for the perfect prospect or conjuring the quiet and natural wonders that her rural home provides, Montagu's epistolary depictions of Sandleford attest to the intertwined moral and aesthetic value she derives from this estate.

One of her earliest renderings of Sandleford occurs in a letter to her sister in the summer of 1743. Having married Edward the previous August, Montagu expresses the excitement of a newlywed.

> You never saw anything so pretty as the view these gardens command, for my part I would not change the situation for any I ever saw; there is nothing in Nature pretty that they have not. The prospect is allegro [. . .]. There is a charming grove where your reveries may wander at pleasure, you may allegorize like Spenser, or pastoralize like the lesser poets, there are roses and honeysuckles hourly dropping [. . .]. Indeed my dear Sall, these pretty things are mere toys, as are all things in this world, but a true friend. I am thankful for the benefits of fortune, and pleased with them, but really attached only to the person who bestows them.[41]

The letter demonstrates how Montagu uses the landscape arts both to express her marital triumph and to temper it with humility. A riot of conflicting emotions infuses this seemingly placid description. Awe and deference compete for prominence as she gropes for the proper emotional pitch for her letter. Her recourse to hyperbole ("I never saw anything so pretty") and shift of praise from the estate to its owner—her husband—suggest that she is still adjusting to the grandeur of her new life and feels anxious to behave in a manner that proves her worthiness.

But when she swerves toward pious gratitude ("these pretty things are mere toys"), Montagu exposes the discomfiting effect of realizing that she may be enjoying her good fortune too much. She senses that acquisitiveness may motivate her enjoyment and so she attenuates that possibility with avowals of a higher motive. This maneuver develops into a signature technique for legitimating her social superiority, anticipating the ethical calculus she will practice in the face of her soaring coal-mine fortune. The movement from the garden to its owner in her thought process evidences the conflation of estate and lord, operative even in Montagu's confessional letter to her sister (one of the few people to whom she would later confide her frustrations with her marriage). Thus, gazing upon the Sandleford gardens engages a visual and implicitly economic process whereby Montagu synthesizes the fact that she is mistress of this property. Such moments emerge as steps in her process of learning how to be a benevolent and deserving landowner. Of course, in this instance she occupies that role only by association, given that the law of coverture makes Edward and not his wife the sole proprietor. Nevertheless, being his wife entails certain privileges and duties, which also accrue to the role she will eventually assume as owner once she is widowed.

Of paramount interest here is the visual component of Montagu's emergent awareness of landownership. The process moves from seeing the land's beauty to recognizing her (albeit indirect) ownership thereof, and then on to acknowledgment of her debt to God for her good fortune. The land's dual function as a source of both aesthetic pleasure and economic value is conflated in the proceedings, as admiration of the garden's beauty precipitates awareness of possession and hence potential greed. Instances such as these disrupt the moral geography of north and south previously discussed. Nevertheless, moral edification is also embedded in the process both within Sandleford and between north and south. Previously when we saw her discussing her Denton properties, Montagu gave the impression of being caught in the middle of these poles, and also indignant at the offensive "middling sort" who live there. Now that we encounter her contemplating her triumphant marriage and marveling at a home like Sandleford, she expresses social anxiety that situates her in the middle relative to her higher-born husband. Traces of her social anxiety recur in the letters preceding her widowhood, and when these traces appear with regard to the Sandleford landscape, they remind us that identity formation occurs through engagement with the land. Gazing on the land instructs Montagu to embrace pious self-censorship, engaging her moral sense and thus closing the circuit uniting aesthetics and economics in her tableau of Sandleford's landscaped beauty.

Lest we lose sight of the landscape arts constructed in Montagu's letter, it bears repeating that her emphasis on visual pleasure encodes her access to the privileges of landscape ("The prospect is allegro [. . .]. There is a charming grove," etc.). Such aesthetic pleasures constitute the eighteenth century's landscape arts and help explain why, in contemplating her garden, Montagu sees it first as a source of sensual delight. The intimations of moral and social anxiety, the sense that she may lack the probity and stature that life at Sandleford requires, play themselves out in her descriptions of the estate, affirming the crucial function of land as a determinant of identity. More broadly speaking, and mindful of landscape's long historical trajectory, I would add that the Sandleford letters also animate the ascendance of the landscape arts, displaying their unique capacity to legitimate a capitalist political economy through rituals of aesthetic and moral sophistication.

Such sophistication is an abiding feature of Montagu's epistolary engagement with her husband, intimating how she learns to cultivate this trait to prove herself worthy of him but then turns elsewhere to exercise her aesthetic talent once relations with him have chilled. In another representation of Sandleford, this one written to rather than about him, she reveals the extent to which she associates Edward and Sandleford with the delights of the landscape arts. The estate comes to serves as an index for her evolving relationship with her husband, and Sandleford gradually surpasses him as the cherished essence of home. Writing from the spa town of Tunbridge Wells in 1749, she reassures her husband that despite the town's charm, and her fine lodgings and garden there, she would rather be with him: "I shall wish I could procure wings to bring me to you on the terrace at Sandleford, where I have passed so many happy hours in the conversation of the best of companions."[42] Having been married for seven years, Montagu continues to express her feelings for Edward primarily in terms of gratitude. Enjoying her garden at Tunbridge Wells evokes a similar scenario at Sandleford, and in the process she realizes and acknowledges her debt to her husband for granting her access to what I have identified as the privileges of landscape. The realization of privilege in turn prompts an awareness that she must prove herself worthy of her good fortune.

Yet in light of Bridget Hill's skeptical interpretation of the Montagu marriage, the emotional gestures toward Edward become merely dutiful expressions of affection rather than intimations of a passionate bond.[43] Having spilled ample ink on the virtues of marrying for money, Montagu more likely flatters her husband in order to maintain marital harmony while engaging in pursuits that might strike him as frivolous. Another crucial factor in the Montagus' marital relations is the death of their son, nicknamed "Punch," in September 1744. Noting Elizabeth Montagu's devastation in the wake of this loss, the *Oxford Dictionary of National Biography* implies the toll it took on her marriage: "She and her husband were frequently apart; they remained friendly but there were no more children."[44] The cumulative evidence that Montagu's was a mercenary marriage, subsequently undermined by tragedy, makes it likely that she derives more pleasure from the Sandleford landscape than from her husband. The husband therefore becomes the index of the estate rather than vice versa.

MARITAL ENNUI, WIDOWHOOD, AND THE CONSOLATIONS OF LANDSCAPE

A letter written about five years later reveals that after more than a decade of marriage, Montagu no longer aligns Edward with the pleasures of landscape. In a sense, she epitomizes my argument that women's independence bears a crucial link to landownership. Her example reveals how marriage subordinates women while widowhood liberates and sometimes elevates them, provided they have sufficient means, with land surpassing all other means to this end. Once Montagu no longer associates Edward with the landscape's pleasures, the latter becomes a consolation for the absence of the former. Thus, Montagu writes in June 1755 to her cousin and close friend, the poet Gilbert West: "Mr. Montagu has been studiously disposed ever since we came to Sandleford, so that I pass seven or eight hours every day entirely alone. Five months are to pass before I return to the land of the living, but I can amuse myself in the regions of the dead. If it rains so that I cannot walk in the garden, Virgil will carry me to the Elysian fields, or Milton into Paradise."

Facing the prospect of spending a rainy day all alone and indoors, she goes on to remind herself of her good fortune in being endowed by God with "the resources of recollection and expectation"; such gifts disallow any temptation to be "discontented and ill humored."[45] Spanning a dozen years, the three Sandleford letters discussed thus far—to her sister, her husband, and her cousin—exemplify how Montagu gropes for her ideal self in the estate's landscape and finds it in the conjoined aesthetic and moral appreciation for her good fortune.

The landscape arts have thus far served as a useful category of analysis for Montagu's aesthetic imagination, whether in reference to her coal mines or her stately home at Sandleford. As a manifestation of capitalism, the category is capacious enough to encompass various iterations of aestheticized land, whether a coal mine landscape or a more conventional one. For several reasons, we need to consider how this classification does and does not intersect with the term *garden*. The reference to the garden as her preferred space for spiritual contemplation (her desired "walk in the garden") exemplifies the adjacent discourses it summons in its wake—the Elysian fields, the garden of Eden, Virgil, Milton, and so forth. A similar usage appears in this chapter's very first letter excerpt, when she writes from Denton to tell Elizabeth Carter, "I never saw a sweeter spot for a garden." The landscape arts encompass the garden but not vice versa, making the distinction between them a matter of scope. Other examples considered thus far, from the images of a coal "harvest" and "sixty [men] in a wheatfield reaping" to the panoramic view of the River Tyne from her hired house in Denton, all constitute instances of aestheticized land that are not gardens. The difference matters if we are to account for the many ways in which Montagu mobilizes the landscape arts in the service of her self-construction. Examples such as "my best object the mouth of a coal mine" demonstrate that her aesthetic imagination extends well beyond the garden, a discrete space of aestheticized land that occasions spiritual contemplation.

We need a distinction between the garden and the landscape arts in order to appreciate how the pious and solitary persona that Bending identifies with the Sandleford garden also transports her aesthetic imagination to many other places. He addresses Montagu's reliance on the rhetoric of retirement, especially in order to counterbalance her image as a metropolitan salon hostess. Noting that "for most of her life Montagu was associated with a spectacular city culture," Bending asks, "How does [she] position herself both physically and ideologically when away from the town?"[46] By widening our critical lens to consider the entire panorama of her aesthetic imagination, from coal mines to pleasure gardens, we see its pervasive scope and recognize how the ideological work that interests Bending also occurs in many other settings and thus has much greater cultural impact. His model proves especially fruitful in conversation with *Prolific Ground* because both projects recognize how entwined her identity is with capitalism.

In various contexts Bending traces Montagu's penchant for meditating on her own "limited significance in the greater scheme of things," which serves her well when humility is called for. But he is struck by her inconsistent views about the kind of garden she wants. In 1764 she writes that "I do not want a fine garden [. . .] I want not Stewart, Adams, or Brown." But a decade later she decides to hire two of these very men, James Stuart and Capability Brown, to undertake extravagant and expensive building projects, including a fashionable remodeling of the Sandleford grounds in the century's signature style.[47] The plans expose Montagu as a woman who absolutely does want a fine garden, one befitting a "fine lady" with her "all-too-fashionable displays of wealth, power, and status." Such contradictions in her persona interest Bending because they capture "the changing significance of retirement and the places both garden and retirement occupy in the thoughts and feelings of Montagu and the culture she inhabits."[48]

This interpretation of the ambiguity and inconsistency in her self-representation builds on an invaluable understanding that the contradictions and apparent hypocrisies in her letters express a comparable ambiguity within the broader culture. Such insight complicates foregoing judgments of the narrative of self-legitimation regarding Montagu's coal mines, wherein she imagines the riches they produce and in turn "the hand of bounty [that] may bestow them in seasonable assistance to distress." Though self-serving, this rationale emerges from a culture that is reckoning with the unanticipated opportunities and troubles that accompany unprecedented economic growth. Within this context, the pious pose in her garden arises from the culture's contradictory confrontations with inordinate wealth. Bending's observations on the tension between the benevolent and indulgent aspects of Montagu's disposition offer a similar, historically nuanced approach to a complex and controversial figure among eighteenth-century women writers. His assessment also attests to the multivalent nature of her commitment to the landscape arts. If her appreciation for these arts early in life was tempered by a sense of indebtedness to Edward for giving her access to them, as she ages she loses this humility. Instead, her devotion to the landscape arts expands, especially after his death.

Montagu's drifting devotion from her husband to an increasing array of philanthropic and other endeavors reveals how personal and historical circumstances converge to make her a compelling figure in the century's history of landscape. Further epistolary evidence regarding her marriage compounds the impression that her investment in various types of landscape increases as her attachment to Edward wanes. Bending notes that she initiated the negotiations with Stuart and Brown "only a few weeks after her husband's death" in 1775.[49] After seven years of widowhood, she muses in a letter to Elizabeth Carter that her need for a husband has long expired: "When a wife I was obedient because it was my duty, [. . .] but it seems to me that a new master and new lessons after ones opinions and habits were formed must be a little awkward, and with all due respect to the superior sex, I do not see how they can be necessary to a woman unless she were to defend her lands and tenements by sword or gun."[50] Montagu's obligatory recognition of Edward as her "superior" presents female subordination as a logical necessity given a young wife's need for guidance from a more authoritative and experienced helpmeet. More striking, however, is the excerpt's bare conflation of husband and property; his primary role is to protect "her lands and tenements." By this logic, second marriages are a remnant of feudal times, and rejecting them frees her in widowhood to embrace her privileged access to the landscape arts. Not faced with the burden of defending Sandleford from invaders, she deigns instead to improve it.

Montagu's comments on marriage reveal a pragmatic approach to her negotiation with patriarchy. More noteworthy is the suggestion that her cooperation is provisional; she submits to marital subordination but sees no need to seek it out again once she has achieved widowhood. This condition gives her the best access to the two iterations of landscape in its ascendant form, i.e., the landscape arts and the landscape of absolute property. Thus, her thirty-three-year marriage to Edward serves her as a kind of training in the latter landscape so that, once widowed, she may have ongoing access to both forms. By learning how to manage the coal trade as his business partner, she eventually comes to command the landscape of absolute property. We have seen her exercise this command primarily in the context of her northern collieries and adjacent lands. Sandleford, by contrast, more often elicits her aesthetic appreciation, as this estate is the locus for her leisure, the place where she might reward herself for her considerable exertions as a businesswoman.

In such a light, we see that Montagu has negotiated the patriarchy through strategic subordination that in turn positions her to rise to a more authoritative and independent stature. Having proven her mettle as a coal magnate and her acumen in the landscape arts, she compels us to interpret these intertwined processes within the context of emergent capitalism. The landscape of absolute property undergirds the landscape arts that she celebrates at Sandleford, and together they render her an exemplar of possessive individualism. The fact that she provoked such criticism (nay, vitriol) in some of her contemporaries and has received censure from more recent scholars accentuates how she sometimes overstepped the bounds of proper female individualism.[51] It is certainly necessary to distinguish individualism from vanity and egotism; nevertheless, the ongoing debate over whether Montagu deserves censure or praise testifies to the provocative nature of her letters and her mode of individuation.

The trials of estate improvement at Sandleford introduce the language of struggle and toil to Montagu's letters, and in a context that has more often brought her tranquility. One letter, written in the wake of Capability Brown's death in February 1783, explains how she continues to execute his plans but finds progress slow given their scope. The letter addresses Frances Reynolds (sister of Sir Joshua), who painted Montagu's portrait and sustained an enduring friendship with her. She explains the situation in ways that expose the disjunction between delighting in a beautiful landscape garden and taking the necessary steps to create it.

> I do not remember any Summer as favourable to rural life, & particularly to ye charms of a River, than this has been. By the direction of the late and celebrated Mr Brown we are making a piece of water at the side of a Wood, which will in time embellish the scene, & at this time w^d have refreshed the eye extremely, if the cool liquid element had flowed through it, but at present it presents only the ideas of drought and labour, a large number of workmen are toiling to encrease a small stream to a large body of water, [. . .] it now is an emblem of a small pittance, by industry & dexterity encreasing itself till it becomes abundant.[52]

Montagu makes adept register shifts here that reveal her frustration while also expressing humor toward the situation. Initially writing in the voice of a leisured gentlewoman, she indicates her habituation to summer's rural pleasures. But her subsequent description discloses how her expectations have been thwarted by the improvements underway, turning her rural idyll into a shambles, and herself into an overseer of sorts, presiding over a throng of laborers. The fey quality of "the cool liquid element" becomes ludicrous in light of "the ideas of drought and labour" that displace the water in her imagination. She creates a bathetic effect by moving from a fanciful tableau of leisure to an actual one of complex maneuvering through seemingly colossal undertakings. In the process, the refined gentlewoman becomes a besieged mistress, navigating the turbulent (though scant) waters of her extravagant—and extravagantly unfinished—landscape garden.

What are the implications of Montagu's subtle self-mockery in this passage? On the one hand, she assumes a lighthearted stance toward trying circumstances, proving her good humor in the face of the indefinitely postponed enjoyment of bucolic serenity. On the other hand, the passage's rhetoric implicitly derides her own outsized ambition, which has undone her quest for refinement by surrounding her instead with dirt and a dry riverbed. The two readings are not mutually exclusive, though the ambiguity contained therein may expose her anxiety over the possible excess of her endeavors. Having encountered endless delays when employing architect James Wyatt to renovate the Sandleford mansion, Montagu was accustomed to the challenges of managing major building projects.[53] The letter to Frances Reynolds reveals the landowner's recourse to humor as a way to cope with a situation that otherwise threatens to unsettle her self-image as a leisured gentlewoman. From a broader perspective, the passage also exposes the cost—the labor—required to produce the landscape arts. Without minimizing the incalculable contributions of "a large number of workmen," we nevertheless also witness her own expenditure of labor in order to attain the rewards she seeks in her property. Thus, we encounter the ironic fate of a woman who presides over a landscape of absolute property; in pursuing such an elaborate, Brownian version of the landscape arts, Montagu must perform considerable emotional and managerial labor in order to access the luxury provided by landownership. The scenario becomes emblematic of the pitfalls that arise in her effort to landscape her identity.

SANDLEFORD AS A WORKING LANDSCAPE

As the site of extravagant landscape improvements, Sandleford emerges in Montagu's oeuvre as a contested site, especially in light of recent scholarship debating what these endeavors tell us about her mode of landownership. As a woman undertaking such grand projects, she ran the risk of inciting imputations of vanity—a charge that appears in James Woodhouse's depictions of her in remarkable and varied detail. In his posthumously published *Life and Lucubrations of Crispinus Scriblerus* (1814/1896), he renames her "Scintilla," deriding her need to be considered beautiful.[54] Over the course of a relationship that spanned from 1767 to 1788, Woodhouse came to pose a significant challenge to Montagu's self-conception as a paragon of virtue. His negative portrait of his mistress cuts deep by maligning her femininity, suggesting that submitting to female authority makes his subjection all the more degrading. The nickname "Scintilla" indicts his patron's fondness for diamonds, as Hester Thrale perhaps did in her witticism that the famous hostess was "brilliant in diamonds, solid in judgment, critical in talk."[55] Woodhouse's depiction of the improvements at Sandleford, where he worked as land bailiff and house steward for nearly twenty years, condemns his mistress through pointed contempt for both the remodeled chapel in what was once a priory and the new, Brownian landscape design.

> But might, in gothic Mansion, on the Plain,
> Through leafy, flowery, fruitful, Seasons, reign;
> That there, her Sylvan votaries all might view
> Her grand achievements, and give glory due!
> There she enlarg'd her antiquated Dome,
> Which worthless Monks long made their idle home;
> [. . .]
> There, to administer more food for Pride,
> With ornaments bedeck'd the fair outside,
> Where she might show her Wealth—her Taste display—
> Expecting praise from all who pass'd that way.[56]

Though Woodhouse ensured that such venom never saw print during his lifetime (a decision that William Christmas attributes to Woodhouse's concern for his children), by now other sources have corroborated that he had reason to be bitter.[57]

He insinuates that Montagu desecrated a sacred space by making domestic grandeur out of the "antiquated Dome, / Which worthless Monks long made their idle home." Considering my previous discussion of Montagu's preoccupation with virtue—not to mention her devout Anglicanism—the poem's imputation of sinful decadence and vainglory would no doubt have rankled.

The question of Montagu's vast wealth and the ways she spent it continues to generate debate to this day, as critics wrestle with the intersection of her gender and socioeconomic status. Woodhouse's emphasis on her womanhood constitutes a potent reminder of the gendered strictures within which she operated and the concomitant risk of transgression she faced as a wealthy female landowner. Regardless of one's view regarding "the Queen of the Blues" as a virtuous philanthropist or a vain and greedy autocrat (or a combination thereof), one must acknowledge her formidable stature as a woman of vast accomplishments. I am struck by how much Montagu's self-perception hinges on the experiences of property ownership. Her self-regard depends on how she is perceived *as* a property owner—and the owner of properties that she aims to improve, just as she wants to maintain (or redeem) her own image. Though one might agree with Betty Rizzo that Montagu was egotistical, Harriet Guest counterbalances that charge by describing how the statesman Sir John Macpherson expressed appreciation for the Bluestocking assemblies. She frames her assessment in terms of how Montagu worked within the social limitations of her time: "Montagu's role in his account is ambiguously poised between active intervention and the more indirect diffusion of polished manners that is a more traditional feminine skill. [. . .] Her assemblies effect political ends because they *remove* men from their political context, reconfirming their identities as what Habermas calls '*human beings pure and simple*,' as private men who participate in the literary public sphere."[58] Guest's assessment of Montagu's quasi-political maneuvering is consistent with my previous claims about how she cooperates with patriarchy so as to advance her own interests. Unlike her marriage, her gender-inclusive salons nourished her sense of independence, of playing a decisive role in facilitating the exchange of ideas. Insofar as feminism and its history constitute political issues, Montagu did participate in politics; her economic and cultural agency makes an important contribution to this history. If egotism furthered this contribution, then so be it.

Montagu's favorite country estate looms large in this analysis, and when we integrate Woodhouse's depiction thereof into the broader portrait of Sandleford provided by her own letters, we confront competing versions of the place. While she seeks to glorify the estate through the landscape arts, Woodhouse exposes the landscape of absolute property undergirding the aesthetic conception that Montagu promotes. My introduction to this chapter claimed that the landscape arts work in Montagu's letters to cover up the landscape of absolute property, and we see a similar process of deception—now, self-deception—in the way she depicts the charity projects she undertook at Sandleford. Self-legitimation through redemptive labor proves an effective strategy for Montagu in multiple contexts; but so, too, could it be marshaled against her. She portrays herself as a benevolent steward, and a connoisseur of the landscape arts, but Woodhouse's poetry exposes how she in fact operates in a landscape of absolute property, wherein profit supersedes any demand for mutual reciprocity with her dependents. Insofar as his hostile portrait of her has complicated (if not uniformly tarnished) her reputation, the mistress described in *Crispinus Scriblerus* proves more coercive and disdainful than the benevolent figure she aspires to be.

Competing landscapes also emerge when we consider the conflicting critical assessments of the charity Montagu undertook at Sandleford. While some scholars detect a note of self-congratulation in the way she describes her charitable efforts, others read these as sincere. In the former camp, Steve Hindle notes that her commitment to charity escalates once she has undertaken the expensive improvement projects: "It is nonetheless striking that her program of subsidized potato sales and livestock purchases was introduced only after she had begun to remodel the estate in the mid-1770s, almost as if she sensed that the laboring poor would suffer collateral damage as a consequence of emparkment."[59] The potato scheme mentioned here was one way Montagu sought to ease her conscience by subsidizing the sale of potatoes to the poor and by restricting the beneficiaries of her largesse to those who truly needed it. Her own description of the scheme reveals a certain self-regard in the project: "I was so pleased to find I had done my poor neighbors service with so little expence, that you may be assured I repeated my pottato cultivation this year, & found all the poor women & children in the neighborhood collecting them. As those who labour deserve to eat, I please myself with preparing supper for these good folks [. . .] My Bailiff here thinks he has made some improvement in the mode of cultivating potatoes, & I believe will publish his method."[60]

My analysis of Sandleford has traced the emergence of both the landscape of absolute property and its counterpart the landscape arts, and suggested how they displace the reciprocal relations that governed a landscape of stewardship. In this context, Montagu's paternalistic approach to charity does come across as compensatory. Under the earlier regime, care for the poor would have been customary. Her self-satisfaction ("I please myself") reveals that custom—a lord's or lady's accountability to her dependents—no longer obtains in a capitalist society. Were she operating by custom, she would have no occasion to congratulate herself. Her self-regard also pales in light of her recognition that the scheme succeeds "with so little expence," implying that charity appeals to her especially when it costs her "so little."

Peter Denney also notices that Montagu's interactions with the poor occur within a capitalist regime, and that this system involved the erosion of custom:

"[T]he kind of charity Montagu praised did not pertain to the customary rights that protected the independence of laborers, but to the spurs to industry that boosted their productivity, ensured their discipline, and intensified their dependence on the market-driven employment arrangements of persons of property."[61] The emphasis on productivity signals a greater concern for profit than for the well-being of all members of a community. A damning portrait of her improvement projects, Denney's article identifies landed property as the locus for her hypocritical indulgence in luxury while counseling her dependents against (and denying them access to) such corruption. He goes on to argue, with reference to the unemployed weavers who resorted to working for Montagu, "[H]er pastoral Arcadia was so saturated in the language of sentiment that by placing the laboring population within her aesthetic vision, she could literally see them as dependent on her refined feelings in the same way that they were now dependent on her employment practices—the acceptance of surveillance, the demonstration of gratitude, and the application of industry. And it was precisely by reforming a potentially unruly populace that she thought her landscape park did, indeed, civilize the countryside."[62] In noting Montagu's "aesthetic vision," Denney identifies the class politics that play out in the "improvement" of her estate.

Building upon Denney's analysis, Adam Bridgen traces the emergence of a working-class consciousness in Woodhouse's poetic depictions of his mistress and her property. Noting a significant transformation in the ethos of estate management during the eighteenth century, Bridgen attributes the change to increasing demands for profit as capitalist social relations gradually displaced quasi-feudal ones. Regarding Montagu's adoption of the Brownian aesthetic for Sandleford, he asserts, "Montagu was an exemplar of this shift from an 'ancient, public, and (implicitly) masculine' ideal of estate management, which stressed the subordination of private desires to the preservation of social harmony, to a more individualistic, commercial outlook, in which 'social relations were reduced to purely economic relations between consumers and producers.'"[63] The shoemaker poet, according to Bridgen, grasped how the new economic system instrumentalized nature in ways that also degraded humanity's relations with one another. The scope of Woodhouse's condemnation proves especially powerful in its attention to the environmental harm caused by the Brownian aesthetic. By connecting the visual and economic components of Montagu's approach to improvement, Bridgen suggests, Woodhouse understood the damage caused by his mistress's mode of landownership.

LABOR VERSUS LEISURE AT SANDLEFORD

In exposing the landscape of absolute property that actually operates at Sandleford, Woodhouse also reveals the misprision that Montagu's philanthropy requires.

The landscape arts as she conceives them necessitate blindness to the toil required to create seemingly natural scenery. To appreciate the contrast in each party's representation of Sandleford, consider the following letter that she wrote to Carter in October 1776, upon returning from France:

> The change of season has made more alteration in the animals around me than place & foreign travel has wrought in me. The nightingale who sung through the night when I was here in May, has ceased to charm us with her lay, the frisking lamb is become grave & distrest; & even ye foolish gosling assumes airs of consequence & discretion waddles in all ye dignity of Goose. The bee has ceased his industrious labours, & having collected honey enough for the winter takes his rest at home. What lessons of prudence, of propriety, of moderation do these animals give and what leisure have I not to attend to them, & yet I shall neither learn ye discreet silence of ye nightingale nor ye increased gravity or assumed importance of the sheep & Goose, & least of all, perhaps, the moderation of ye bee. I shall talk & laugh every day, & any day, if it offers, dig further & deeper in my mines. Yet my winter is at hand, my summer as well as theirs is over, my time of life is fallen into ye sere & yellow leaf.[64]

Montagu congregates the industrious bee, frisking lamb, dignified goose, and the rest in order to create a tableau of bustling animal energy at work on her farm. But strikingly, she embraces her liminal status in relation to this thriving landscape. A tour de force in pastoral reverie, the passage crafts a harmonious natural world for Montagu either to emulate or defy as the mood suits her. By identifying the seasonal rhythms at work in both the animal kingdom and her own life ("my winter is at hand"), she implies a kinship between herself and them.

Evidence of the landscape of absolute property appears in this playful foray into nature's rhythms as they manifest among the fauna at Sandleford. Yet, in a beguiling twist on the typical georgic tableau, she situates herself as part of the natural order and yet at liberty to depart from it at will. The fanciful refusal to abide by nature's rhythms when they thwart her mood and ambition ("I shall talk & laugh every day [&] dig further & deeper in my mines") elevates her above natural law. She resists the agrarian calendar only to embrace industrial production, thus attenuating any inclination to emulate nature's fauna. Laughing on her way to the mines, Montagu emerges as a kind of manic businesswoman who eventually grows bored by natural serenity. An order observed from above, nature inspires her to wax philosophical and to contemplate her mortality ("my time of life is fallen into ye sere & yellow leaf"). But she embraces the privilege of abandoning this order as the occasion suits her. Such visions of nature, and of work, prove more accessible to someone of Montagu's stature than they are to her dependents.

However poetic and whimsical the passage may be, its link to the estate's calendar of productivity as portrayed by its steward, Woodhouse, is tenuous at best.

A landscape of leisure for the patron proves to be one of labor for her charge; Montagu enjoys the landscape arts while Woodhouse suffers the one of absolute property. In *Crispinus Scriblerus*, he charts the schedule of agrarian tasks at Sandleford in the following way:

> In sunshine hours his six days' labor sped,
> While countless projects occupied his head;
> To plan improvement, or contrive defense—
> To heighten profit, or reduce expense—
> To mark each wood and field—each mound and mead
> Fair herds and flocks that batten—milk—or breed—
> And reconnoit'ring Teams, and Hinds, the while,
> To help their purpose, and appoint their toil.[65]

The accumulation of infinitive phrases produces a sense of the relentless demands of agricultural work. The person performing these tasks has no time to express affection or kinship for the animals he tends, or to observe beauty in the woods and fields he oversees. The implied pressure exerted by the owner for him "To heighten profit, or reduce expense" further intensifies his labors, suggesting that any lessening of exertion will incur her disapproval. As Christmas and others have shown, Montagu did in fact censure Woodhouse for failing to meet her standards, though the reasons have less to do with his productivity than with his insufficiently deferential conduct. Christmas explains that "according to both Woodhouse and Montagu, Sandleford prospered under his oversight, yet there was still palpable friction between them throughout his tenure."[66] In the absence of aesthetic observations about the estate in Woodhouse's portrayal, we are left with images of toil—a stark landscape of absolute property fraught with demands for yet further toil. His "six days' labor" implies that a servant's work is perpetual, and the passage thus throws into relief the luxury that Montagu enjoys with her exemption from nature's calendar of labors. And this very landscape makes it possible for Montagu to enjoy the landscape arts. Ultimately, even though the latter landscapes prevail in Montagu's oeuvre, the specter of the former one haunts these letters because of how Woodhouse contests his mistress's self-regard.

We encounter a much different version of Sandleford in Bending's most recent assessment of this estate, one that questions the denigration of labor that Hindle, Denney, and Bridgen detect in her landownership practices. Bending is struck by Montagu's insistence on calling the renovated grounds at Sandleford a "Brown landscape" even though Brown died well before the execution of his plans was complete. In this interpretation, she downplays her improved Berkshire abode despite the great expenditure it required, thus exposing her awareness that some might find such expenditure excessive: "Montagu's emphasis on the 'humble' landscape of her pleasure grounds also becomes a means of sidestepping the very obvious expense of turning an old abbey into a fashionable new house, and of doing so with the aid of some of the most famous architects and designers of her day."[67] The pastoral rhetoric that Montagu favors in her depictions of Sandleford enables her to cultivate humility in an estate that differs, Bending notes, from many others that favor "the fashionable use of temples and monuments as markers for intellectual and emotional engagement, or—less generously—as the markers of a pleasurable vision unconcerned by utility or productivity."[68]

Also unlike the foregoing critics, Bending is willing to accept Montagu at her word when she claims to undertake her elaborate improvement projects in order to help the local poor. He argues that her attention to the laborers is at the crux of her Sandleford story. Crucially, this interpretation recognizes a certain self-deception on Montagu's part; she eases her conscience by justifying her indulgence in luxury since it employs the needy: "The use of these poor laborers is not simply mentioned in passing but plays a central role in the story that Montagu is able to create. [. . .] Rather than announcing the purchase of a commodity, Montagu insists on highlighting the payment of laborers, and that insistence in turn enables her to characterize financial exchanges as moral transactions."[69] This way of thinking is essential to her self-conception because it has the capacity to license any number of luxuries. Regardless of the conflicting conclusions they draw, it is striking that all the critics under consideration notice Montagu's tendency to justify the use of her wealth by treating her indulgence in luxury as a form of generosity, even when acquisitiveness is at the root of her ambition.

This chapter has demonstrated how Montagu's prolific letter-writing affords us access to the quotidian and seasonal rhythms of life among the English elite while also revealing the dynamic relation among her many roles, and her participation in broader cultural phenomena such as fashionable estate improvement. A tendency to value the visual over the productive landscape, witnessed not only in Montagu and her peers but also in many scholars today, testifies to the ascendance of the landscape arts and the occlusion of other eighteenth-century landscapes. My aim has been to recuperate the significance of the alternative, working landscape in order to expose the labor that Montagu may have preferred to remain unnoticed—both her own and others'. The ambivalence she expresses in her letters about the Denton collieries suggests that although they exhausted her, she also valued the wealth they produced and the occasion they gave her to exercise benevolence for her dependents. Her reliance on landscape rhetoric in both agricultural and industrial contexts, I argue, provides a means for her to legitimate work that might otherwise seem improper for someone of her gender and station. Contradictory reactions to her compel me to qualify my claim for the interdependence of landscape and women's agency in that the value of said agency proves dubious when it prescribes conservative standards of femininity.

Ultimately, the multiplicity of roles Montagu played, landscapes she presided over or visited, and reactions she provoked demonstrate the deeply entangled histories of landscape and eighteenth-century British women's writing. Taking stock of Barker, Finch, Scott, and Montagu turns out to be an ongoing exercise in balancing remarkable female accomplishment with the unsettling accommodation of patriarchy. Based on the evidence of these four women writers, we cannot dismiss the conclusion that such accommodation was unavoidable—and furthermore, not necessarily experienced as burdensome by the women themselves. My previous comments about Montagu and Scott's misprision regarding their philanthropy further expose the chasm between their proto-feminism and our own modern feminist values, on which there remains no consensus. The discontinuities should, I believe, both provoke our interest and guarantee that the debate continues because in the end, it is both necessary and salutary. The alchemical process that I have identified in the various ways these women turn land into landscape (or coal into cash) suggests the power of literary imagination in the face of seemingly intransigent gender inequality. So, too, this process proves subversive vis-à-vis gender but conservative in its perpetuation of social inequality. Montagu stands apart from Barker, Finch, and Scott insofar as she cannot compel the world to deliver her ideal landscape in the way that their poetic and fictional practices do. Finally, a certain female solidarity seems plausible, especially when women writers enlist the land in their efforts for female uplift.

CONCLUSION

Girls were roses, and their season was as short as the flowers'.
—Virginia Woolf, *Orlando: A Biography*

THE DIFFERENCE BETWEEN A ROSE and a landscape is negligible when we consider the metaphorical woman who inhabits both entities. Whether as a blossom or a hillside, figurations of the female body animate British literature in the long eighteenth century, and two centuries later, such imagery endures. This book has traced the manifestation of this rhetoric in British women's writing over the course of a century that saw the unprecedented proliferation of both literary and material landscapes in British culture. As Jane Barker, Anne Finch, Sarah Scott, and Elizabeth Montagu attest, land and landscape are through-lines in the representation of a gentlewoman's life. Virginia Woolf's *Orlando* (1928) offers a provocative affirmation of this premise in her fictional biography of a man-turned-woman, a novel that famously interrogates what it means to write a woman's life and to be a woman writer. A matter of cliché by now, the figuration nevertheless makes it worthwhile to interrogate a literary tradition that treats women as landscape adornments (flowers) and land as evocative of the female body (mother nature).

Woolf's observation implies that a girl's fertility is seasonal, making her body an extension of the earth's rhythms and fruits. Of course, there is nothing new, in the eighteenth century, about the gendered division of roles, as Rebecca Bushnell demonstrates in her history of sixteenth- and seventeenth-century English garden manuals, which "paint[ed] women as flowers, the object of green desire, rather than [depicting] them as those who cultivate them."[1] My book builds on Bushnell's by tracing female agency in British women's writing during the subsequent century. *Orlando* offers a felicitous example of what *Prolific Ground* explores in terms of the landscapes of stewardship and custom, and their subsequent eradication by—or transformation into—the landscape arts and their corollary, the landscape of absolute property. Building on my key term's unstable meaning, I conclude with a brief study of Woolf's novel because it refracts the significance of landscape in ways that reveal the topic's ongoing and fascinating relationship to gender and to the history of British women's writing.

Analyzing the pervasiveness of landscape in Woolf's *Orlando* also offers a focused way to redress the absence of women from eighteenth-century landscape studies. It may seem esoteric to locate reparation for this exclusion in a modernist experimental novel. Yet, Orlando's experiences as a landowning aristocrat, as both a man and a woman, whose lifespan subsumes the long eighteenth century, makes the novel surprisingly serviceable, indeed tailor-made, for concluding the present study. Reading the novel through the lens of landscape, one comes away with the impression that Woolf integrated this specific topic because of its capacity to address the material and aesthetic concerns that coalesce in the ownership and representation of land; moreover, she links these concerns to female autonomy and creativity in ways that reveal a sensitivity to the interdependence of landownership and female self-determination. From the beginning, set during the Elizabethan era, Orlando's identity is embedded in his (and later her) country estate, and her self-realization hinges, to some extent, on whether she may rightfully inherit and bequeath it to her heirs.

Throughout the novel, Orlando's aesthetic appreciation of his/her estate is conflated with questions of ownership. Six pages prior to Woolf's equation of girls and roses, she stages a scene of landscape contemplation that enmeshes her hero's aesthetic and proprietary sensibilities.

> He had walked very quickly uphill through ferns and hawthorn bushes, startling deer and wild birds, to a place crowned by a single oak tree. It was very high, so high indeed that nineteen English counties could be seen beneath, and on clear days thirty, or forty perhaps, if the weather was very fine. [. . .] For a moment Orlando stood counting, gazing, recognising. That was his father's house; that his uncle's. His aunt owned those three great turrets among the trees there. The heath was theirs and the forest; the pheasant and the deer, the fox, the badger, and the butterfly.[2]

Orlando contemplates an expansive view of English counties receding on the horizon, settling eventually into thoughts of how much of that horizon belongs to his family. Capturing how easily the contemplation of rural beauty shades into its possession, Woolf exposes how enjoyment of the landscape may be indistinguishable from the pleasure of ownership. Likewise significant, the aunt who owns a piece of the landscape foretells a future wherein Orlando, too, will be a female landowner. With playful ambiguity, Woolf invites readers to share Orlando's pleasure and to laugh at the absurd notion of owning butterflies. The author's technique reveals how, for Britain's elite, identity emerges through ownership of a rural estate and the exercise of an aesthetic sensibility prone to appreciate it.

Yet Woolf is engaging in literary-historical sleight of hand here, depicting a moment set during the Elizabethan era with a slightly anachronistic trope, for the prospect view flourished only later in the seventeenth century.[3] On the page following Orlando's landscape meditation, the Queen arrives. The novel's annotator,

Maria DiBattista, glosses the scene with a note registering that Orlando's home is based on Knole, the ancestral estate of the woman who inspired Woolf's hero(ine), Vita Sackville-West—also her lover. Unlike Orlando, however, Sackville-West famously lost the estate to her male cousin in a widely publicized lawsuit over its inheritance, the outcome of which affirmed the longevity of primogeniture.

As DiBattista's note explains, "Queen Elizabeth visited Knole in 1573."[4] A purposeful compression of literary and chronological time, the scene also reveals how Woolf links questions of landscape contemplation, property ownership, and female authority. Orlando almost offends his Queen by arriving late to her reception at his home, a near-disaster occasioned by his enchantment with the landscape. Had he been more concerned to pay homage to the monarch rather than lingering over the sunset, he would not have risked such a breach in protocol. Thus, Woolf constructs her hero's competing loyalties, to his queen on the one hand and to himself and his passion for nature, and its possession, on the other. Added to this scenario are intimations of how the novel confronts the uneasy position of women in possession of authority. Queen Elizabeth, famous for defying male constructions of monarchical authority, nevertheless occupies a subordinate position in relation to Orlando, a beautiful young man who does not reciprocate her passion for him. Yet the emotional imbalance does not hinder the monarch's dispensation of patronage, for "it was on this same night, so tradition has it, when Orlando was sound asleep, that she made over formally, putting her hand and seal finally to the parchment, the gift of the great monastic house that had been the Archbishop's and then the King's to Orlando's father" (18).

Woolf orchestrates the scene of the royal visit, moving from landscape contemplation to a nearly missed formal reception, to a briefly glimpsed and aging female body, and finally to the momentous bequest of the very estate that prompted the heir nearly to forget his duty. Together, the linked components reveal ineffable connections among aesthetic pleasure, property ownership, and female power. Though the queen's passion goes unrequited, it nevertheless precipitates the property transfer that equips Orlando with a patrimony that will go on to be contested after his gender transformation. These issues evolve over the course of the novel as Orlando transforms from a nobleman beholden to a female monarch to a noblewoman beset by a troubled inheritance in a monarchy that proscribes women's landownership (albeit not in the heroine's case).

Woolf handles these matters in a way that calls attention to the law's absurdity. Orlando's gender transformation prompts Woolf to consider the bureaucratic dimension of the momentous change. Upon the protagonist's return to England—now a woman—after having lived abroad, she encounters "the iron countenance of the law"; "three major suits [. . .] had been preferred against her during her absence [. . .]. The chief charges against her were (1) that she was dead, and therefore could not hold any property whatsoever; (2) that she was a woman, which amounts to much the same thing; (3) that she was an English Duke who had married one Rosina Pepita, a dancer; and had had by her three sons, which sons now declaring that their father was deceased, claimed that all his property descended to them" (124). The marriage in question remains mysterious, for readers learned about "a deed of marriage" only when Orlando's secretaries inspected the papers by his bedside as their lord slept for days on end before awaking, for the first time, as a woman (98). Readers learn nothing else about the marriage to Rosina Pepita or the heirs who stake a claim to Orlando's estate. The legal battle stretches across decades but remains a matter of satirical bemusement: "Thus it was in a highly ambiguous condition, uncertain whether she was alive or dead, man or woman, Duke or nonentity, that [Orlando] posted down to her country seat, where, pending the legal judgment, she had the Law's permission to reside in a state of incognito or incognita, as the case might turn out to be" (125). The narrator's playful derision of the law's absurdity trivializes Orlando's legal troubles, though when they eventually get resolved in her favor, it's clear that women's legal access to landownership is not a trivial matter.

Woolf's treatment of the law may be satirical, but she vests her heroine with a love of nature that is serious and steady. Such a defining trait unites the male and female versions of Orlando, who draws poetic inspiration from the land where s/he lives, making the land an essential component of his, and then her, identity. A signature site for contemplating the land, the oak tree at the top of the hill is where his poetic avocation first germinates. By having Orlando "attach his floating heart to" this oak tree, Woolf signals her profound understanding of the elements that comprise the most emblematic British landscapes (15). Orlando's oak tree, and the poem it inspires, echo the Jacobite oak from Anne Finch's "Upon My Lord Winchilsea" as well as the avenue of oaks that entices the travelers toward Millenium Hall in Sarah Scott's novel of that name. (Jane Barker's arboreal commitments manifest in lime and ash trees instead.)[5] In their own ways, Finch, Barker, Scott, and Woolf acknowledge the unique resonance of the oak tree and its belonging in the British landscape. As Orlando lingers on the hilltop and stills his beating heart beneath the oak tree, Woolf describes what he sees: "The sun was rapidly sinking, the white clouds had turned red, the hills were violet, the woods purple, the valleys black" (16). The proliferation of color, the changes in the refraction of light, the composition of a scene through varied elements of sky and land, hills and wood, all demonstrate Woolf's expertise in the conventions of landscape description. Such description drives the text's production of aesthetic pleasure, and Woolf exploits this technique to illustrate her hero's aesthetic refinement and to reveal how this sensibility is enmeshed with material considerations such as ownership of the objects providing that visual pleasure. By creating a hero so acutely attuned to the natural environment that s/he devotes centuries to writing a poem titled "The Oak Tree," Woolf concocts a plot with ample occasion to elaborate on

Britain's (and as we will see, Turkey's) visual pleasures, and to link these indelibly to landownership.

It is not coincidental that *Orlando* features well-worn landscape tropes that simultaneously mark his status, her gender, and the historical period in question. By imagining an ageless hero(ine) whose relationship to property changes along with her gender, Woolf recognizes that landscape, landownership, and gender are not only deeply entangled but also historically contingent. Gazing on the horizon, Orlando exercises the prospect view in part because he is a man with a patrimony. Once he becomes a she, Woolf has occasion to consider the difference gender makes, and she does so explicitly through the language of landscape. As the novel nears its end, the narrator wrestles with the constancy of Orlando's essential self: "Through all these changes she had remained, she reflected, fundamentally the same. She had the same brooding meditative temper, the same love of animals and nature, the same passion for the country and the seasons. [. . .] 'After all,' she thought, getting up and going to the window, 'nothing has changed. The house, the garden are precisely as they were. [. . .] There are the same walks, the same lawns, and the same pool, with, I dare say, the same carp in it'" (173).

Looking out the window is something Orlando does habitually, signaling how Woolf constructs her protagonist by depicting her frequently looking at the land. And in the process of contemplating the passage of time, Orlando gropes for evidence of changelessness by turning to the landscape. Yet, Woolf treats its components as proof of a constancy that proves elusive. The scene goes on to describe "an extraordinary tingling and vibration all over her," which settles into her ring finger and introduces a question whose significance is greater for a woman than for a man—the question being, of course, whether and whom she will marry (175). Equally significant, though easily overlooked and tinged with ambiguity, is the observation that "she was about to bear a child" (171). Standing at the window gazing upon her estate, Orlando contemplates her sameness even as she embodies a fundamental fact of female biology that has made her decisively different from her male self. The juxtaposition of a seemingly timeless landscape and an inhabitant facing momentous change suggests that landscapes evolve as they are filtered through a specific—and gendered—consciousness. Orlando's gender transformation changes her in (at least) two significant ways: her marital and soon-to-be-maternal status and her eligibility to inherit and bequeath property now signify in fundamentally different ways, and these changes in turn produce a different landscape.

As the foregoing chapters have demonstrated, Garrett Sullivan's framework for historicizing landscape consists of three iterations. Woolf's novel focuses on Orlando's ancestral estate in a way that animates this historical array of landscapes over the course of her protagonist's centuries-long life. Not only does Orlando's identity hinge on estate ownership, but significant aspects of his interaction with the estate introduce concerns belonging to what we have come to recognize as the intertwined landscapes of stewardship and custom. Whether he performs his proper role as the landowner comes into focus at times when Orlando fails to follow the protocol of landownership. During the Jacobean phase of the story, a crisis ensues after the hero, having slept for a week straight, loses all interest in stewarding his estate as formerly: "How he spent his time, nobody quite knew. The servants, of whom he kept a full retinue, though much of their business was to dust empty rooms and to smooth the coverlets of beds that were never slept in, watched, in the dark of the evening, as they sat over their cakes and ale, a light passing along the galleries, through the banqueting halls, up staircases, into the bedrooms, and knew that their master was perambulating the house alone" (51–52). Though Woolf does not frame Orlando's dereliction of duty in terms of a failure to oversee the estate's agriculture or husbandry, focusing instead on the house servants, the scene still demands to be read in terms of disintegrating customary relations between lord and dependents. When he eventually escapes his melancholy, he does so in terms that recuperate a landscape of custom.

Awaking, beneath the oak tree, from a reverie on the nature of fame (to which he aspired in fantasies of becoming a writer), Orlando sees his house with news eyes, realizing the arrogance of his aspiration. It dawns on him: "Never had the house looked more noble and humane" (78). Woolf locates the nobility and humanity of Orlando's estate in the customary relations of the anonymous ancestors and laborers who lived there before him.

> Why, then, had he wished to raise himself above them? For it seemed vain and arrogant in the extreme to try to better that anonymous work of creation; the labours of those vanished hands. Better was it to go and leave behind you an arch, a potting shed, a wall where peaches ripen, than to burn like a meteor and leave no dust. For after all, he said, kindling as he looked at the great house on the greensward below, the unknown lords and ladies who lived there never forgot to set aside something for those who come after; for the roof that will leak; for the tree that will fall. There was always a warm corner for the old shepherd in the kitchen; always food for the hungry. (78)

One could hardly wish for a more lucid expression of the intertwined landscapes of stewardship and custom. Orlando acknowledges the privilege of being able to contribute to the legacy of an estate so beautifully harmonious. Imagining the dependents whose labor made it possible, he figures their work in terms of the landscape they create: "an arch, a potting shed, a wall where peaches ripen."

Woolf thus imagines a culture in which social relations exemplify the first two of Sullivan's three categories of landscape; Orlando enacts a landscape of stewardship, and his servants participate in a landscape of custom. A complicating factor is that authentic landscapes of custom (as Sullivan delineates them) treat such relations as the natural order of things rather than a cause for celebration.

The distinction exposes Woolf's retrospective gaze as she re-creates a bygone era and tweaks it for her own purposes. From her twentieth-century vantage, the landscape of custom proves more quaint than authentic. For all her rhapsodizing over the estate's grandeur, and evocation of the pleasures of landownership, she also subverts her portrait of social privilege, for example observing, when Orlando wanders the estate's crypt, that "all pomp is built upon corruption" (53). In more ways than one, she disrupts the harmony of Orlando's estate, making it dissipate over the centuries as its stability falters through entanglement in the expensive lawsuit. But as Orlando muses on the value of his home—"kindling as he looked at the great house"—he does so in terms of both its beauty and the social relations it sustains. Despite moments of irony and ambiguity, the novel stakes its claim to a literary tradition that conflates owner and estate; Orlando's identity evolves through ongoing engagement with the meaning and value of his/her ancestral home.

Orlando's aesthetic sensibility distinguishes him as belonging to an elite whose tastes evolve through the contemplation of rural land. Immediately following the gender transformation, Woolf concocts an episode with a female Orlando living among gypsies in Turkey, sometime in the early eighteenth century. The episode occurs after his stint (as a man) as the British ambassador to Turkey and his subsequent transformation into a woman, when she retreats to the countryside in "the high mountains above Broussa" (124). The scenario emphasizes her facility with the landscape arts, which in turn prompt her return to native soil. A conflict over the significance of land arises when the aesthetically astute heroine encounters suspicion from the gypsies who have taken her in but reject her affinity for the beautiful. The scene foregrounds the contrasting experiences of land represented by the gypsies, on the one hand, and Orlando on the other. During her sojourn with the gypsies, she shifts from inhabiting a world defined by the landscape arts to one defined by nonvisual experience of the land. Woolf renders the shift in terms of Orlando's welcome liberation from the demands of ambassadorship: "The pleasure of having no documents to seal, or sign, no flourishes to make, no calls to pay was enough. The gipsies followed the grass; when it was grazed down, on they moved again. [Orlando] washed in streams if she washed at all [. . .]. She milked the goats; she collected brushwood" (104). Like the gypsies, Orlando relates to the land primarily as a source of sustenance rather than visual pleasure. But even while following their ways, her aesthetic sensibility persists, provoking suspicion in her hosts.

> One evening, when they were all sitting round the camp fire and the sunset was blazing over the Thessalian hills, Orlando exclaimed:
>
> "How good to eat!"
> (The gipsies have no word for 'beautiful.' This is the nearest.)
>
> All the young men and women burst out laughing uproariously. The sky good to eat indeed! (105)

The cultural difference between the British and the gypsies interests Woolf in this scene, and she renders it in terms of aesthetic perception and the lack thereof.[6] Living apart from other aesthetes provides the heroine with a fleeting freedom from the burdens of being an aristocrat and a diplomat, but eventually she grows weary.

Like her predecessor Galesia in the Jane Barker trilogy, Orlando sees what she desires imprinted on the land before her, thus enacting her attachment to the landscape arts. Woolf explains the heroine's shifting mood among the gypsies in terms of her perception of landscape: "It was now midsummer, and if we must compare the landscape to anything it would have to be a dry bone. [. . .] Suddenly, a shadow, though there was nothing to cast a shadow, appeared on the bald mountain-side opposite. It deepened quickly and soon a green hollow showed where there had been a barren rock before. As she looked, the hollow deepened and widened, and a great park-like space opened in the flank of the hill. Within, she could see an undulating, grassy lawn; she could see oak trees dotted here and there" (111). Woolf expresses Orlando's desire for home by superimposing a British landscape over the Turkish one. Visual imagery permeates the entire passage (almost a page in length), suggesting that aesthetic appreciation comes more naturally to Orlando than a subsistence-driven relation to the land.

A turning point in *Orlando* occurs when, after an expensive and decades-long legal battle, sometime in the mid- to late-nineteenth century, the lawsuit's settlement legitimates her status as a female landowner; her estates "which are now desequestrated in perpetuity descend and are tailed and entailed upon the heirs male of [her] body" (187). Woolf satirizes a legal system that takes decades to decide, finally, that she is female, and that she may exercise the legal rights that for men are considered innate. The settlement restores the traditional order of things insofar as Orlando may once again preside over her estate. Yet, the trouble induced by turning the lord of the manor into a lady suggests Woolf's awareness that "the traditional order of things" remains, to the end, patriarchal. Orlando's legal status as a woman, and her severely depleted coffers, underscore how women's landownership differs decisively from the standard male model. The difference proves costly; in sum, Orlando pays a penalty for being a woman: "The cost of the lawsuits had been prodigious, [and] though she was infinitely noble again, she was also excessively poor" (187).

Orlando's contested landownership exemplifies one of several ways in which the landscape of absolute property illuminates the novel's yoking of women's writing and property ownership. Understood as a modern capitalist regime wherein the only views of land that matter belong to the landed elite, this landscape lays the foundation for Orlando's life as a woman writer. The experience of landownership, and its proscription for women, constitute fundamental aspects of the character's identity formation. It comes as no surprise that Vita Sackville-West won a prize for a poem called *The Land* (1927), which among other concerns charts her troubled access to landownership. Regardless of the differences between the real woman's disinheritance from Knole and the novelistic restitution of her patrimony, what matters here is that landownership is at the crux of a gentlewoman's identity. These matters grow somewhat ambiguous in the novel's virtuosic final chapter, set in the 1920s, as the heroine's multiple selves navigate rural and urban spaces for self-realization. London exerts its power as the site for the publication and celebration of *The Oak Tree* ("'The Burdett Coutts' Memorial Prize [. . .] she had won" [228]). But questions about the heroine's multiplicity dissipate as if by alchemy once she leaves the city and drives onto her own soil: "And it was at this moment, when she had ceased to call 'Orlando' and was deep in thoughts of something else that the Orlando whom she had called came of its own accord; as was proved by the change that now came over her as she passed through the lodge gates into the park" (229). Such passages affirm the heroine's preternatural identification with her landed estate.

But Woolf infuses even the chapter's climax with uncertainty, staging its final scene at the hill-top oak tree, where Orlando's hallucinatory landscape visions reveal her to be more dazzled by her own imagination than by visual or actual sovereignty over the estate. Prior to this scene, the chapter builds momentum with the heroine's meditative and memory-drenched perambulation through her mansion's interior, then out to the garden, past the gardener Joe Stubbs in his shop, and gradually up the hill to the tree. An embodiment of those without access to the landscape of absolute property, Stubbs troubles his mistress's reverie when she glimpses his "pink flesh where the nail should have been" (236). Like James the porter, Mrs. Grimsditch the housekeeper, and Mr. Dupper the chaplain, Stubbs belongs to the estate staff who, though much appreciated by Orlando, perform ceaseless labor so that she may fulfill her proper role as their mistress.

Once at the summit, she briefly observes the panoramic view of Snowdon and the Hebrides (itself fanciful). But then her sight gives way to a palimpsest landscape in which "the bare mountains of Turkey" overtake her vision, only to collapse once darkness falls so that she now sees "only misty fields, lamps in cottage windows, [and] the slumbering bulk of a wood" (239). Thus, while bringing her heroine full circle, honoring the tree that inspired her poetry, Woolf does not conclude the novel with the same rhapsody of triumphant possession that Orlando expressed as a young man surveying his vast estate. Instead, the author vests the heroine with a contemplative and less possessive outlook. Now, rather than enumerating the landed possessions on the horizon, Orlando thinks, "And that [. . .] was my land once" (239). Such an open-ended conclusion intimates that as a woman, Orlando relates to her property differently than she did as a man. The scene does not eradicate the value of women's landownership so much as attenuate it. Questions about perception and the self's multiplicity now supersede the visual pleasures of landownership in Orlando's consciousness. The husband who has made fleeting appearances since the previous chapter returns, introducing the prospect of intimacy; yet, the fact of Orlando's landownership endures, an abiding, if tenuous, foundation for her future selves.

Prolific Ground has confronted the fact that British landscape is so deeply entwined with an overwhelmingly male-dominated practice—landownership—that the women writers who appropriate its conventions cannot avoid accommodating this institution at least to some degree. Woolf's irreverent pseudobiography exposes these facts in a way that revels in their absurdity without overturning them. For this reason, a bittersweetness mingles with Orlando's triumphant return to the status of a noblewoman. A similar effect results from the way Woolf sustains the social privilege that prevailed among the proto-feminists who preceded her—a feature that likewise exposes a chasm between early twentieth- and early twenty-first-century feminists. Ultimately, the preservation and naturalization of the social hierarchy establishes continuity among Barker, Finch, Scott, Montagu, and Woolf. The resonance among their various texts demonstrates how landscape is if anything an exceedingly malleable discourse, and this quality makes it attractive to women writers who grasp how representations of land serve as a reservoir for an array of beliefs, aspirations, and affiliations in which identity is embedded. The writers featured herein ground their agency in innovative approaches to landscape that question and sometimes subvert their culture's patriarchal foundations. Their creativity, wisdom, and artful negotiation of various social constrictions leave a lasting impression of the possibilities for female self-invention in and through the land.

ACKNOWLEDGMENTS

Prolific Ground has been so long in the making that I fear overlooking the many colleagues and friends who helped bring it to fruition. Since its inception, the book benefited from the rigorous and steady feedback of William Worden, Rasma Lazda-Cazers, and Richard Gordon. Bill has proven especially supportive not only during multiple rounds of manuscript submission and revision, but also throughout the book's final phase. During writing workshops with these fellow scholars, we thrived with the support of Deirdre Worden and Gunars Cazers. Writing under pressure proved less onerous with the critical acumen and good humor of this treasured scholarly community.

Early on in my engagement with Anne Finch, I had the good fortune to receive feedback from Barbara McGovern, whose insights corrected my course as I reckoned with a monumental figure in eighteenth-century British women's writing. Since then, Claudia Kairoff and Jennifer Keith have generously shared their expertise well in advance of the publication of *The Cambridge Edition of the Works of Anne Finch, Countess of Winchilsea*. Kathryn King offered encouragement and advice in the even more arduous process of identifying how Jane Barker figures into the book. I needed to get Barker "right" before I could feel confident in moving forward, and Kathy's feedback proved invaluable at an important juncture.

I also thank J. J. Wilson, a model academic whom I've known since childhood, and who shared her expertise on Virginia Woolf and offered sound advice to energize my writing. Betty Press shared her expertise with digital images; I thank her for this as well as her enduring friendship.

I have benefited from various kinds of institutional support. I thank the University of Southern Mississippi for a sabbatical and an Aubrey Keith and Ella Ginn Lucas Grant. Further afield, I thank the Huntington Library for providing access to the Elizabeth Robinson Montagu Papers and the Chawton House Library for a visiting fellowship.

Just out of graduate school and somewhat adrift regarding my scholarly agenda, I was lucky to work briefly at Southern Methodist University alongside Rajani Sudan, who kindly served as a reference and introduced me to another valuable mentor, Robert Markley. I am grateful to them both. Several other colleagues in eighteenth-century studies offered feedback on essays wherein ideas about *Prolific Ground* germinated: Elizabeth Heckendorn Cook, Giulia Pacini, and

Laura Runge. I also thank Daniel Lehman for guidance during my time at Ashland University and for supporting my move to the University of Southern Mississippi, where I could grow more as a scholar in my field.

Most recently, I thank Miriam Wallace for her expertise and guidance during critical stages in the process of completing and publishing my manuscript. Prior to then, Emily Shelton read and reread these chapters, offering insight and inspiration that proved crucial to strengthening my argument. Anne Sanow deserves thanks, too, for introducing me to Emily, for sharing her own publishing expertise, and for being a great friend. Similarly, David Cochran read portions of the manuscript and offered sound advice; his generosity and inimitable sense of humor kept me going. In the bigger picture, I could not have completed the book without the unstinting support of Andrew Berman, Nicholas and Rachel Ciraldo, Miranda Grieder, Rory Kerber, Marie-Chantal Killeen, Jeanne Ross, Heather Songster, and Andrew Zionts. I dedicate the book to Michele Anna Jordan, who got me started, and Thomas V. O'Brien, whose patience I tested and who nevertheless kept me going.

NOTES

INTRODUCTION

1. Elizabeth Montagu, unpublished letter to Elizabeth Vesey, September 27, 1783, MO 6579, Huntington Library, San Marino, California.
2. On women's landownership during Montagu's era, see Judith S. Lewis, *Sacred to Female Patriotism: Gender, Class, and Politics in Late Georgian Britain* (New York: Routledge, 2003).
3. Isis Brook, "Aesthetic Appreciation of Landscape," in *The Routledge Companion to Landscape Studies*, 2nd ed., ed. Peter Howard, Ian Thompson, Emma Waterton, and Mick Atha (New York: Routledge, 2019), 40.
4. Tom Williamson, *Polite Landscapes: Gardens & Society in Eighteenth-Century England* (Stroud, Gloucestershire: Sutton Publishing, 1995) and *The Transformation of Rural England: Farming and the Landscape, 1700–1870* (Exeter: University of Exeter Press, 2002); Timothy Mowl, *Gentlemen and Players: Gardeners of the English Landscape* (Stroud, Gloucestershire: The History Press, 2000).
5. Briony McDonagh, *Elite Women and the Agricultural Landscape, 1700–1830* (New York: Routledge, 2017).
6. Nicola Verdon, "The 'Lady Farmer': Gender, Widowhood, and Farming in Victorian England," in *The Farmer in England, 1650–1980*, ed. Richard W. Hoyle (Ashgate, 2013; Routledge, 2016), 241–262.
7. Bridget Hill, *Women, Work, and Sexual Politics in Eighteenth-Century England* (Oxford: Basil Blackwell Press, 1989); and Amanda Vickery, *Behind Closed Doors: At Home in Georgian England* (New Haven, CT: Yale University Press, 2009).
8. Carol Barash, *English Women's Poetry, 1649–1714: Politics, Community, and Linguistic Authority* (New York: Oxford University Press, 1996); Elaine Chalus, *Elite Women in English Political Life, c. 1754–1790* (New York: Oxford University Press, 2005); Harriet Guest, *Small Change: Women, Learning, Patriotism, 1750–1810* (Chicago: University of Chicago Press, 2000); and Emma Major, *Madam Britannia: Women, Church, and Nation, 1712–1812* (New York: Oxford University Press, 2012).
9. Garrett Sullivan, *The Drama of Landscape: Land, Property, and Social Relations on the Early Modern Stage* (Stanford, CA: Stanford University Press, 1998), 26.
10. John Barrell, "The Public Prospect and the Private View: The Politics of Taste in Eighteenth-Century Britain," in *The Birth of Pandora and the Division of Knowledge* (Philadelphia: University of Pennsylvania Press, 1992), 41–61; Denis Cosgrove, *Social Formation and Symbolic Landscape* (Madison: University of Wisconsin Press, 1984); and W.J.T. Mitchell, "Imperial Landscape," in *Landscape and Power*, ed. W.J.T. Mitchell (Chicago: University of Chicago Press, 1994), 5–34.
11. Douglas Chambers, *The Planters of the English Landscape Garden: Botany, Trees, and the Georgics* (New Haven, CT: Yale University Press, 1993).
12. Cynthia Wall, *Grammars of Approach: Landscape, Narrative, and the Linguistic Picturesque* (Chicago: University of Chicago Press, 2019), 18.
13. Stephen Bending, *Green Retreats: Women, Gardens, and Eighteenth-Century Culture* (New York: Cambridge University Press, 2013).

14. On female agency and literary form, see Betty Schellenberg, *The Professionalization of Women Writers in Eighteenth-Century Britain* (New York: Cambridge University Press, 2005).
15. Lisa L. Moore, *Sister Arts: The Erotics of Lesbian Landscapes* (Minneapolis: University of Minnesota Press, 2011). For related queer readings, see also J. David Macey , "Eden Revisited: Re-visions of the Garden in Astell's *Serious Proposal*, Scott's *Millenium Hall*, and Graffigny's *Lettres d'une peruvienne*," *Eighteenth-Century Fiction* 9, no. 2 (January 1997): 161–182. Sarah Scott's *Millenium Hall*, in particular, has been importantly read as a Sapphic text; see for example Sally O'Driscoll, "Lesbian Criticism and Feminist Criticism: Readings of *Millenium Hall*," *Tulsa Studies in Women's Literature* 22, no. 1 (Spring 2003): 57–80.
16. Bridget Hill, "A Tale of Two Sisters: The Contrasting Careers and Ambitions of Elizabeth Montagu and Sarah Scott," *Women's History Review* 19, no. 2 (April 2010): 215–229; and Betty Rizzo, "Two Versions of Community: Montagu and Scott," *Huntington Library Quarterly* 65 no. 1/2 (2003): 193–214.
17. Liz Griffiths, review of *Elite Women and the Agricultural Landscape, 1700–1830*, by Briony McDonagh, *Agricultural History Review* 66, no. 1 (2018): 157–158.
18. McDonagh, *Elite Women*, 164. See also Ruth Perry, "Mary Astell and the Feminist Critique of Possessive Individualism," *Eighteenth-Century Studies* 23, no. 4, (Summer 1990): 444–457.
19. McDonagh, *Elite Women*, 143.
20. Bridget Hill, *Eighteenth-Century Women: An Anthology* (New York: Routledge, 1984), 48.
21. Felicity Nussbaum, *Torrid Zones: Maternity, Sexuality, and Empire in Eighteenth-Century English Narratives* (Baltimore, MD: Johns Hopkins University Press, 1995); Jason Farr, "Disability as Metaphor and Lived Experience in Samuel Richardson's *Pamela* and Sarah Scott's *Millenium Hall*," *Studies in Eighteenth-Century Culture* 50 (2021): 309–312.
22. Bridget Hill, "Women's History: A Study in Change, Continuity, or Standing Still?" in *Women's Work: The English Experience 1650–1914*, ed. Pamela Sharpe (New York: Oxford University Press, 1998), 52.
23. Patricia Crawford, "Women and Property: Women as Property," *Parergon* 19, no. 1 (January 2002): 165.
24. Crawford, "Women and Property," 156.
25. Judith Broome: *Fictive Domains: Body, Landscape, and Nostalgia, 1717–1770* (Lewisburg, PA: Bucknell University Press, 2007).
26. Carole Fabricant, "Binding and Dressing Nature's Loose Tresses: The Ideology of Augustan Landscape Design," *Studies in Eighteenth-Century Culture* 8 (1979): 109–135.
27. Jennifer Keith, *Poetry and the Feminine from Behn to Cowper* (Newark: University of Delaware Press, 2005).
28. Kathryn King, "Constructions of Femininity," in *A Companion to Eighteenth-Century Poetry*, ed. Christine Gerrard (Malden, MA: Wiley-Blackwell, 2006), 438–439.
29. Barrell, "The Public Prospect," 47.
30. Malcolm Andrews, *Landscape and Western Art* (Oxford: Oxford University Press, 1999), 157.
31. Jacqueline Labbe, *Romantic Visualities: Landscape, Gender, and Romanticism* (New York: St. Martin's Press, 1998), 30–31.

CHAPTER 1 — JANE BARKER'S LIMINAL LANDSCAPES

1. Jane Spencer, "Creating the Woman Writer: The Autobiographical Works of Jane Barker," *Tulsa Studies in Women's Literature* 2, no. 2 (Autumn 1983): 167; Kathryn King and Jeslyn Medoff, "Jane Barker and Her Life (1652–1732): The Documentary Record," *Eighteenth-Century Life* 21, no. 3 (November 1997): 97.
2. King and Medoff, "Jane Barker," 22; Leigh A. Eicke, "Jane Barker's Jacobite Writings," *Women's Writing and the Circulation of Ideas: Manuscript Publication in England, 1550–1800*, ed. George L. Justice and Nathan Tinker (New York: Cambridge, 2002), 137–157; and

Kathryn King, *Jane Barker, Exile: A Literary Career 1675–1725* (New York: Oxford University Press, 2000), 147–179.

3. Victoria Joule sees an ongoing project of revision as central to Barker's work: see "'She Did But Take Up Old Stories': Generic Fluidity and Women's Life-Writing of the Early Eighteenth Century," *Bulletin of the John Rylands University Library of Manchester* 90, no. 2 (September 2014): 61.
4. On Barker's navigation of manuscript and print, see King, *Jane Barker*, 29–67; and Rachel Mann, "Jane Barker, Manuscript Culture, and the Epistemology of the Microscope," *Eighteenth-Century Life* 43, no. 1 (January 2019): 50–75.
5. King argues that Barker most likely had publication foisted upon her by the male coterie, thus "cautioning against uncritical use of the printed volume in accounts of women's print-world involvements and self-representational strategies." *Jane Barker, Exile*, 34. Cf. King, "Cowley among the Women; or, Poetry in the Contact Zone," in *Women and Literary History: 'For There She Was,'*" ed. Katherine Binhammer and Jeanne Wood (Newark: University of Delaware Press, 2003), 43–63.
6. William McBurney, "Edmund Curll, Mrs. Jane Barker, and the English Novel," *Philological Quarterly* 37, no. 4 (1958): 385–399; Jane Spencer, *The Rise of the Woman Novelist* (Oxford: Blackwell, 1986), 62–67; King, *Jane Barker*, 169–179; and Nicole Horejsi, *Novel Cleopatras: Romance Historiography and the Dido Tradition in English Fiction, 1688–1785* (Toronto: University of Toronto Press, 2019), 25–53.
7. Nathaniel Paradise, "Interpolated Poetry, the Novel, and Female Accomplishment," *Philological Quarterly* 74, no. 1 (Winter 1995): 57–76. Also referencing Barker, Margaret Ezell observes that "[women's] prose texts very often include the writer's verses." See "From Manuscript to Print: A Volume of Their Own?" in *Women and Poetry, 1660–1750*, ed. Sarah Prescott and David E. Shuttleton (New York: Palgrave, 2003), 146. In addition to Joule, "Generic Fluidity," see Kathryn King, "Genre Crossings," in *The Cambridge Companion to Women's Writing in Britain, 1660–1789*, ed. Catherine Ingrassia (New York: Cambridge University Press, 2015), 97–99.
8. Kathryn King, "Of Needles and Pins and Women's Work," *Tulsa Studies in Women's Literature* 14, no. 1 (Spring 1995): 77–93; Misty Anderson, "Tactile Places: Materializing Desire in Margaret Cavendish and Jane Barker," *Textual Practice* 13, no. 2 (1999): 329–352; Rivka Swenson, "Representing Modernity in Jane Barker's *Galesia Trilogy*: Jacobite Allegory and the Patch-Work Aesthetic," *Studies in Eighteenth-Century Culture* 34 (2005): 55–80; Samara Anne Cahill, "Realist Latitudes: Textilic Nationalism and the Global Fiction of the 1720s," *Digital Defoe: Studies in Defoe & His Contemporaries* 7, no. 1 (Fall 2015): 66–91; and Alice Tweedy McGrath, "Unaccountable Form: Queer Failure and Jane Barker's Patchwork Method," *The Eighteenth Century: Theory and Interpretation* 60, no. 4 (Winter 2019): 353–373.
9. On Barker and the history of the novel, see (in addition to McBurney, "Edmund Curll") Josephine Donovan, "Women and the Rise of the Novel: A Feminist-Marxist Theory," *Signs* 16 no. 3 (Spring 1991): 441–462. On Barker and Catholicism, see Tonya Moutray McArthur, "Jane Barker and the Politics of Catholic Celibacy," *Studies in English Literature* 47 no. 3 (Summer 2007): 595–618; Bridget Keegan and Libby Hallgren Hoxmeier, eds., "Jane Barker's Catholic Poems: An Edition of 'Poems Refering to the Times' from the Magdalen Manuscript, Part One," *Tulsa Studies in Women's Literature* 31 no. 1/2 (Spring/Fall 2012): 181–228; Karen Gevirtz, "Recent Developments in 17th and 18th-Century English Catholic Studies," *Literature Compass* 12/2 (2015): 47–58; and Joanne Myers, "Jane Barker's Conversion and the Forms of Religious Experience," *Eighteenth-Century Fiction* 30 no. 3 (Spring 2018): 369–393. On lesbian sexuality, see Anderson "Tactile Places," 345–348; McGrath, "Unaccountable Form"; and Kathryn King, "The Unaccountable Wife and Other Tales of Female Desire in Jane Barker's *A Patch-Work Screen for the Ladies*," *The Eighteenth Century: Theory and Interpretation* 35, no. 2 (Summer 1994): 155–172. On adjacent histories, see Chloe Wigston Smith, *Women, Work, and Clothes in the Eighteenth-Century Novel* (New York: Cambridge

University Press, 2013), 47–80; Karen Gevirtz, *Women, the Novel, and Natural Philosophy* (New York: Palgrave, 2015), 71–100; Heather Meek, "Jane Barker, Medical Discourse, and the Origins of the Novel," *Literature and Medicine Volume 1: The Eighteenth Century*, ed. Clark Lawlor and Andrew Mangham (New York: Cambridge University Press, 2021), 51–69; and Carolin Boettcher, "Cooking Up Knowledge: Materiality, Recipes, and Jane Barker's *A Patch-Work Screen for the Ladies*," *ABO: Interactive Journal for Women in the Arts, 1640–1830* 12, no. 2 (Winter 2022): 1–17.

10. King traces the notorious publisher Edmund Curll's "unsolicited" 1713 publication of *Bosvil and Galesia* and Barker's subsequent involvement in the 1719 version, which appeared in *Entertaining Novels* alongside her second novel, *Exilius or The Banished Roman* (first edition 1715). See *Jane Barker*, 181–183. My analysis uses the 1719 version of the first novel.
11. On the economic transformations of the Augustan Age, see J. G. A. Pocock, *The Machiavellian Moment: Florentine Political Thought and the Atlantic Republican Tradition* (Princeton, NJ: Princeton University Press, 1975), 423–461.
12. Carly Watson discusses *A Patch-Work Screen* as the first instance of the form's adaptation specifically for women. See *Miscellanies, Poetry, and Authorship, 1680–1800* (New York: Palgrave Macmillan, 2021), 227.
13. Jane Barker, *Love Intrigues: or, The Amours of Bosvil and Galesia*, in *The Galesia Trilogy and Selected Manuscript Poems of Jane Barker*, ed. Carol Shiner Wilson (New York: Oxford University Press, 1997), 47. Kristina Straub traces the imagery of rising and falling in the first two Galesia novels; see "Frances Burney and the Rise of the Woman Novelist," in *The Columbia History of the British Novel*, ed. John Richetti (New York: Columbia University Press, 1994), 199–219.
14. *The Lining of the Patch Work Screen*, in *The Galesia Trilogy*, ed. Carol Shiner Wilson (New York: Oxford University Press, 1997), 290.
15. For a historical analysis of the bark inscription topos, see Nicolle Jordan, "'I Writ These Lines on the Body of the Tree': Jane Barker's Arboreal Poetics," in *Invaluable Trees: Cultures of Nature, 1660–1830*, ed. Laura Auricchio, Elizabeth Heckendorn Cook, and Giulia Pacini (Oxford: Voltaire Foundation, 2012): 251–263.
16. See for example Crawford, "Women and Property"; April London, *Women and Property in the Eighteenth-Century English Novel* (Cambridge: Cambridge University Press, 1999); Susan Staves, *Married Women's Separate Property in England, 1660–1833* (Cambridge, MA: Harvard University Press, 1990); and McDonagh, *Elite Women*.
17. Other examples of the 'woman writing a woman writer'—in both fiction and verse—include Lady Mary Wroth's *The Countess of Montgomery's Urania* (1621), Margaret Cavendish, Elizabeth Singer Rowe's *Friendship in Death, in Twenty Letters from the Dead to the Living* (1728), and Charlotte Smith.
18. Bronwen Price, "Verse, Voice, and Body: The Retirement Mode and Women's Poetry 1680–1723," *Early Modern Literary Studies* 12, no. 3 (January 2007): 8. She quotes Barker, *A Patch-Work Screen for the Ladies*, in *The Galesia Trilogy*, ed. Carol Shiner Wilson (New York: Oxford University Press, 1997), 76. Throughout the chapter, I have deliberately retained Barker's spelling and capitalization.
19. Price, "Verse," 1.
20. It proves challenging to identify the most relevant definition of *topography*. Price's usage corresponds most closely to *Oxford English Dictionary* (*OED*), s.v. "topography, 1.b.": "A detailed description or delineation of the features of a locality." Accessed June 10, 2022.
21. In defining *landscape* as a noun, *OED* emphasizes visual perception: "A picture representing natural inland scenery, as distinguished from a sea picture, a portrait, etc." (definition 1.a.), accessed July 2, 2022.
22. The son of James II, known as the Old Pretender (James Francis Edward Stuart), inspired the so-called Fifteen, which attempted to overturn the Hanoverian succession of George I (who reigned 1714–1727). See John Roach Young, "The Fifteen," in *Britain in the Hanoverian Age 1714–1837: An Encyclopedia*, ed. Gerald Newman (New York: Garland, 1997), 254.

23. Geoff Berry, "Modernism, Climate Change, and Dystopia: An Ecocritical Reading of Light Symbology in Conrad's *Heart of Darkness* and Eliot's *The Waste Land*," *COLLOQUY: Text Theory Critique* 21 (2011): 82.
24. Stephen Daniels, "Marxism, Culture, and the Duplicity of Landscape," in *New Models in Geography: The Political-Economy Perspective*, ed. Richard Peet and N. J. Thrift (London: Unwin Hyman, 1989), 207.
25. Raymond Williams, *Keywords* (New York: Oxford University Press, 1976), 164–165.
26. Sullivan, *The Drama*; Andrews, *Landscape*; and Cosgrove, *Social Formation*, 13.
27. For evidence of the pastoral as prone to conceptual drift of the sort that gives landscape a likewise unstable meaning, see Barash, *English Women's Poetry*, 185; and London, *Women and Property*, 5.
28. Sullivan, *The Drama*, 13–16.
29. It is important to acknowledge the unstable meaning of the term *absolute* in reference to authority and landed property. For my purposes, references to absolute property involve a landlord's absolute self-interest rather than his conformity to customary relations. Ursula Vogel's usage of the term illustrates its common affiliation with proto-capitalist narratives of liberalism, which theorize private property in opposition to the customs of feudal landownership: "To the extent that ownership thus postulates the individual's *absolute* command over things, the essential meaning of property must be sought in each person's power to exclude all others from making any claim to his goods" [Vogel's emphasis]. See "When the Earth Belonged to All: The Land Question in Eighteenth-Century Justifications of Private Property," *Political Studies* 36 (1988): 102–103.
30. Barker, *Bosvil and Galesia*, 40. All poetic lines are italicized in the first novel but not in the sequels.
31. For a survey of British political partisanship, see Christine Gerrard, "Poetry, Politics, and the Rise of Party," in *A Companion to Eighteenth-Century Poetry*, ed. Christine Gerrard (Malden, MA: Blackwell, 2006), 7–22. Cf. Nigel Everett, *The Tory View of Landscape* (New Haven, CT: Yale University Press, 1994.
32. Joseph Addison, *The Spectator* 2, no. 414 (1712), accessed May 30, 2020, https://www.gutenberg.org/cache/epub/12030/pg12030-images.html#chap02.
33. Scholarship on rural retirement and the pastoral is vast. See especially James Turner, *The Politics of Landscape: Rural Scenery and Society in English Poetry 1630–1660* (Cambridge, MA: Harvard University Press, 1979); and Annabel Patterson, *Pastoral and Ideology: Virgil to Valéry* (Berkeley: University of California Press, 1987), 133–192.
34. Ezell, "From Manuscript to Print," 146.
35. King identifies Barker the novelist as "A Writer for Pay" and traces her effort to reach an elevated readership; see *Jane Barker*, 180–217. William Warner positions Barker within a history of the novel that valorizes reading for virtue above reading for pleasure; regrettably, he offers no detailed analysis. See *Licensing Entertainment: The Elevation of Novel Reading in Britain, 1684–1750* (Berkeley: University of California Press, 1998), 42, 160, 193.
36. King, *Jane Barker*, 207.
37. An earlier version of Galesia's first poem, entitled "The contract with the muses / writ on the bark of a shady ash-tree," appeared in Part Two of *Poetical Recreations*. See Barker, *The Galesia Trilogy*, 324–325.
38. The first quotation appears in Barker, *Bosvil and Galesia*, 13.
39. The final quotation appears in Barker, *Bosvil and Galesia*, 13.
40. See also Cahill, "Realist Latitudes," 72.
41. Gevirtz, *Women*, 75.
42. Felicity Heal, "The Crown, the Gentry, and London: The Enforcement of Proclamation, 1596–1640," in *Law and Government under the Tudors*, ed. Claire Cross et al. (New York: Cambridge University Press, 1988), 211–226. Heal cites Charles I's 1632 proclamation and then evaluates seventeen prior proclamations issued by Elizabeth I, James I, and Charles himself.

43. Samara Anne Cahill, "Novel 'Modes' and 'Indian Goods': Textilic Nationalism in *A Patch-Work Screen for the Ladies* and *The Lining of the Patch Work Screen*," *Studies in Eighteenth-Century Culture* 44 (2015): 167.
44. On bigamy as an allegory through which Barker addresses "questions of legitimacy, fidelity, and troubled conscience facing" Jacobites, see King, *Jane Barker*, 166–169.
45. The text shifts the spelling of the heroine's name from *Galesia* to *Galecia* without explanation.
46. King, *Jane Barker*, 217.
47. See Eicke, "Jane Barker's Jacobite Writings," 151–153; King *Jane Barker*, 214–217; and Carol Shiner Wilson, "Jane Barker (1652–1732): From Galesia to Mrs Goodwife," in *Women and Poetry 1660–1750*, ed. Sarah Prescott and David Shuttleton (New York: Palgrave, 2003), 44.
48. Swenson, "Representing Modernity," 71, 70.
49. Constance Lacroix, "Wicked Traders, Deserving Peddlers, and Virtuous Smugglers: The Counter-Economy of Jane Barker's Jacobite Novel," *Eighteenth-Century Fiction* 23, no. 2 (Winter 2011–12): 281.
50. Lacroix, "Wicked Traders," 282.

CHAPTER 2 — STEWARDING THE COUNTRY HOUSE

1. See "The Miseries of St. Germains" in *The Galesia Trilogy and Manuscript Poems of Jane Barker*, ed. Carol Shiner Wilson (New York: Oxford University Press, 1997), 302–307.
2. Barbara McGovern, *Anne Finch and Her Poetry: A Critical Biography* (Athens: University of Georgia Press, 1992), 10.
3. McGovern, *Anne Finch*, 98–99.
4. McGovern, *Anne Finch*, 13.
5. McGovern, *Anne Finch*, 14, 20, 29, 64.
6. Paula Backscheider, *Women Poets and Their Poetry: Inventing Agency, Inventing Genre* (Baltimore, MD: Johns Hopkins University Press, 2005), 28–79. See also Susan Staves, *A Literary History of Women's Writing in Britain, 1660–1789* (New York: Cambridge University Press, 2006), 138–144.
7. On these dates, see *The Cambridge Edition of the Works of Anne Finch*, ed. Jennifer Keith and Claudia Kairoff, vol. 1, *Early Manuscript Books* (New York: Cambridge University Press, 2019), 531 and 704–705.
8. Jennifer Keith, "The Reach of Translation in the Works of Anne Finch," *Philological Quarterly* 95, no. 3/4 (June 2016): 482.
9. Michael Gavin, "Critics and Criticism in the Poetry of Anne Finch," *ELH* 78, no. 3 (Fall 2011): 642.
10. Gavin, "Critics and Criticism," 643.
11. Sullivan, *The Drama*, 10.
12. Sullivan, *The Drama*, 15.
13. The Whig ascendancy originates in the 1689 ouster of James II and the subsequent coronation of William III and Mary II (James's daughter by his first wife, Anne Hyde). The Whigs come to dominate Parliament with Sir Robert Walpole, considered the first prime minister, a post he held 1721–1742.
14. Gavin, "Critics and Criticism," 641.
15. Gavin, "Critics and Criticism," 644.
16. Tom Williamson and Liz Bellamy, *Property and Landscape: A Social History of Land Ownership and the English Countryside* (London: Butler and Tanner, 1987), 124.
17. Heather Dubrow, "The Politics of Aesthetics: Recuperating Formalism and the Country House Poem," in *Renaissance Literature and Its Engagements with Form*, ed. Mark David Rasmussen (New York: Palgrave, 1994), 74.
18. Claudia Kairoff, Jennifer Keith, and Jean Marsden, "General Introduction," *The Cambridge Edition of the Works of Anne Finch* (New York: Cambridge University Press, 2019), 1:lix.

19. Gillian Wright, *Producing Women's Poetry, 1600–1730: Text and Paratext, Manuscript and Print* (New York: Cambridge University Press, 2013), 186.
20. Keith, "The Reach of Translation," 468–469.
21. Charles Molesworth, "Property and Virtue: The Country-House Poem of the Seventeenth Century," *Genre* 1 (1968): 141–157.
22. Ben Jonson, "To Penshurst," in *The Poems of Ben Jonson*, ed. George Burke Johnston (Cambridge, MA: Harvard University Press, 1962), 76–79, line 19.
23. McGovern, *Anne Finch*, 27–28.
24. McGovern, *Anne Finch*, 27.
25. Kairoff and Keith, *Works* 1:531.
26. See Jennifer Keith, "Anne Finch in the Twenty-First Century: Finding the Artist in History," *Literature Compass* (2018), 3. https://doi.org/10.1111/lic3.12441.
27. Simon Schama, *Landscape and Memory* (New York: Knopf, 1995), 153–170.
28. Jim Casey argues persuasively for the political subtext of any imagery or language used in country-house poetry that relates to leveling, which he links to the egalitarian Levellers, who agitated during the English Civil Wars. "'Equall Freedome, Equall Fare': The Illusion of Egalitarianism in the Country House Poem," *Early English Studies* 3 (2010): 1–29.
29. Erin Drew, *The Usufructuary Ethos: Power, Politics, and Environment in the Long Eighteenth Century* (Charlottesville: University of Virginia Press, 2021), 1. She quotes *The OED*, definition 1.a. One exemplary usage here, from William Blackstone's *Commentaries on the Laws of England* (1766), offers further insight: "A subject therefore hath only the usufruct, and not the absolute property of the soil."
30. *Oxford English Dictionary*, s.v. "usufruct."
31. Drew, *The Usufructuary Ethos*, 2.
32. Drew, *The Usufructuary Ethos*, 82.
33. Drew, *The Usufructuary Ethos*, 110.
34. Drew, *The Usufructuary Ethos*, 18.
35. Portions of chapter 2 previously appeared in "Anne Finch and the Fallen Country House," in *The Intellectual Culture of the English Country House*, ed. Matthew Dimmock, Andrew Hadfield, and Margaret Healy (Manchester: Manchester University Press, 2015), 129–145.
36. Mark Girouard, *Life in the English Country House: A Social and Architectural History* (New Haven, CT: Yale University Press, 1994).
37. Finch's editors note the poem's uncertain date of composition; see *Works* 1:648. On the political orientation of "The Petition," see Melissa Schoenberger, *Cultivating Peace: The Virgilian Georgic in England, 1650–1750* (Lewisburg, PA: Bucknell University Press, 2019), 91–103.
38. The poem never specifies the grove as oak trees, but the *Works* editors quote antiquarian John Aubrey's *The Natural History and Antiquities of the County of Surrey*, which records the episode and affirms the species in question. See *Works* 1:532n87, lines 23–44. For analysis of the oak as an emblem for the royalist cause, see Chambers, *The Planters*, 37–38.
39. Wes Hamrick, "Trees in Anne Finch's Jacobite Poems of Retreat," *SEL Studies in English Literature 1500–1900* 53, no. 3 (Summer 2013): 549.
40. Drew, *The Usufructuary Ethos*, 84.
41. Addison, *The Spectator*.
42. Nicolle Jordan, "'Where Power Is Absolute': Royalist Politics and the Improved Landscape in a Poem by Anne Finch, Countess of Winchilsea," *The Eighteenth Century: Theory and Interpretation* 46, no. 3 (Fall 2005): 262.
43. David Burnett, *Longleat: The Story of an English Country House* (London: William Collins, 1978), 70.
44. McGovern, *Anne Finch*, 112. See also Laura Tallon, "Ekphrasis and Gender in Anne Finch's Longleat Poems," *Eighteenth-Century Life* 40, no. 1 (January 2016): 84–107.
45. Portions of this chapter previously appeared in "'Those Stately Palaces': Tribute and Estates in the Work of Anne Finch and Jane Barker," in *The Circuit of Apollo: Women's Tributes to*

Women in the Eighteenth Century, ed. Laura Runge and Jessica Cook (Newark: University of Delaware Press, 2019), 36–53.

46. McGovern, *Anne Finch*, 86.
47. *Oxford English Dictionary* definition 1.a., s.v. "landscape," accessed July 2, 2022.
48. According to Neus Ribas San Emeterio, some Catalonian textile experts refer to an Eastern flower as the Assyrian rose. See "Frederic Marès Deulovol, lace collector," *Datatèxtil* No. 23 (2010): 24.
49. Burnett, *Longleat*, 77.
50. According to Burnett, Weymouth "spent £30,000 (at least £200,000 in modern figures) on earth removal, planting and construction work of almost epic proportion." *Longleat*, 76.
51. Jonson, *Poems*, 79, lines 93–94.
52. Mary Louise Pratt, *Imperial Eyes: Travel Writing and Transculturation* (New York: Routledge, 1992), 201, 205–206.

CHAPTER 3 — "AND THE COUNTRY ADJACENT"

1. David Oakleaf, "At the Margins of Utopia: Jamaica in Sarah Scott's *Millenium Hall*," *Eighteenth-Century Fiction* 28, no. 1 (Fall 2015): 135; and Julie McGonegal, "The Tyranny of Gift Giving: The Politics of Generosity in Sarah Scott's *Millenium Hall* and *Sir George Ellison*," *Eighteenth-Century Fiction* 19, no. 3 (Spring 2007): 300, 305.
2. Robin Runia, "'Knights of Matrimony,' Christian Duty and *Millenium Hall*," in *After Marriage in the Long Eighteenth Century: Literature, Law and Society*, ed. Jenny DiPlacidi and Karl Leydecker (New York: Palgrave, 2018), 92. In a related reading, Judith Broome observes that "the women of Scott's model community sacrifice actual motherhood and sexuality in their quest for agency." *Fictive Domains: Body, Landscape, and Nostalgia, 1717–1770* (Lewisburg, PA: Bucknell University Press, 2007), 143.
3. Nanette Morton, "'A Most Sensible Oeconomy': From Spectacle to Surveillance in Sarah Scott's *Millenium Hall*," *Eighteenth-Century Fiction* 11, no. 2 (January 1999): 185–204.
4. Katherine Nolan, "Sarah Scott's Narrative 'No Place': Gazing and Utopia in *Millenium Hall*," *Eighteenth-Century Fiction* 33, no. 4 (Summer 2021): 520; Vincent Carretta, "Utopia Limited: Sarah Scott's *Millenium Hall* and *The History of Sir George Ellison*," *The Age of Johnson* 5 (1992): 309–311; Broome, *Fictive Domains*, 156.
5. Alison Conway, *Private Interests: Women, Portraiture, and the Visual Culture of the English Novel, 1709–1791* (Toronto: University of Toronto Press, 2001), 3. Janine Barchas offers a reading of *Millenium Hall*'s frontispiece that complements Conway's insights into visuality: "[The frontispiece] is a portrait, not because it offers an image of the ostensible gentleman narrator of the piece, but because it depicts the title 'character' of the novel, Millenium Hall." Yet, this reading ignores how the novel's visual dynamics develop more extensively in relation to the landscape than to the manor house. See "Prefiguring Genre: Frontispiece Portraits from *Gulliver's Travels* to *Millenium Hall*," *Studies in the Novel* 30, no. 2 (Summer 1998): 279.
6. Sarah Scott, *Millenium Hall*, ed. Gary Kelly (Peterborough, ON: Broadview Press, 1995), 59.
7. Lisa L. Moore, *Dangerous Intimacies: Toward a Sapphic History of the British Novel* (Durham, NC: Duke University Press, 1997), 22–48; Nolan, "Sarah Scott's Narrative," 513–529.
8. Gary Kelly, "Sarah Scott 1720–1795," in *Oxford Dictionary of National Biography*, ed. Colin Matthew, Brian Harrison, and Lawrence Goldman (Oxford: Oxford University Press, 2006), 469, accessed December 9, 2021.
9. Felicity Nussbaum, *The Limits of the Human: Fictions of Anomaly, Race, and Gender in the Long Eighteenth Century* (New York: Cambridge University Press, 2003), 118–119; and David Shuttleton, *Smallpox and the Literary Imagination, 1660–1820* (New York: Cambridge University Press, 2007), 135.

10. Kelly, "Sarah Scott," 469.
11. Nicole Pohl, "Sarah Scott, *Millenium Hall* (1762)," in *Handbook of the British Novel in the Long 18th Century*, ed. Katrin Berdt and Alessa Johns (Boston: De Gruyter 2022), 296.
12. Broome offers a provocative interpretation of visual agency in *Millenium Hall.* She observes its distinctive "relation to the fictive domains of body and landscape," reading the Hall women's self-enclosure in their estate as evidence of their ability "to assume the [typically male] invisibility of the unmarked category." *Fictive Domains*, 154.
13. Scott, *Millenium Hall*, 56.
14. Broome, *Fictive Domains*, 149.
15. The estate tour has prompted critics to explore the role of domestic tourism in Scott's novel. See for example Crystal B. Lake, "Redecorating the Ruin: Women and Antiquarianism in Sarah Scott's *Millenium Hall*," *ELH* 76, no. 3 (Fall 2009): 661–686.
16. Elizabeth Bohls, *Women Travel Writers and the Language of Aesthetics, 1716–1818* (New York: Cambridge University Press, 1995), 87.
17. Fabricant, "Binding and Dressing Nature's Loose Tresses," 148.
18. *Oxford English Dictionary*, s.v. "landscape," definition 1a, accessed November 1, 2021.
19. Gary Kelly, "Introduction," in *Millenium Hall* (Peterborough, ON: Broadview Press, 1997), 11.
20. Oakleaf, "At the Margins," 135.
21. *Oxford English Dictionary*, s.v. "entail, n.2."
22. Major, *Madam Britannia*, 156.
23. Scott, *Millenium Hall*, 243.
24. Sullivan, *The Drama*, 16.
25. Nicola Whyte, *Inhabiting the Landscape: Place, Custom, and Memory, 1500–1800* (Barnsley, UK: Oxbow Books, 2009), 93.
26. Karen Gevirtz, *Life after Death: Widows and the English Novel, Defoe to Austen* (Newark: University of Delaware Press, 2005), 105–106.
27. Felicity Nussbaum, *Torrid Zones*, 135.
28. Nicolle Jordan, "Gentlemen and Gentle Women: The Landscape Ethos in *Millenium Hall*," *Eighteenth-Century Fiction* 24, no. 1 (Fall 2011): 31–54.
29. Sullivan, *The Drama*, 10.
30. London, *Women and Property*, 118, 121.
31. Scott, *Millenium Hall*, 110.
32. For a similar argument, see Dorice Williams Elliott, "Sarah Scott's *Millenium Hall* and Female Philanthropy," *SEL: Studies in English Literature, 1500–1900* 35, no. 3 (June 1995): 545.
33. For a complementary interpretation of how *Millenium Hall* is riven by paradox, see Moore, *Dangerous Intimacies*, 44.
34. McGonegal, "The Tyranny," 302. She quotes Raymond Williams, *The Country and the City* (New York: Oxford University Press, 1973), 59.
35. McGonegal, "The Tyranny," 292.
36. The novel uses inconsistent honorifics when referring to the character in question. It often uses "Miss Mancel" when recounting her past and "Mrs. Mancel" when describing her in the present; yet, this pattern is not entirely consistent.
37. Jennie Batchelor, "Fictions of the Gift in Sarah Scott's *Millenium Hall*," in *The Culture of the Gift in Eighteenth-Century England*, ed. Linda Zionkowski and Cynthia Klekar (New York: Palgrave Macmillan, 2009), 168.
38. Batchelor, "Fictions of the Gift," 167.
39. Batchelor, "Fictions of the Gift," 168.
40. See for example G. J. Barker-Benfield, *The Culture of Sensibility: Sex and Society in Eighteenth-Century Britain* (Chicago: University of Chicago Press, 1992).

41. McGonegal, "The Tyranny," 297.
42. McGonegal, "The Tyranny," 291.
43. McGonegal, "The Tyranny," 300–301.
44. McGonegal, "The Tyranny," 301.
45. Sullivan, *The Drama*, 27.
46. Alistair Fowler, *The Country House Poem: A Cabinet of Seventeenth-Century Estate Poems and Related Items* (Edinburgh: Edinburgh University Press, 1994), 21.
47. Nicole Pohl makes a similar point; see "'Sweet place, where virtue then did rest': The Appropriation of the Country-House Ethos in Sarah Scott's *Millenium Hall*," *Utopian Studies* 7, no. 1 (1996): 56.
48. Bellamy and Williamson, *Property and Landscape*, 124.
49. Barker, *A Patch-Work Screen*, 73.
50. Alexander Pope, "Epistle to Burlington," in *The Poems of Alexander Pope*, ed. John Butt (New Haven, CT: Yale University Press, 1963), 586–596, line 179.
51. Pope, "Epistle to Burlington," line 57.
52. Williamson, *Polite Landscapes*, 113.
53. Stephen Bending, "Mrs. Montagu's Contemplative Bench: Bluestocking Gardens and Female Retirement," *Huntington Library Quarterly* 69, no. 4 (December 2006): 577.
54. Lisa L. Moore, *Sister Arts*, 68–73; and Linda Dunne, "Mothers and Monsters in Sarah Robinson Scott's *Millenium Hall*," in *Utopian and Science Fiction by Women: Worlds of Difference*, ed. Carol Kolmerten (Syracuse, NY: Syracuse University Press, 1994), 57–58.
55. Williamson and Bellamy, *Property and Landscape*, 150–151.
56. James Thompson, *Models of Value: Eighteenth-Century Political Economy and the Novel* (Durham, NC: Duke University Press, 1996), 60.
57. Thompson, *Models of Value*, 71.

CHAPTER 4 — ELIZABETH MONTAGU, BLUESTOCKING LANDSCAPER

1. Betty Schellenberg, *Literary Coteries and the Making of Modern Print Culture* (New York: Cambridge University Press, 2016), 153–180.
2. Schellenberg, *Literary Coteries*, 96.
3. Nicole Pohl et al., *Elizabeth Montagu Correspondence Online*, https://emco.swansea.ac.uk/project/about/, accessed April 21, 2023.
4. Elizabeth Eger, "Elizabeth Montagu Biography," *Elizabeth Montagu Correspondence Online*, https://emco.swansea.ac.uk/montagu/bio/, accessed April 21, 2023.
5. Elizabeth Montagu, unpublished letter to Sarah Scott, December 26, 1767, MO 5871, Huntington Library, San Marino.
6. Pohl, "Introduction: 'The Commerce of Life': Elizabeth Montagu (1718–1800)," *Huntington Library Quarterly* 81, no. 4 (Winter 2018): 446. See also Major, *Madam Britannia*, 75.
7. Elizabeth Montagu, unpublished letter to Elizabeth Carter, June 27, 1766, MO 3174, Huntington Library, San Marino. I have deliberately retained Montagu's spelling and capitalization throughout the chapter.
8. Les Turnbull, "Elizabeth Montagu: 'A Critick, a Coal Owner, a Land Steward, a Sociable Creature,'" *Huntington Library Quarterly* 18, no. 4 (Winter 2018): 669.
9. On Edward Montagu's bequest, see J. V. Beckett, "Elizabeth Montagu: Bluestocking Turned Landlady," *Huntington Library Quarterly* 49, no. 2 (Spring 1986): 150, 159.
10. McDonagh, *Elite Women*, 139.
11. Rizzo, "Two Versions of Community," 194–195.
12. McDonagh, *Elite Women*, 26. See also Rita J. Dashwood and Karen Lipsedge, "Women and Property in the Long Eighteenth Century," *Journal for Eighteenth-Century Studies* 44, no. 4 (2021): 335–341.

13. W. Powell Jones, "The Romantic Bluestocking, Elizabeth Montagu," *Huntington Library Quarterly* 12, no. 1 (November 1948): 85–98; Ian Ross, "A Bluestocking over the Border: Mrs. Montagu's Aesthetic Adventures in Scotland, 1766," *Huntington Library Quarterly* 28, no. 3 (May 1965): 213–233.
14. Emma Major, "Femininity and National Identity: Elizabeth Montagu's Trip To France," *ELH* 72, no. 4 (Winter 2005): 910.
15. Stephen Bending, "Mrs. Montagu's Contemplative Bench," 555–580; and *Green Retreats*, 135–172.
16. McDonagh, *Elite Women*, 91.
17. Elizabeth Child, "Elizabeth Montagu, Bluestocking Businesswoman," *Huntington Library Quarterly* 65, no. 1/2 (May 2002): 165.
18. Turnbull, "Elizabeth Montagu," 673. He quotes an unpublished letter from Montagu to Sarah Scott, December 26, 1767, MO 5871, Huntington Library, San Marino.
19. Turnbull, "Elizabeth Montagu," 672.
20. Turnbull, "Elizabeth Montagu," 683.
21. Nicole Pohl, "General Introduction from the Editor-in-Chief," *Elizabeth Montagu Correspondence Online*, https://emco.swansea.ac.uk/edition/introduction/, accessed October 7, 2023.
22. Elizabeth Montagu, unpublished letter to Elizabeth Carter, July 28, 1766, MO 3178, Huntington Library, San Marino.
23. Child, "Elizabeth Montagu," 168.
24. "The Bookshelf," *The Elizabeth Montagu Correspondence Online*, http://emco.swansea.ac.uk/emco/works, accessed April 23, 2023.
25. Stephen Bending, "Literature and Landscape in the Eighteenth Century," in *Oxford Handbook Topics in Literature* (Oxford Academic Edition, 2015), 3, https://doi.org/10.1093/oxfordhb/9780199935338.013.133.
26. Montagu in *Bluestocking Feminism*, 1:146. Eger identifies Arthur's as "an exclusive gentleman's club in London," 222. She has not regularized Montagu's spelling or punctuation.
27. Montagu in *Bluestocking Feminism*, 1:146.
28. Major, *Madam Britannia*, 158–159.
29. Lawrence Stone and Jeanne C. Fawtier Stone, *An Open Élite? England 1540–1880* (Oxford: Clarendon Press, 1984).
30. Paul Langford, *Public Life and the Propertied English Gentleman, 1689–1798* (New York: Oxford University Press, 1991), 59, 61.
31. Elizabeth Montagu, unpublished letter to Elizabeth Vesey, September 27, 1783, MO 6579, Huntington Library, San Marino.
32. Child makes a similar point; see "Elizabeth Montagu," 159.
33. Elizabeth Montagu, unpublished letter to George, Lord Lyttelton, July 23, 1766, MO 1445, Huntington Library, San Marino.
34. Major, *Madam Britannia*, 76.
35. See for example "Part II: Consuming Arts" in *Women, Writing, and the Public Sphere, 1700–1830*, ed. Elizabeth Eger et. al. (Cambridge: Cambridge University Press, 2001), 75–162.
36. Elizabeth Montagu, unpublished letter to Elizabeth Carter, June 27, 1766, MO 3174, Huntington Library, San Marino.
37. On Montagu in relation to urban sociability, consumption, and the public sphere, see for example Elizabeth Eger, *Bluestockings: Women of Reason from Enlightenment to Romanticism* (New York: Palgrave Macmillan, 2010); and Sylvia Harcstark Myers, *The Bluestocking Circle: Women, Friendship, and the Life of the Mind in Eighteenth-Century England* (New York: Oxford University Press, 1990).
38. Eger, *Bluestockings*, 62.
39. See also Eger, *Bluestockings Displayed: Portraiture, Performance, and Patronage, 1730–1830* (New York: Cambridge University Press, 2013).
40. Bending, *Green Retreats*, 145.

41. Emily J. Climenson, ed., *Elizabeth Montagu: The Queen of the Bluestockings* (London: John Murray, 1906), 1.149–50.
42. Matthew Montagu, ed., *The Letters of Mrs. Elizabeth Montagu: With Some of the Letters of Her Correspondents, Part the Second* (London: T. Cadell and W. Davies, 1809–1813), 118–119.
43. Bridget Hill, "The Course of the Marriage of Elizabeth Montagu: An Ambitious and Talented Woman Without Means," *Journal of Family History* 26, no. 1 (January 2001): 3–17.
44. Barbara Brandon Schnorrenberg, "Elizabeth Montagu," in *The Oxford Dictionary of National Biography*, ed. Colin Matthew, Brian Harrison, and Lawrence Goldman (Oxford: Oxford University Press, 2004–13), accessed October 4, 2014.
45. Climenson, *Elizabeth Montagu*, 2:294–2:295.
46. Bending, *Green Retreats*, 139, 141.
47. Bending, *Green Retreats*, 143, 144.
48. Bending, *Green Retreats*, 144, 145.
49. Bending, *Green Retreats*, 144.
50. Blunt, *Mrs. Montagu*, 2:119–2:120.
51. Romantic writers like Byron, Coleridge, and Hazlitt heaped contempt upon the Bluestockings; see Eger, *Bluestockings*, 206–207.
52. Richard Wendorf and Charles Ryskamp, "A Blue-Stocking Friendship: The Letters of Elizabeth Montagu and Frances Reynolds in the Princeton Collection," *Princeton University Library Chronicle* 41, no. 3 (Spring 1980): 197.
53. Rosemary Baird, *Mistress of the House: Great Ladies and Grand Houses 1670–1830* (London: Phoenix, 2003), 214.
54. For details about Woodhouse's partial publication of this text, see William Christmas, *The Lab'ring Muses: Work, Writing, and the Social Order in English Plebeian Poetry, 1730–1830* (Newark: University of Delaware Press, 2001), 183–210.
55. Quoted in Eger, *Bluestockings*, 110.
56. *The Life and Poetical Works of James Woodhouse (1735–1820)*, ed. R. I. Woodhouse (London: Leadenhall Press, 1896), 1.166.
57. Linda J. Van Netten Blimke, "'The Tranquility of a Society of Females': Mary Morgan's *A Tour to Milford Haven*, Elizabeth Montagu, and the Transformative Politics of Female Governance," *ABO: Interactive Journal for Women in the Arts, 1640–1830* 9, no. 2 (Fall 2019): 8–10.
58. Harriet Guest, "Bluestocking Feminism," in *Reconsidering the Bluestockings*, ed. Nicole Pohl and Betty A. Schellenberg (San Marino, CA: Huntington Library, 2003), 64. Emphasis in original.
59. Steve Hindle, "Representing Rural Society: Labor, Leisure, and the Landscape in an Eighteenth-Century Conversation Piece," *Critical Inquiry* 41, no. 3 (Spring 2015): 646.
60. Elizabeth Montagu, unpublished letter to Leonard Smelt, November 15, 1776, MO 5012, Huntington Library, San Marino.
61. Peter Denney, "'Unpleasant, tho' Arcadian Spots': Plebeian Poetry, Polite Culture, and the Sentimental Economy of the Landscape Park," *Criticism* 47, no. 4 (Fall 2005): 503.
62. Denney, "'Unpleasant, tho' Arcadian Spots,'" 509.
63. Adam Bridgen, "A World of Fire and Drought': Ecosocialism, Improvement, and Apocalypse in James Woodhouse's *Crispinus Scriblerus*," *Romantic Environmental Sensibility: Nature, Class, and Empire*, ed. Ve-Yin Tee (Edinburgh: Edinburgh University Press, 2022), 182. He quotes Denney's "'Unpleasant, tho' Arcadian Spots.'"
64. Elizabeth Montagu, unpublished letter to Elizabeth Carter, October 25, 1776, MO 3406, Huntington Library, San Marino.
65. Woodhouse, quoted in Christmas, *The Lab'ring Muses*, 201.
66. Christmas, *The Lab'ring Muses*, 184.

67. Stephen Bending, "Negotiating Men: Elizabeth Montagu, 'Capability' Brown, and the Construction of Pastoral," in *Women and the Land, 1500–1900*, ed. Amanda L. Capern, Briony McDonagh, and Jennifer Aston (Martlesham, England: Boydell Press, 2019), 186.
68. Bending, "Negotiating Men," 185.
69. Bending, "Negotiating Men," 195.

CONCLUSION

1. Rebecca Bushnell, *Green Desire: Imagining Early Modern English Gardens* (Ithaca, NY: Cornell University Press, 2003), 131.
2. Virginia Woolf, *Orlando: A Biography* (New York: Harcourt, 2006), 14–15.
3. Turner, *The Politics of Landscape*.
4. Maria DiBattista, "Notes to *Orlando: A Biography*," in *Orlando*, general ed. Mark Hussey (New York: Harcourt, 2006), 258.
5. For lime trees see Barker, *A Patch-Work Screen*, 73; and for an ash tree see Barker, *Bosvil and Galesia*, 14.
6. On racial and ethnic difference in the novel, see Julie Vandivere, "The Bastard's Contention: Race, Property, and Sexuality in Virginia Woolf's *Orlando*," *Modernism/modernity* 28, no. 1 (January 2021): 91–116, https://doi.org/10.1353/mod.2021.0012.

BIBLIOGRAPHY

Addison, Joseph. *The Spectator* 2, no. 414 (1712), accessed May 30, 2020, https://www.gutenberg.org/cache/epub/12030/pg12030-images.html.

Anderson, Misty. "Tactile Places: Materializing Desire in Margaret Cavendish and Jane Barker." *Textual Practice* 13, no. 2 (1999): 329–352.

Andrews, Malcolm. *Landscape and Western Art.* Oxford: Oxford University Press, 1999.

Backscheider, Paula. *Women Poets and Their Poetry: Inventing Agency, Inventing Genre.* Baltimore, MD: Johns Hopkins University Press, 2005.

Baird, Rosemary. *Mistress of the House: Great Ladies and Grand Houses 1670–1830.* London: Phoenix, 2003.

Barash, Carol. *English Women's Poetry, 1649–1714: Politics, Community, and Linguistic Authority.* New York: Oxford University Press, 1996.

Barchas, Janine. "Prefiguring Genre: Frontispiece Portraits from *Gulliver's Travels* to *Millenium Hall.*" *Studies in the Novel* 30, no. 2 (Summer 1998): 260–286.

Barker-Benfield, G. J. *The Culture of Sensibility: Sex and Society in Eighteenth-Century Britain.* Chicago: University of Chicago Press, 1992.

Barker, Jane. *The Galesia Trilogy*, edited by Carol Shiner Wilson. New York: Oxford University Press, 1997.

Barrell, John. *The Birth of Pandora and the Division of Knowledge.* Philadelphia: University of Pennsylvania Press, 1992.

Batchelor, Jennie. "Fictions of the Gift in Sarah Scott's *Millenium Hall.*" In *The Culture of the Gift in Eighteenth-Century England*, edited by Linda Zionkowski and Cynthia Klekar, 159–175. New York: Palgrave Macmillan, 2009.

Beckett, J. V. "Elizabeth Montagu: Bluestocking Turned Landlady." *Huntington Library Quarterly* 49, no. 2 (Spring 1986): 149–164.

Bending, Stephen. *Green Retreats: Women, Gardens, and Eighteenth-Century Culture.* New York: Cambridge University Press, 2013.

———. "Literature and Landscape in the Eighteenth Century." *Oxford Handbook Topics in Literature.* Oxford Academic, 2015. https://doi.org/10.1093/oxfordhb/9780199935338.013.133.

———. "Mrs. Montagu's Contemplative Bench: Bluestocking Gardens and Female Retirement." *The Huntington Library Quarterly* 69, no. 4 (December 2006): 555–580.

———. "Negotiating Men: Elizabeth Montagu, 'Capability' Brown, and the Construction of Pastoral." In *Women and the Land, 1500–1900*, edited by Amanda L. Capern, Briony McDonagh, and Jennifer Aston, 176–200. Martlesham, England: Boydell Press, 2019.

Berry, Geoff. "Modernism, Climate Change, and Dystopia: An Ecocritical Reading of Light Symbology in Conrad's *Heart of Darkness* and Eliot's *The Waste Land.*" *COLLOQUY: Text Theory Critique* 21 (2011): 81–100.

Blimke, Linda J. Van Netten. "'The Tranquility of a Society of Females': Mary Morgan's *A Tour to Milford Haven*, Elizabeth Montagu, and the Transformative Politics of Female Governance." *ABO: Interactive Journal for Women in the Arts, 1640–1830* 9, no. 2 (Fall 2019): 3–27.

Blunt, Reginald, ed. *Mrs. Montagu, "Queen of the Blues": Her Letters and Friendships.* 2 vols. New York: Houghton Mifflin, 1923.

Boettcher, Carolin. "Cooking Up Knowledge: Materiality, Recipes, and Jane Barker's *A Patch-Work Screen for the Ladies*." *ABO: Interactive Journal for Women in the Arts, 1640–1830* 12, no. 2 (Winter 2022): 1–17. https://digitalcommons.usf.edu/abo/vol12/iss2/4.

Bohls, Elizabeth. *Women Travel Writers and the Language of Aesthetics, 1716–1818*. New York: Cambridge University Press, 1995.

Bridgen, Adam J. "A World of Fire and Drought': Ecosocialism, Improvement, and Apocalypse in James Woodhouse's *Crispinus Scriblerus*." In *Romantic Environmental Sensibility: Nature, Class, and Empire*, edited by Ve-Yin Tee, 172–194. Edinburgh: Edinburgh University Press, 2022.

Brook, Isis. "Aesthetic Appreciation of Landscape." In *The Routledge Companion to Landscape Studies*, edited by Peter Howard, Ian Thompson, Emma Waterton, and Mick Atha, 2nd ed., 39–50. New York: Routledge, 2019.

Broome, Judith. *Fictive Domains: Body, Landscape, and Nostalgia, 1717–1770*. Lewisburg, PA: Bucknell University Press, 2007.

Burnett, David. *Longleat: The Story of an English Country House*. London: William Collins, 1978.

Bushnell, Rebecca. *Green Desire: Imagining Early Modern English Gardens*. Ithaca, NY: Cornell University Press, 2003.

Cahill, Samara Anne. "'Novel Modes' and 'Indian Goods': Textilic Nationalism in *A Patch-Work Screen for the Ladies* and *The Lining of the Patch Work Screen*." *Studies in Eighteenth-Century Culture* 44 (2015): 163–184.

———. "Realist Latitudes: Textilic Nationalism and the Global Fiction of the 1720s." *Digital Defoe: Studies in Defoe & His Contemporaries* 7, no. 1 (Fall 2015). http://digitaldefoe.org/2015/10/28/realist-latitudes-textilic-nationalism-and-the-global-fiction-of-the-1720s/.

Carretta, Vincent. "Utopia Limited: Sarah Scott's *Millenium Hall* and *The History of Sir George Ellison*." *The Age of Johnson* 5 (1992): 303–325.

Casey, Jim. "'Equall Freedome, Equall Fare': The Illusion of Egalitarianism in the Country House Poem." *Early English Studies* 3 (2010): 1–29.

Chalus, Elaine. *Elite Women in English Political Life, c. 1754–1790*. New York: Oxford University Press, 2005.

Chambers, Douglas. *The Planters of the English Landscape Garden: Botany, Trees, and the Georgics*. New Haven, CT: Yale University Press, 1993.

Child, Elizabeth. "Elizabeth Montagu, Bluestocking Businesswoman." In *Reconsidering the Bluestockings*, edited by Nicole Pohl and Betty A. Schellenberg, 153–173. San Marino, CA: The Huntington Library, 2003.

Christmas, William. *The Lab'ring Muses: Work, Writing, and the Social Order in English Plebeian Poetry, 1730–1830*. Newark: University of Delaware Press, 2001.

Climenson, Emily J., ed. *Elizabeth Montagu: The Queen of the Bluestockings*. 2 vols. London: John Murray, 1906.

Conway, Alison. *Private Interests: Women, Portraiture, and the Visual Culture of the English Novel, 1709–1791*. Toronto: University of Toronto Press, 2001.

Cosgrove, Denis. *Social Formation and Symbolic Landscape*. Madison: University of Wisconsin Press, 1984.

Crawford, Patricia, "Women and Property: Women as Property." *Parergon* 19, no. 1 (January 2002): 151–171.

Daniels, Stephen. "Marxism, Culture, and the Duplicity of Landscape." In *New Models in Geography: The Political-Economy Perspective*, edited by Richard Peet and N. J. Thrift, 196–220. London: Unwin Hyman, 1989.

Dashwood, Rita J., and Karen Lipsedge. "Women and Property in the Long Eighteenth Century." *Journal for Eighteenth-Century Studies* 44, no. 4 (2021): 335–341.

Denney, Peter. "'Unpleasant, tho' Arcadian Spots': Plebeian Poetry, Polite Culture, and the Sentimental Economy of the Landscape Park." *Criticism* 47, no. 4 (Fall 2005): 493–514.

DiBattista, Maria. "Notes to *Orlando: A Biography*." In *Orlando*, edited by Mark Hussey, 247–310. New York: Harcourt, 2006.

Digital Humanities Team at Swansea University. *Elizabeth Montagu Correspondence Online.* Accessed April 21, 2023. https://emco.swansea.ac.uk/project/about/.

Donovan, Josephine. "Women and the Rise of the Novel: A Feminist-Marxist Theory." *Signs* 16, no. 3 (Spring 1991): 441–462.

Drew, Erin. *The Usufructuary Ethos: Power, Politics, and Environment in the Long Eighteenth Century.* Charlottesville: University of Virginia Press, 2021.

Dubrow, Heather. "The Politics of Aesthetics: Recuperating Formalism and the Country House Poem." In *Renaissance Literature and Its Engagements with Form*, edited by Mark David Rasmussen, 67–88. New York: Palgrave, 1994.

Dunne, Linda. "Mothers and Monsters in Sarah Robinson Scott's *Millenium Hall.*" In *Utopian and Science Fiction by Women: Worlds of Difference*, edited by Carol Kolmerten, 54–72. Syracuse, NY: Syracuse University Press, 1994.

Eger, Elizabeth. *Bluestockings: Women of Reason from Enlightenment to Romanticism.* New York: Palgrave Macmillan, 2010.

———. *Bluestockings Displayed: Portraiture, Performance, and Patronage, 1730–1830.* New York: Cambridge University Press, 2013.

Eger, Elizabeth, ed. *Bluestocking Feminism: Writings of the Bluestocking Circle, 1738–1791.* Vol. 1. London: Pickering & Chatto, 1999.

———. "Elizabeth Montagu Biography," *Elizabeth Montagu Correspondence Online.* Accessed April 21, 2023. https://emco.swansea.ac.uk/montagu/bio/.

Eger, Elizabeth, Charlotte Grant, and Clíona Ó Gallchoir, eds. *Women, Writing, and the Public Sphere, 1700–1830.* Cambridge: Cambridge University Press, 2001.

Eicke, Leigh. "Jane Barker's Jacobite Writings." In *Women's Writing and the Circulation of Ideas: Manuscript Publication in England, 1550–1800*, edited by George L. Justice and Nathan Tinker, 137–157. New York: Cambridge University Press, 2002.

Elliott, Dorice Williams. "Sarah Scott's *Millenium Hall* and Female Philanthropy." *SEL: Studies in English Literature, 1500–1900* 35, no. 3 (June 1995): 535–553.

Everett, Nigel. *The Tory View of Landscape.* New Haven, CT: Yale University Press, 1994.

Ezell, Margaret. "From Manuscript to Print: A Volume of Their Own?" In *Women and Poetry, 1660–1750*, edited by Sarah Prescott and David E. Shuttleton, 140–160. New York: Palgrave, 2003.

Fabricant, Carole. "Binding and Dressing Nature's Loose Tresses: The Ideology of Augustan Landscape Design." *Studies in Eighteenth-Century Culture* 8 (1979): 109–135.

Fowler, Alistair. *The Country House Poem: A Cabinet of Seventeenth-Century Estate Poems and Related Items.* Edinburgh: Edinburgh University Press, 1994.

Gavin, Michael. "Critics and Criticism in the Poetry of Anne Finch." *English Literary History* 78, no. 3 (Fall 2011): 633–655.

———. *The Invention of English Criticism 1650–1760.* New York: Cambridge University Press, 2015.

Gerrard, Christine. "Poetry, Politics, and the Rise of Party." In *A Companion to Eighteenth-Century Poetry*, edited by Christine Gerrard, 7–22. Malden, MA: Blackwell, 2006.

Gevirtz, Karen. *Life after Death: Widows and the English Novel, Defoe to Austen.* Newark: University of Delaware Press, 2005.

———. "Recent Developments in 17th and 18th-Century English Catholic Studies." *Literature Compass* 12/2 (2015): 47–58.

———. *Women, the Novel, and Natural Philosophy, 1660–1727.* New York: Palgrave Macmillan, 2014.

Girouard, Mark. *Life in the English Country House: A Social and Architectural History.* New Haven, CT: Yale University Press, 1994.

Griffiths, Liz. Review of *Elite Women and the Agricultural Landscape, 1700–1830,* by Briony McDonagh. *Agricultural History Review* 66, no. 1 (2018): 157–158.

Guest, Harriet. "Bluestocking Feminism." In *Reconsidering the Bluestockings*, edited by Nicole Pohl and Betty A. Schellenberg, 58–80. San Marino, CA: Huntington Library, 2003.

———. *Small Change: Women, Learning, Patriotism, 1750–1810*. Chicago: University of Chicago Press, 2000.

Hamrick, Wes. "Trees in Anne Finch's Jacobite Poems of Retreat." *SEL Studies in English Literature 1500–1900* 53, no. 3 (Summer 2013): 541–563.

Heal, Felicity. "The Crown, the Gentry, and London: The Enforcement of Proclamation, 1596–1640." In *Law and Government under the Tudors*, edited by Claire Cross, David Loades, and J. J. Scarisbrick, 211–226. New York: Cambridge University Press, 1988.

Hill, Bridget. "The Course of the Marriage of Elizabeth Montagu: An Ambitious and Talented Woman Without Means." *Journal of Family History* 26, no. 1 (January 2001): 3–17.

———. *Eighteenth-Century Women: An Anthology*. New York: Routledge, 1984.

———. "A Tale of Two Sisters: The Contrasting Careers and Ambitions of Elizabeth Montagu and Sarah Scott." *Women's History Review* 19, no. 2 (April 2010): 215–229.

———. *Women, Work, and Sexual Politics in Eighteenth-Century England*. Oxford: Basil Blackwell Press, 1989.

———. "Women's History: A Study in Change, Continuity, or Standing Still?" In *Women's Work: The English Experience 1650–1914*, edited by Pamela Sharpe, 42–58. New York: Oxford University Press, 1998.

Hindle, Steve. "Representing Rural Society: Labor, Leisure, and the Landscape in an Eighteenth-Century Conversation Piece." *Critical Inquiry* 41, no. 3 (Spring 2015): 615–654.

Jones, W. Powell. "The Romantic Bluestocking, Elizabeth Montagu." *Huntington Library Quarterly* 12, no. 1 (November 1948): 85–98.

Jonson, Ben. *The Poems of Ben Jonson*. Edited by George Burke Johnston. Cambridge, MA: Harvard University Press, 1962.

Jordan, Nicolle. "Anne Finch and the Fallen Country House." In *The Intellectual Culture of the English Country House*, edited by Matthew Dimmock, Andrew Hadfield, and Margaret Healy, 129–145. Manchester: Manchester University Press, 2015.

———. "Gentlemen and Gentle Women: The Landscape Ethos in *Millenium Hall*." *Eighteenth-Century Fiction* 24, no. 1 (Fall 2011): 31–54.

———. "'Those Stately Palaces': Tribute and Estates in the Work of Anne Finch and Jane Barker." In *The Circuit of Apollo: Women's Tributes to Women in the Eighteenth Century*, edited by Laura Runge and Jessica Cook, 36–53. Newark: University of Delaware Press, 2019.

———. "'Where Power Is Absolute': Royalist Politics and the Improved Landscape in a Poem by Anne Finch, Countess of Winchilsea." *Eighteenth Century: Theory and Interpretation* 46, no. 3 (Fall 2005): 255–275.

Joule, Victoria. "'She Did But Take Up Old Stories': Generic Fluidity and Women's Life-Writing of the Early Eighteenth Century." *Bulletin of the John Rylands University Library of Manchester* 90, no. 2 (September 2014): 47–66.

Kairoff, Claudia, and Jennifer Keith, eds. *The Cambridge Edition of the Works of Anne Finch, Countess of Winchilsea*. 2 vols. New York: Cambridge University Press, 2019–2021.

Kairoff, Claudia, Jennifer Keith, and Jean Marsden. "General Introduction." *The Cambridge Edition of the Works of Anne Finch, Countess of Winchilsea*, 1: xvii–cxii. New York: Cambridge University Press, 2019.

Keegan, Bridget, and Libby Hallgren Hoxmeier, eds. "Jane Barker's Catholic Poems: An Edition of 'Poems Refering to the Times' from the Magdalen Manuscript, Part One." *Tulsa Studies in Women's Literature* 31, no. 1/2 (Spring/Fall 2012): 181–228.

Keith, Jennifer, "Anne Finch in the Twenty-First Century: Finding the Artist in History." *Literature Compass* (2018), 1–11. doi.org/10.1111/lic3.12441.

———. *Poetry and the Feminine from Behn to Cowper*. Newark: University of Delaware Press, 2005.

———. "The Reach of Translation in the Works of Anne Finch." *Philological Quarterly* 95, no. 3/4 (June 2016): 467–493.

Kelly, Gary. "Introduction: Sarah Scott, Bluestocking Feminism, and *Millenium Hall*." In *Millenium Hall*, edited by Gary Kelly, 11–43. Peterborough, ON: Broadview Press, 1997.

———. "Sarah Scott (1720–1795)." In *Oxford Dictionary of National Biography*, edited by Colin Matthew, Brian Harrison, and Lawrence Goldman. Oxford: Oxford University Press, 2006. Accessed December 9, 2021.

King, Kathryn. "Constructions of Femininity." In *A Companion to Eighteenth-Century Poetry*, edited by Christine Gerrard, 431–443. Malden, MA: Wiley-Blackwell, 2006.

———. "Cowley Among the Women; or, Poetry in the Contact Zone." In *Women and Literary History*, edited by Katherine Binhammer and Jeanne Wood, 43–63. Newark: University of Delaware Press, 2003.

———. "Genre Crossings." In *The Cambridge Companion to Women's Writing in Britain, 1660–1789*, edited by Catherine Ingrassia, 86–100. New York: Cambridge University Press, 2015.

———. *Jane Barker, Exile: A Literary Career 1675–1725*. New York: Oxford University Press, 2000.

———. "Of Needles and Pins and Women's Work." *Tulsa Studies in Women's Literature* 14, no. 1 (Spring, 1995): 77–93.

———. "The Unaccountable Wife and Other Tales of Female Desire in Jane Barker's *A Patchwork Screen for the Ladies*." *Eighteenth Century: Theory and Interpretation* 35, no. 2 (Summer 1994): 155–172.

King, Kathryn, and Jeslyn Medoff. "Jane Barker and Her Life (1652–1732): The Documentary Record." *Eighteenth-Century Life* 21, no 3 (November 1997): 16–38.

Labbe, Jacqueline. *Romantic Visualities: Landscape, Gender, and Romanticism*. New York: St. Martin's Press, 1998.

Lacroix, Constance. "Wicked Traders, Deserving Peddlers, and Virtuous Smugglers: The Counter-Economy of Jane Barker's Jacobite Novel." *Eighteenth-Century Fiction* 23, no. 2 (Winter 2011–2012): 269–294.

Lake, Crystal B. "Redecorating the Ruin: Women and Antiquarianism in Sarah Scott's *Millenium Hall*." *ELH* 76, no. 3 (Fall 2009): 661–686.

Langford, Paul. *Public Life and the Propertied English Gentleman, 1689–1798*. New York: Oxford University Press, 1991.

Lewis, Judith S. *Sacred to Female Patriotism: Gender, Class, and Politics in Late Georgian Britain*. New York: Routledge, 2003.

London, April. *Women and Property in the Eighteenth-Century English Novel*. Cambridge: Cambridge University Press, 1999.

Major, Emma. "Femininity and National Identity: Elizabeth Montagu's Trip To France." *ELH* 72, no. 4 (Winter 2005): 901–918.

———. *Madam Britannia: Women, Church, and Nation, 1712–1812*. New York: Oxford University Press, 2012.

Mann, Rachel. "Jane Barker, Manuscript Culture, and the Epistemology of the Microscope." *Eighteenth-Century Life* 43, no. 1 (January 2019): 50–75.

McArthur, Tonya Moutray. "Jane Barker and the Politics of Catholic Celibacy." *SEL: Studies in English Literature* 47, no. 3 (Summer 2007): 595–618.

McBurney, William. "Edmund Curll, Mrs. Jane Barker, and the English Novel." *Philological Quarterly* 37, no. 4 (1958): 385–399.

McDonagh, Briony. *Elite Women and the Agricultural Landscape, 1700–1830*. New York: Routledge, 2018.

McGonegal, Julie. "The Tyranny of Gift Giving: The Politics of Generosity in Sarah Scott's *Millenium Hall* and *Sir George Ellison*." *Eighteenth-Century Fiction* 19, no. 3 (Spring 2007): 291–306.

McGovern, Barbara. *Anne Finch and Her Poetry: A Critical Biography*. Athens: University of Georgia Press, 1992.

McGrath, Alice Tweedy. "Unaccountable Form: Queer Failure and Jane Barker's Patchwork Method." *Eighteenth Century: Theory and Interpretation* 60, no. 4 (Winter 2019): 353–373.

Meek, Heather. "Jane Barker, Medical Discourse, and the Origins of the Novel." In *Literature and Medicine*. Vol. 1, *The Eighteenth Century*, edited by Clark Lawlor and Andrew Mangham, 51–69. New York: Cambridge University Press, 2021.

Mitchell, W.J.T. "Imperial Landscape." In *Landscape and Power*, edited by W.J.T. Mitchell, 5–34. Chicago: University of Chicago Press, 1994.

Molesworth, Charles. "Property and Virtue: The Country-House Poem of the Seventeenth Century." *Genre* 1 (1968): 141–157.

Montagu, Elizabeth (Robinson). Correspondence. Huntington Library, San Marino, CA.

Montagu, Matthew, ed. *The Letters of Mrs. Elizabeth Montagu: With Some of the Letters of Her Correspondents*, Part the First and Part the Second. London: T. Cadell and W. Davies, 1809–1813.

Moore, Lisa L. *Dangerous Intimacies: Toward a Sapphic History of the British Novel*. Durham, NC: Duke University Press, 1997.

———. *Sister Arts: The Erotics of Lesbian Landscapes*. Minneapolis: University of Minnesota Press, 2011.

Morton, Nanette. "'A Most Sensible Oeconomy': From Spectacle to Surveillance in Sarah Scott's *Millenium Hall*." *Eighteenth-Century Fiction* 11, no. 2 (January 1999): 185–204.

Mowl, Timothy. *Gentlemen and Players: Gardeners of the English Landscape*. Stroud, Gloucestershire: The History Press, 2000.

Myers, Joanne. "Jane Barker's Conversion and the Forms of Religious Experience." *Eighteenth-Century Fiction* 30, no. 3 (Spring 2018): 369–393.

Myers, Sylvia Harcstark. *The Bluestocking Circle: Women, Friendship, and the Life of the Mind in Eighteenth-Century England*. New York: Oxford University Press, 1990.

Nolan, Katherine. "Sarah Scott's Narrative 'No Place': Gazing and Utopia in *Millenium Hall*." *Eighteenth-Century Fiction* 33, no. 4 (Summer 2021): 513–529.

Nussbaum, Felicity. *The Limits of the Human: Fictions of Anomaly, Race, and Gender in the Long Eighteenth Century*. New York: Cambridge University Press, 2003.

———. *Torrid Zones: Maternity, Sexuality, and Empire in Eighteenth-Century English Narratives*. Baltimore, MD: Johns Hopkins University Press, 1995.

Oakleaf, David. "At the Margins of Utopia: Jamaica in Sarah Scott's *Millenium Hall*." *Eighteenth-Century Fiction* 28, no. 1 (Fall 2015): 109–137.

Paradise, Nathaniel. "Interpolated Poetry, the Novel, and Female Accomplishment." *Philological Quarterly* 74, no. 1 (Winter 1995): 57–76.

Patterson, Annabel. *Pastoral and Ideology: Virgil to Valéry*. Berkeley: University of California Press, 1987.

Perry, Ruth. "Mary Astell and the Feminist Critique of Possessive Individualism." *Eighteenth-Century Studies* 23, no. 4 (Summer 1990): 444–457.

Pocock, J.G.A. *The Machiavellian Moment: Florentine Political Thought and the Atlantic Republican Tradition*. Princeton, NJ: Princeton University Press, 1975.

Pohl, Nicole. "Introduction: 'The Commerce of Life': Elizabeth Montagu (1718–1800)." *Huntington Library Quarterly* 81, no. 4 (Winter 2018): 443–463.

———. "Sarah Scott, *Millenium Hall* (1762)." In *Handbook of the British Novel in the Long 18th Century*, edited by Katrin Berdt and Alessa Johns, 295–309. Boston: De Gruyter 2022.

———. "'Sweet place, where virtue then did rest': The Appropriation of the Country-House Ethos in Sarah Scott's *Millenium Hall*." *Utopian Studies* 7, no. 1 (1996): 49–60.

Pope, Alexander. *The Poems of Alexander Pope*. Edited by John Butt. New Haven, CT: Yale University Press, 1963.

Pratt, Mary Louise. *Imperial Eyes: Travel Writing and Transculturation*. New York: Routledge, 1992.

Price, Bronwen. "Verse, Voice, and Body: The Retirement Mode and Women's Poetry 1680–1723." *Early Modern Literary Studies* 12, no. 3 (January 2007): 5.1–5.44.

Rizzo, Betty. "Two Versions of Community: Montagu and Scott." *Huntington Library Quarterly* 65, no. 1–2 (2003): 193–214.

Ross, Ian. "A Bluestocking over the Border: Mrs. Montagu's Aesthetic Adventures in Scotland, 1766." *Huntington Library Quarterly* 28, no. 3 (May 1965): 213–233.

Runia, Robin. "'Knights of Matrimony,' Christian Duty, and *Millenium Hall.*" In *After Marriage in the Long Eighteenth Century: Literature, Law, and Society*, edited by Jenny DiPlacidi and Karl Leydecker, 91–105. New York: Palgrave, 2018.

San Emeterio, Neus Ribas. "Frederic Marès Deulovol, Collector." *Datatèxtil* no. 23 (2010): 4–21.

Schama, Simon. *Landscape and Memory*. New York: Knopf, 1995.

Schellenberg, Betty. *Literary Coteries and the Making of Modern Print Culture: 1750–1790.* New York: Cambridge University Press, 2016.

———. *The Professionalization of Women Writers in Eighteenth-Century Britain*. New York: Cambridge University Press, 2005.

Schnorrenberg, Barbara Brandon. "Elizabeth Montagu." In *The Oxford Dictionary of National Biography*, edited by Colin Matthew, Brian Harrison, and Lawrence Goldman. Oxford. Oxford: Oxford University Press, 2004–13. Accessed October 4, 2014.

Schoenberger, Melissa. *Cultivating Peace: The Virgilian Georgic in England, 1650–1750.* Lewisburg, PA: Bucknell University Press, 2019.

Scott, Sarah. *Millenium Hall*. Edited by Gary Kelly. Peterborough, ON: Broadview Press, 1995.

Shuttleton, David. *Smallpox and the Literary Imagination, 1660–1820.* New York: Cambridge University Press, 2007.

Smith, Chloe Wigston. *Women, Work, and Clothes in the Eighteenth-Century Novel*. New York: Cambridge University Press, 2013.

Spencer, Jane. "Creating the Woman Writer: The Autobiographical Works of Jane Barker." *Tulsa Studies in Women's Literature* 2, no. 2 (Autumn, 1983): 165–181.

———. *The Rise of the Woman Novelist*. Oxford: Blackwell, 1986.

Staves, Susan. *A Literary History of Women's Writing in Britain, 1660–1789.* New York: Cambridge University Press, 2006.

———. *Married Women's Separate Property in England, 1660–1833.* Cambridge, MA: Harvard University Press, 1990.

Stone, Lawrence, and Jeanne C. Fawtier Stone. *An Open Élite? England 1540–1880.* Oxford: Clarendon Press, 1984.

Straub, Kristina. "Frances Burney and the Rise of the Woman Novelist." In *The Columbia History of the British Novel*, edited by John Richetti, 199–219. New York: Columbia University Press, 1994.

Sullivan, Garrett, *The Drama of Landscape: Land, Property, and Social Relations on the Early Modern Stage*. Stanford, CA: Stanford University Press, 1998.

Swenson, Rivka. "Representing Modernity in Jane Barker's *Galesia Trilogy*: Jacobite Allegory and the Patch-Work Aesthetic." *Studies in Eighteenth-Century Culture* 34 (2005): 55–80.

Tallon, Laura. "Ekphrasis and Gender in Anne Finch's Longleat Poems." *Eighteenth-Century Life* 40, no. 1 (January 2016): 84–107.

Thompson, James. *Models of Value: Eighteenth-Century Political Economy and the Novel.* Durham, NC: Duke University Press, 1996.

Turnbull, Les. "Elizabeth Montagu: 'A Critick, a Coal Owner, a Land Steward, a Sociable Creature.'" *Huntington Library Quarterly* 18, no. 4 (Winter 2018): 657–686.

Turner, James. *The Politics of Landscape: Rural Scenery and Society in English Poetry, 1630–1660.* Cambridge, MA: Harvard University Press, 1979.

Vandivere, Julie. "The Bastard's Contention: Race, Property, and Sexuality in Virginia Woolf's *Orlando.*" *Modernism/modernity* 28, no. 1 (January 2021): 91–116. https://doi.org/10.1353/mod.2021.0012.

Verdon, Nicola. "The 'Lady Farmer': Gender, Widowhood, and Farming in Victorian England." In *The Farmer in England, 1650–1980*, edited by Richard W. Hoyle, 241–262. New York: Routledge, 2013.

Vickery, Amanda. *Behind Closed Doors: At Home in Georgian England*. New Haven, CT: Yale University Press, 2009.

Vogel, Ursula. "When the Earth Belonged to All: The Land Question in Eighteenth-Century Justifications of Private Property." *Political Studies* 36 (1988): 102–122.

Wall, Cynthia. *Grammars of Approach: Landscape, Narrative, and the Linguistic Picturesque*. Chicago: University of Chicago Press, 2019.

Warner, William. *Licensing Entertainment: The Elevation of Novel Reading in Britain, 1684–1750*. Berkeley: University of California Press, 1998.

Watson, Carly. *Miscellanies, Poetry, and Authorship, 1680–1800*. New York: Palgrave Macmillan, 2021.

Wendorf, Richard, and Charles Ryskamp. "A Blue-Stocking Friendship: The Letters of Elizabeth Montagu and Frances Reynolds in the Princeton Collection." *Princeton University Library Chronicle* 41, no. 3 (Spring 1980): 173–207.

Whyte, Nicola. *Inhabiting the Landscape: Place, Custom, and Memory, 1500–1800*. Barnsley, UK: Oxbow Books, 2009.

Williams, Dorice. "Sarah Scott's *Millenium Hall* and Female Philanthropy." *SEL: Studies in English Literature, 1500–1900* 35, no. 3 (June 1995): 535–553.

Williams, Raymond. *The Country and the City*. New York: Oxford University Press, 1973.

———. *Keywords*. New York: Oxford University Press, 1976.

Williamson, Tom. *Polite Landscapes: Gardens & Society in Eighteenth-Century England*. Stroud, Gloucestershire: Sutton Publishing, 1995.

———. *The Transformation of Rural England: Farming and the Landscape, 1700–1870*. Exeter: University of Exeter Press, 2002.

Williamson, Tom, and Liz Bellamy. *Property and Landscape: A Social History of Land Ownership and the English Countryside*. London: Butler and Tanner, 1987.

Wilson, Carol Shiner. "Jane Barker 1652–1732: From Galesia to Mrs Goodwife." In *Women and Poetry 1660–1750*, edited by Sarah Prescott and David Shuttleton, 40–49. New York: Palgrave, 2003.

Woodhouse, R. I., ed. *The Life and Poetical Works of James Woodhouse (1735–1820)*. London: Leadenhall Press, 1896.

Woolf, Virginia. *Orlando: Annotated and with an Introduction by Maria DiBattista*, edited by Mark Hussey. New York: Harcourt, 2006.

Wright, Gillian. *Producing Women's Poetry, 1600–1730: Text and Paratext, Manuscript and Print*. New York: Cambridge University Press, 2013.

Young, John Roach. "The Fifteen." In *Britain in the Hanoverian Age 1714–1837: An Encyclopedia*, edited by Gerald Newman, 254. New York: Garland, 1997.

INDEX

Addison, Joseph, 27–28, 32, 72
aesthetics: in landscape arts, 75–76, 78–79, 103, 138; politics and, 76
agriculture and industry discord, 117–118, 127
Andrews, Malcolm, 12, 22
Anne, Queen of Great Britain, 69
Ardelia. *See* Finch, Anne (née Kingsmill)
aristocratic ideology, 113
Austen, Jane, 5; *Mansfield Park,* 28

Barchas, Janine, 172n5
Barker, Jane: biblical imagery of, 48; communal knowledge, 37; depiction of landscape, 5, 6, 7, 152; experimentation with genres, 17–18, 167n7; "The *Grove,*" 35, 36, 37, 39; hostility to bourgeois ideology, 51; Jacobitism of, 16, 27, 55; *The Lining of the Patch Work Screen,* 14, 17; literary career of, 13, 16–17, 169n35; *A Patch-Work Screen for the Ladies,* 17; *Poetical Recreations,* 16, 29; proto-feminism of, 55; rural ideal of, 131; "The *Rivulet,*" 35. See also *Galesia Trilogy, The* (Barker)
Barrell, John, 10, 11, 12
Batchelor, Jennie, 98, 102
Bathurst, Henry Bathurst, 4
Bellamy, Liz, 58, 104, 110, 111
Bending, Stephen, 109, 120, 135, 136, 140–141, 149–150; *Green Retreats,* 7; "Literature and Landscape in the Eighteenth Century," 125
benevolent stewardship, 47, 49, 90, 91, 131, 146
Blackett, John, 122
Bluestocking society, 9, 15, 114, 119, 124, 136, 145, 176n51
Bohls, Elizabeth, 85
Bosvil (character), 18, 19, 24, 29–30
Bowes, Mary, 122
Bridgen, Adam, 147, 149
Brook, Isis, 2
Broome, Judith, 84, 172n2, 173n12
Brown, Capability: design for Sandleford Priory, 1, 117, 119, 141, 142, 144, 147, 149; landscape style of, 4, 5, 108, 109
Burlington, Richard Boyle, 4
Burnett, David, 76
Burney, Frances, 5
Bushnell, Rebecca, 152

Cahill, Samara Anne, 43
Cambridge Edition of the Works of Anne Finch, The (Kairoff and Keith), 65
capitalism: gender and, 9, 17; landownership and, 87, 108, 126, 147; landscape arts and, 4, 8, 29, 54, 56, 76, 86, 88, 91, 95–99, 101–102, 108, 110, 119, 125, 140, 142
Carew, Thomas: "To Saxham," 59
Carter, Elizabeth, 118, 122, 132, 140, 141, 148
Casey, Jim, 171n28
Chambers, Douglas: *The Planters of the English Landscape Garden,* 4
Charles I (king of England), 42, 169n42
Child, Elizabeth, 121, 123
Christmas, William, 135, 144, 149
Church of England, 87
Clavering, Thomas, 122
coal mining industry, 118, 121, 122, 126, 128
Cobham, Richard Temple, 4
commodification: of coal, 126; of land, 90, 109, 115
commodity, 47, 49, 56, 90, 150
Conway, Alison, 81, 172n5
country estates: as microcosm of the state, 104; patriarchy in, 53; women in, 10, 106, 136, 145, 153
country-house poetry: conventions of, 59–60, 62, 65, 66, 77; deviation from rules of, 63, 66, 69; examples of, 62; female voice in, 62–63; hierarchical social relations in, 14; landscape and, 56, 57; political subtext, 171n28; rhetoric of hospitality, 59–60
country houses, 15, 52, 54, 70

Cowley, Abraham, 31, 75
Cowper, William: "The Solitude of Alexander Selkirk," 78
Crawford, Patricia, 9–10, 11; "Women and Property: Women as Property," 9
Cromwell, Oliver, 71
Curll, Edmund, 168n10
customary landscapes, 88, 89

Daniels, Stephen, 21
Denham, John, 75
Denney, Peter, 135, 146, 147, 149
Denton Estates: landscape of absolute property in, 129–130, 135; monetary value of, 129; Montagu's epistolary depictions of, 122–123, 129, 134, 138, 150
Description of Millenium Hall, A (Scott): agricultural labor in, 111; artistic activity in, 105; beauty of grounds in, 84, 106, 107; Christian ethos of, 87–88, 111; comparison to Finch's poems, 86–87; deception, 86, 87, 92, 93, 97, 112, 113; depiction of landscape, 15, 85, 86, 88–90, 93–95, 97, 98, 102–103, 105–109, 112, 124; depiction of patriarchy, 84–86; emergent capitalism in, 88, 91, 95, 96, 97, 98, 99, 101, 102, 108; eroticism of language, 84; estate as "political and moral microcosm" in, 104; estate tour scene, 92, 110, 111–112, 173n15; ethical inconsistency in, 93; exploitation as selfless care, 102; female agency in, 86, 87, 96, 98; female characters of, 14, 81–82, 83, 84, 98, 100, 105, 109, 111; female independence in, 85, 87, 88, 94, 99, 103; feminist reading of, 9, 81, 87; form and content of, 6, 90; gift economy in, 97, 98; ideological subtext, 98–99, 109, 111; landscape park in, 108, 109, 110, 111, 112; literary history embedded in, 104; male narrator in, 81–82, 84–85, 86–87, 105–107, 109; mystification in, 85, 97–98; objectification in, 83, 84, 85–86, 105, 107, 113; opening paragraphs, 84; outdoor scenes, 105, 107; paradoxical purpose of, 96–97; passage about the wood, 110–111; philanthropy theme, 88, 89–90, 99, 100–101, 105, 108, 113; political subtext in, 108; publication of, 108; reciprocal relations in, 86, 89, 90–91, 92, 93, 97, 98, 99, 100, 101; sexuality in, 166n15; sisterhood in, 92, 93, 94; social and gender relations in, 87, 88; treatment of the working poor, 94–96, 101, 109–110, 111; utopianism of, 86, 88, 90, 91, 94, 97, 102, 104, 106, 126, 172n2; value system, 98, 108, 113; visual agency in, 82, 83–84, 85, 86–87, 90, 98, 172n5, 173n12
DiBattista, Maria, 153–154
Drew, Erin, 68–69; *Usufructuary Ethos,* 71
Dubrow, Heather, 59
Dunham Massey: image of mount at, *64*
Dyer, John: *The Fleece,* 69

Eastwell estate: oak trees, 71; patriarchal landscape of, 57, 60–61; photograph, *58*; poetic depiction of, 62, 63, 64–65, 67, 69, 70
Eger, Elizabeth, 114, 135, 136
Elizabeth I (queen of England), 154, 169n42
Elizabeth Montagu Correspondence Online, The, 124
Emerson, Ralph Waldo, 12
enclosure of land, 89, 102, 120
English Civil Wars, 67, 69
experiential landscape, 23, 26, 32, 90
Ezell, Margaret, 29, 167n7

Fabricant, Carole, 10, 11, 85
Fairfax, Mary, 77
Fairfax, Thomas Fairfax, 3rd baron of, 77
femininity: codes of, 3; forms of, 132, 133–134, 144, 145, 150; ideal, 99; morality and, 125
"feminotopia," 90
Finch, Anne (née Kingsmill): Anglicanism of, 52; country-house poems of, 54; depression of, 53; engagement with patriarchy, 14, 53, 54–55, 57–58, 60, 61, 62, 66, 70, 74, 79–80, 134; estate poems, 60; exile form London, 59, 69–70, 73; father-in-law of, 65–66; inheritance, 69; Jacobitism of, 55, 60, 71, 79; landscape in poetry of, 7, 14, 54, 55–57, 61–62, 94; life in Eastwell, 60–61; literary career of, 13, 14, 56; marriage of, 65; "Miscellany Poems with Two Plays by Ardelia," 57; pen-name of, 2, 53; political subtext in poetry of, 71; proto-feminism of, 10, 55, 63; relationship to landed property, 5, 56, 57, 59, 69, 152; relationship to nature, 53–54; religious views of, 52; reputation of, 53; rhetoric of hospitality, 73; rural retreat of, 52; social status of, 52–53, 69; "The Introduction," 10; "The Petition for an Absolute Retreat," 70; "To the Honorable the Lady Worsley

at Longleat," 14, 54, 72, 73–79; translations of, 60; "Upon My Lord Winchilsea Converting the Mount in His Garden to a Terras," 14, 54
Finch, Charles (4th Earl of Winchilsea), 53, 62, 64, 65, 66, 67, 68, 74
Finch, Heneage (3rd Earl of Winchilsea) (Finch's father-in-law), 65, 68, 71–72
Finch, Heneage (5th Earl of Winchilsea) (Finch's husband), 52, 53, 57, 59, 73
Finch, William (Viscount Maidstone), 65
Fowler, Alistair, 104

Galesia (character): aesthetic sensibility, 28; approach to Parnassus, 48; communitarian values, 19; courtship of, 19, 24–25, 27, 29, 40; engagement with the land, 18, 20, 21, 23, 29–30, 32, 33, 37, 38, 46–48; as estate manager, 18, 19, 25, 26, 27, 38, 42–43; family history, 31–32; identity of, 18, 20–21, 24, 26, 29, 32, 34, 37, 51; involvement in monetary exchange, 47; Jacobite views of, 50; life in London, 39, 40–42, 44–45, 49, 94; nostalgia for "ancient times," 44; poetry of, 27, 29, 30–31, 32–33, 34, 45, 169n37; political affiliation of, 31–32, 40; return to the country, 26, 28, 34, 35, 50–51; social position, 27; stagecoach journey, 38; visual imagination of, 40, 42, 44–45
Galesia Trilogy, The (Barker): competing landscapes in, 2, 18–24, 29, 51; critique of social order in, 17, 27; formal hybridity of, 29; genre of, 17–18; heroine in, 131; historical and political context of, 17, 21, 23, 24, 27–28, 31; imagery of rising and falling, 168n13; overview, 14; plot of, 18; proto-feminist implications of, 19; publication of, 17; references to land, 18–19
garden: vs. landscape arts, 140. *See also* landscape gardening
Gavin, Michael, 55, 57
gazing upon the land, 84
gender inequality, 134, 151
gentry capitalism, 87
georgic, 57, 69, 97, 148, 165n11, 171n37
Gevirtz, Karen, 37, 89
Gilpin, William, 5
Girouard, Mark, 70
Glorious Revolution of 1688, 57, 58–59, 69, 70, 73
Grainger, James: *The Sugar-Cane,* 69
grotto, 110, 111
Guest, Harriet, 145
gypsies, 158–159

Habermas, Jürgen, 145
Hamrick, Wes, 71
Haslewood, William, 53
Heal, Felicity, 169n42
Hill, Bridget, 2, 9, 139
Hindle, Steve, 146, 149
Hintman, Mr. (character), 98
Huntington Library, 120, 121

ideology of benevolence, 102
ideology of domesticity, 98–99
improvement: aestheticized representations of, 136; economic components of, 121, 130, 147, 150; landscape of ownership and, 1, 142–143, 144, 146; landscape of stewardship and, 62, 65, 71–72, 74, 75, 76, 109; moralized discourse of, 131; satirical view of, 28; social status and, 117, 119, 120, 135–136
individual/collective binary, 20
individualism, 4, 8, 28, 89, 132, 142, 147
industrial landscaping, 118, 120–125

Jacobite rising of 1715, 21
James I (king of England), 169n42
James II (king of England), 16, 27, 53, 168n22, 170n13
Johnson, Samuel, 114
Jonson, Ben, 76, 77; "To Penshurst," 59, 63

Kairoff, Claudia, 65
Keith, Jennifer, 11, 54–55, 60, 65; *Poetry and the Feminine from Behn to Cowper,* 10
Kelly, Gary, 83, 87
Kent, William, 4
King, Kathryn, 16–17, 29, 47, 168n10, 169n35; "Constructions of Femininity," 10–11
Kingsmill, Bridget, 53
Kip, Johannes, *64, 82*
Knight, Richard Payne, 5
Knole country house, 154
Knyff, Leendert, *64, 82*

Labbe, Jacqueline, 12–13; *Romantic Visualities,* 12
Lacroix, Constance, 50, 51
Lamont (character), 84, 92, 94, 98, 109

land: aesthetic cultivation of, 90, 127, 138; economic value of, 128–129, 138; management of, 69, 147; as model of value, 113; sexuality and, 84; social identity in relation to, 19; transmutation into landscape, 33, 35
landownership: coal industry and, 128, 135; individualistic forms of, 4, 132; male-dominated practice of, 161; political authority and, 3–4, 58–59, 129; proto-feminist agenda and, 113; Roman property law and, 68; social identity and, 2–3, 17, 127–130; as source of wealth, 49; study of, 3; women and, 2, 13, 17, 18, 98, 104–105, 119, 120, 132, 139, 147, 153, 155, 159–160
landscape: aesthetic of, 3, 4; alchemy of, 103, 113, 126, 151; definition of, 2, 19, 21–22, 75, 85; as dreamscape, 40, 44–45; elusiveness of the term, 57, 169n27; evolving meaning of, 22, 54, 56; experiential, 23, 26, 32, 90; female identity and, 23, 115, 152; feminization of, 6, 10, 12; geography and, 134; historical evolution of, 2, 28, 62; institutionalization of, 57; literature and, 5, 152, 161; as mark of social status, 108; moral dimension of, 125, 136; vs. nature, 21; scholarship on, 2, 3, 9, 15, 152–153; as social construct, 2, 3, 22; social inequality and, 9, 151; taxonomy of, 36, 37; theories of, 3–4, 54; vs. topography, 20; visual, 15, 23, 34, 35, 40, 44, 75–76; Whig approaches to, 28, 32
landscape arts: aesthetic pleasures in, 105, 138; agriculture and, 118; alchemy of, 103; ascendance of, 138, 142, 150; association with the south, 134, 135; definition of, 22; development of, 4–6, 56–57, 150; exclusion of industry, 130; vs. garden, 140; gendered exclusivity of, 5, 11–12; landscape of absolute property and, 99, 103, 107, 109, 119, 125, 126, 127, 142, 146, 152; vs. landscapes of custom and stewardship, 3–4, 6, 7, 23–24, 37, 111, 152; as manifestation of wealth, 110, 116–117; poetry and, 11, 57; prospect view of, 10–13; sexuality in, 7; women's value of, 105, 135
landscape ethos, 90
landscape gardening, 4, 6, 57, 103, 143
landscape of absolute property: capitalism and, 99, 125, 132, 159; definition of, 169n29; dominance in social relations, 56, 69, 91, 111; economic interest and, 8, 49, 116; landscape arts and, 76, 103, 107, 115–116, 117, 119, 125, 126, 127, 142, 146; vs. landscapes of stewardship and custom, 25, 28, 69, 93, 94, 101, 102, 132, 146, 152; literary depictions of, 86
landscape of custom: authentic nature of, 158; conception of, 22–23, 94–95; vs. landscape arts, 3; vs. landscape of absolute property, 28, 69; literary depictions of, 26, 95, 157–158; obsolescence of, 69, 88–89, 90, 152
landscape of stewardship: communal values of, 4, 27–28; conception of, 22–23; vs. landscape arts, 3–4, 23–24; liminal quality of, 72; literary depictions of, 25, 26, 54, 86, 106, 157; nostalgia for, 44, 130–132; obsolescence of, 96, 97; as paradise, 45; principles of reciprocity in governance of, 4; transition to landscape of absolute property, 25, 28, 69, 102, 152
Langford, Paul, 128, 129
"lesbian genres," 7
Liddell, Henry, 122
Lining of the Patch Work Screen, The (Barker): celebration of terrestrial Paradice, 48; criticism of social order in, 48–49; depiction of landscape, 46–48, 49; dream episode, 46–48; ending of, 50; in-set narratives of, 45–46; Jacobite propensities, 50; opening scene, 45; plot and characters, 18; scenes of urban vice, 49
London, April, 91, 160
London, UK: urban inequity, 49
Longleat estate: engraved image of, *73*; Finches in, 72–73; gardens of, 75, 76, 77; owners of, 72, 74, 76; poetic depiction of, 56, 57, 62, 73, 74–76, 78–79; view of, *77*
Love Intrigues, or The History of the Amours of Bosvil and Galesia (Barker): conception of land in, 25; depiction of landscape in, 25–26, 27, 33–34; estate management scene, 38, 42; genres of, 18; plot and characters, 18, 24; poetry in, 27, 30–31, 33; politics in, 31; publication of, 168n10; rural scenery, 30; social order in, 17
Lyttelton, George, 130

Macpherson, John, 145
Major, Emma, 87, 88, 120, 128, 131
male poets, 10–11
Mancel, Louisa, Mrs. (character), 92, 98, 100, 105, 111, 173n36
"man of taste" theory, 11
Mansfield Park (Austen), 28

Marvell, Andrew, 63; *Upon Appleton House,* 59, 77
Mary of Modena, consort of James II, 53
Maynard, Mrs. (character), 2, 82, 89, 92, 93, 94, 105
McDonagh, Briony, 2, 8, 9, 119, 120, 121
McGonegal, Julie, 98, 99, 102; "The Tyranny of Gift Giving," 97
McGovern, Barbara, 73, 75
"Miscellany Poems with Two Plays by Ardelia" (Folger Manuscript), 57, 60, 61, 65
mobile property, 44, 97, 128
Montagu, Barbara, 83
Montagu, Edward, 15, 114, 119, 137, 138, 139, 141, 142
Montagu, Elizabeth (née Robinson): accomplishments of, 151; Anglican identity, 115, 145; background of, 114–115; as Bluestocking leader, 15, 114, 119, 124, 136, 145; business affairs of, 117, 118, 120–122, 123, 127, 129, 132, 142, 143–144, 148; charity work, 146–147; compared to other female coal magnates, 121–122; correspondence of, 15; death of the son of, 139; engagement with patriarchy, 142, 145, 151; estate improvements, 117, 120, 121, 135, 142, 146, 147, 150; female independence, 114, 115, 117, 119, 120, 132, 139, 145; friends of, 130; humor of, 143; identity of, 115, 117, 119, 124, 131, 135–136, 138, 140; imagination of, 125, 126, 129, 140; importance of landscape for, 2, 6, 7, 124, 125, 139–140, 141, 152; interactions with the poor, 130, 146–147; as landowner, 1–2, 8, 15, 115–117, 119–120, 128–130, 131, 137, 138, 144, 147; life and literary career, 13, 15; marital relations, 114, 115, 137, 138–139, 141–142; moral values, 136; parents of, 128; personality of, 120, 121, 145; philanthropy of, 141, 145, 147, 151; portrait of, *116*; potato scheme, 146; as proto-feminist figure, 117, 120; reading preferences, 139; relatives of, 83; reliance on notions of reciprocity, 132, 146; scholarship on, 120–122, 135, 136, 146–147, 149–150; self-legitimation of, 123, 132–133, 137, 141, 146, 150; self-perception of, 115, 117, 120–121, 122, 130, 140–141, 144, 145, 150; Shakespeare, 115, 124; social status of, 114–115, 127, 128, 130, 138; trip to France, 120; use of wealth, 114, 124–125, 145, 150; view of proper femininity, 133–134; widowhood, 130, 139, 141, 142; as woman of taste, 118, 119
Montagu's letters: aesthetic of land in, 125, 127; agriculture and industry discord in, 117–118, 127, 128, 129; circulation of, 114; corpus of, 114, 119, 120; on Denton properties, 118, 119, 122–123, 126, 129, 130, 134, 138, 150; description of coal mines, 121, 122–123, 127, 129, 132–133; image of industrial waste, 118; landscape arts in, 118, 134, 136, 137–138, 140, 141, 143, 145, 148; moral issues in, 125–126, 138; on Northumberland's middle-class women, 133, 135; publication and digitization of, 122, 124; rhetoric of stewardship in, 129, 130–132; on rural pleasures, 143; on Sandleford Priory, 1, 117, 129, 135, 136–138, 143, 145–146, 148, 150; social anxieties in, 115, 123–124, 126, 127–128; visual rhetoric of, 1, 138
Moore, Lisa L., 82; *Sister Arts,* 7
moral economy, 56, 90–91
moral geography, 132, 134, 135, 138
Morgan, Mrs. (character), 84, 91, 100, 105, 111
Mount Morris estate, 82, *82*
Mowl, Timothy, 2

nature: vs. landscape, 21–22
Nolan, Katherine, 82
North of England Institute of Mining and Mechanical Engineers, 121
Northumberland: middle-class women of, 135; social and gender hierarchy, 132–133
Nussbaum, Felicity, 90

Oakleaf, David, 87
oak trees, 71, 84, 105, 106, 155, 157, 160, 171n38
Orlando (character): aesthetic sensibility of, 153, 154, 158–159; estate of, 154, 156–157; frequent gazing at the land, 156; gender transformation, 154, 156, 158, 161; hallucinatory landscape visions, 159–160; landscape arts in, 157, 158; legal troubles, 154–155, 159; life among gypsies in Turkey, 158–159; marriage of, 155
Orlando (Woolf): estate servants and laborers in, 157, 160; final chapter, 160; historical era of, 153–154; landownership in, 153, 156–158, 159–161; landscape tropes, 152–153, 155, 156; oak tree motif, 155, 157, 160; open-ended conclusion, 160; satire of legal system, 159; scene of the royal visit to Knole, 153–154

pastoral, 15, 18, 20, 22, 53, 59, 118, 169n27, 169n33, 177n67
Patch-Work Screen for the Ladies, A (Barker): allusion to the 1720 financial disaster, 43–44; conclusion of, 50; genres of, 18; landownership and social order in, 17; landscape depiction, 21, 27, 32, 34–40, 106; London cityscape in, 41–42, 44; natural imagery, 40–41; plot of, 36–37; poetry in, 20, 32, 33, 34, 35–36; rural retreat in, 39, 50; structure of, 35, 36
patriarchy: institution of, 85–86; landownership and, 53, 134; virtues of, 57–58; women's collaboration with, 2, 7–10, 13, 14, 53–55, 60, 62, 66, 70, 74, 79–80, 86, 134, 142, 145, 151, 161
patrilineal inheritance, 91
"Petition for an Absolute Retreat, The" (Finch), 70
philanthropy, 8, 89–90, 99, 102, 105, 108, 141, 145, 147, 151
Philips, Katherine, 31
picturesque, 5, 120
Poetry and the Feminine from Behn to Cowper (Keith), 10
Pohl, Nicole, 83, 115
Pope, Alexander: "Epistle to Burlington," 107
Pratt, Mary Louise, 90; *Imperial Eyes,* 78
"Preface, The" (Finch), 57, 60–61, 65
Price, Bronwen, 20, 168n20
Price, Uvedale, 5
prospect views, 10, 11, 12–13, 110, 153–154, 156
proto-feminism, 9, 60, 151

Radcliffe, Ann, 5
reciprocal services, 92, 97
Repton, Humphry, 5
Reynolds, Frances, 143
Reynolds, Joshua, *116,* 143
Rizzo, Betty, 145

Sackville-West, Vita, 154, 159–160; *The Land,* 159
Sandleford Priory: agricultural work at, 149; animals at, 148; design of, 1; garden of, 140; labor and leisure at, 144, 147–151; landscape improvement projects, 117, 119, 120, 135–139, 141, 142–143, 144–147, 148, 149–150; landscape of absolute property, 145, 148, 149; owners of, 119; seasonal rhythms at, 148–149, 150; social relations, 136
Schellenberg, Betty, 114
Scott, George Lewis, 83
Scott, Sarah (née Robinson): Anglicanism of, 87; Bab Montagu and, 83; *A Description of Millenium Hall,* 6, 14; financial uncertainty of, 83; *The History of Cornelia,* 83; *The History of Sir George Ellison,* 83, 112; illness of, 82–83; interest in spectatorship, 81, 84; life and literary career, 13, 14, 82–83; marriage of, 83; Mount Morris estate and, 82; perception of landscape, 6, 7, 152; social status of, 128; *The Test of Filial Duty,* 13, 83; view of patriarchy, 80, 103, 134
Siberechts, Jan, *77*
Sidney, Barbara (née Gamage), 63
Sidney, Robert, 63, 77
Smith, Charlotte: *Beachy Head,* 13
Smith, John Raphael, *116*
social geography, 135
social hierarchy, 26, 27, 33, 37, 51, 56, 87, 95, 110, 127–128, 132–133, 161
social inequality, 9, 88, 119, 151, 155
stewardship, 7, 72. *See also* landscape of stewardship
Stewart, Mary, 122
Stillingfleet, Benjamin, 126
Stone, Lawrence and Jeanne, 128
Straub, Kristina, 168n13
Stuart, James, 141
Sullivan, Garrett: *The Drama of Landscape,* 3; on landscape arts, 103; on landscape of custom, 94–95; on landscape of stewardship, 86, 88; study of early modern English drama, 56–57; theory of landscape, 3, 4, 8, 22, 23, 28, 54, 69, 83, 88, 90, 115, 125, 156, 157
Swenson, Rivka, 50, 51

"terraced landscapes," 75
Thompson, James, 113
Thynne, Frances (née Finch), 57, 72, 73, 74
Thynne, Henry, 77
Thynne, James, 77
topography: vs. landscape, 20, 168n20
"To the Honorable the Lady Worsley at Long-Leate" (Finch): comparison to "Upon My Lord Winchilsea," 62, 74, 79; creation of, 73–74; description of Longleat, 62, 72, 74–75; deviation from literary convention, 72–73, 74; emphasis on aesthetic experience, 75–76; estate stewardship in, 14, 62; as example of country-house poetry, 62; female agency

in, 74, 79–80; landscape arts in, 75; landscape in, 54, 72, 75, 76, 79; paradoxical commitment to patriarchy and women's writing, 14, 54–55, 61, 74, 80; passage describing Lady Worsley, 75; patriarchy in, 74; visual agency in, 76, 78–79, 86
trees: personification of, 67. *See also* oak trees
Trentham, Mrs. (character), 83, 109
Tunbridge Wells town, 138, 139
Turnbull, Les, 119, 121, 122

"Upon My Lord Winchilsea Converting the Mount in His Garden to a Terras" (Finch): act of stewardship in, 62–65, 69; description of Eastwell, 62; deviation from poetic convention, 63, 65, 66, 69; estate stewardship in, 14, 62; as example of country-house poetry, 62; female agency in, 63; Jacobite subtext in, 67, 70; landscape in, 54, 66, 67–68; models of masculinity, 66–67; oak tree motif, 69, 155, 171n38; opening stanza of, 63; patriarchy in, 66; patron celebrated by, 63; political context of, 71; subtext embedded in, 67; tree-felling episode, 67, 68, 69, 70; war imagery, 67
usufructuary ethos, 68, 71

Verdon, Nicola, 2
Vesey, Elizabeth, 1, 129
Vickery, Amanda, 2, 8
visual landscape, 15, 23, 34, 35, 40, 44, 150, 158
Vogel, Ursula, 169n29

Wall, Cynthia: *Grammars of Approach,* 5
Walpole, Robert, 170n13
Warner, William, 169n35
West, Gilbert, 139
Weymouth, Thomas Thynne, Viscount of, 57, 64, 72, 73, 75, 76, 78
Whig ascendancy, 27, 28, 57, 170n13
Whyte, Nicola, 89
William III (king of England), 5, 79
Williams, Raymond, 22
Williamson, Tom, 2, 58, 104, 108, 110, 111
Winde, William, 65
Windsor, Alice, 122
Wise, Henry, 4
woman of taste, 12, 118, 119
women: beauty standards, 83; capitalism and, 9, 117; charitable work, 100–101; collaboration with patriarchy, 2, 7–10, 13, 14, 53–55, 60, 62, 66, 70, 74, 79–80, 134; desire for independence, 9, 48; distribution of money by, 100, 101; estate management, 4, 8, 14, 101, 112; fertility of, 152; identity formation, 3, 20–21, 52, 131; as kind of property, 87; landownership, 2, 13, 17, 18, 104–105, 119, 120, 132, 139, 159–160; in landscape studies, 152–153; legal status of, 159; poetic portrayal of, 10–11, 19; relation to land, 2–3, 10, 12, 131–132; risk-taking, 101; self-determination of, 6, 14, 87, 92, 93, 98, 153; self-realization of, 52; social status of, 9, 10, 12–13; widowhood, 139
women writers: appropriation of the prospect view, 11; contributions to landscape discourse, 5; as intruders on the rights of men, 10; patriarchal social order and, 2, 7–9
Woodhouse, James, 117, 145, 147, 148; *Life and Lucubrations of Crispinus Scriblerus,* 144, 146, 149
Woolf, Virginia: depiction of landscape, 161; on girl's fertility, 152; *Orlando,* 152–161; treatment of the law, 154–155
working-class consciousness, 147
Worsley, Frances (née Thynne), 62, 72, 73, 74, 75
Worsley, Robert, 74
Wright, Gillian, 60
Wyatt, James, 1, 143

ABOUT THE AUTHOR

NICOLLE JORDAN is an associate professor of English at the University of Southern Mississippi in Hattiesburg, where she has also served as director of women's and gender studies. She previously taught at universities in Texas and Ohio. Her other publications on British women's writing explore the intersection of politics and nature in works by Lady Mary Wortley Montagu and Maria Graham.